THE

POWER

AND THE

EVIL

THE
POWER
AND THE
EVIL

BLITZ EDITIONS

Published by Blitz Editions
an imprint of Bookmart Ltd
Registered Number 2372865
Trading as Bookmart Ltd
Desford Road
Enderby
Leicester LE9 5AD

ISBN 1 85605 208 7

This material has previously appeared in *Inside Stories*.

Every effort has been made to contact the copyright holders for the pictures.
In some cases they have been untraceable, for which we offer our apologies.
Special thanks to the Hulton-Deutsch Collection, who supplied the majority of pictures,
and thanks also to the following libraries and picture agencies:
Aerospace/Midsummer Books, Anglia Press Limited, Bilderdienst Suddeutscher Verlag,
Fortean Picture Library, Peter Newark, Popperfotos, Press Association, Rex Features,
Frank Spooner Pictures, Syndication International, Topham Picture Source.

The Author
Allan Hall is the American correspondent for a major U.K. newspaper.
He has written several books on crime, the paranormal and the unexplained.

This book was produced by Amazon Publishing Limited
Designed by Cooper Wilson Design
Edited by Graham McColl

Printed in the Slovak Republic
51730

Contents

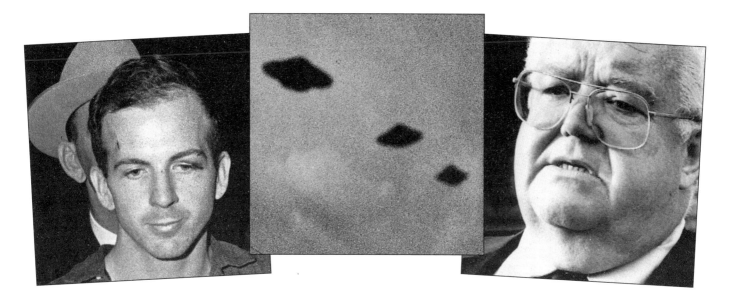

THE POWER AND THE EVIL

Each and every one of us is vulnerable when greater powers than ourselves come into play and touch on our daily lives. Such powers can range from the sleazy workings of organised crime to the (sometimes literally) uplifting experience of a visitation from beings from another world.

Some of the most compelling tales of extraterrestrial visits have been told by very ordinary people who just happened to be in a certain place at a certain time. And ghosts have haunted royalty just as effectively as they have haunted the common man. The terrifying Nazi concentration camps, where doctors such as Karl Babor carried out horrific experiments on their victims, were composed of ordinary people who became subject to the power-crazed madness of Hitler, which swept Germany in the 1930s. And when serial killers, gangsters and mad dictators are on the rampage, the victims of their twisted minds tend to be well-adjusted individuals or groups who wish only to be left alone to live decent lives.

Possibly even more disturbing than evil being perpetrated by those who are clearly seen to be evil is when those who should represent all that is good in society, such as doctors and nurses, turn out to be preying on those in their care. When nurse Beverly Allitt was revealed as a serial killer of babies in her hospital, confidence in nursing took a knock. When charismatic preachers were revealed as hypocrites, confidence in religious organisations took a knock. When Winnie Mandela was at the centre of a murder trial, confidence in the ANC took a knock.

This book shows how the lives of many ordinary, respectable people have been drastically altered by coming into contact with powers over which they have had little control. With some phenomena, such as ghosts and UFOs, there is little an individual can do to control the experience. With others, such as dishonest doctors, the stories in this book should serve as a strong reminder to look and listen carefully before entrusting someone with power over your own and your loved ones' lives.

NEW
FRANKENSTEINS

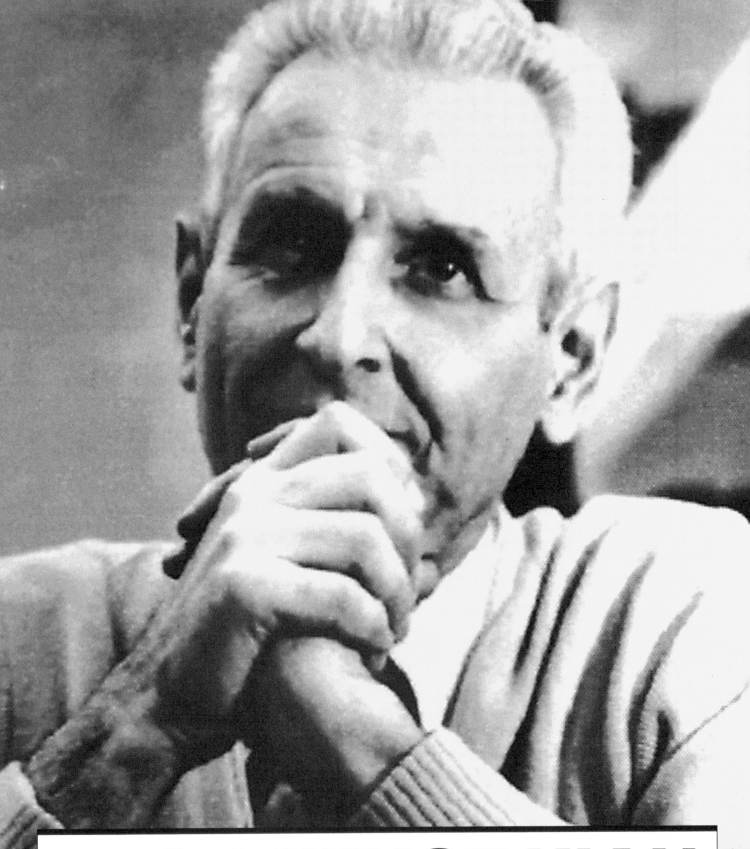

JACK KEVORKIAN
Doctor Death

Jack Kevorkian is an American doctor who helps the terminally ill to die. His activities have caused great controversy in the US. Is he an angel of mercy or an angel of death? Is he an enlightened humanitarian or someone who, but for legal loopholes, would already be behind bars?

Left: *The creature Frankenstein as played by Boris Karloff. Kevorkian likes to compare himself to the mythical doctor who created the monster.*

Opposite: *Dr Jack Kevorkian. To many he is a saint who relieves suffering. But the authorities have branded him a 'ghoul'.*

Below: *The doctor with his 'suicide machine', which brings death to users within a minute.*

America knows him simply as 'Doctor Death'. But Jack Kevorkian, a 64-year-old retired physician, prefers to compare himself to that other misunderstood medical genius – Doctor Frankenstein. But where Frankenstein sought to give life, Kevorkian seeks to take it.

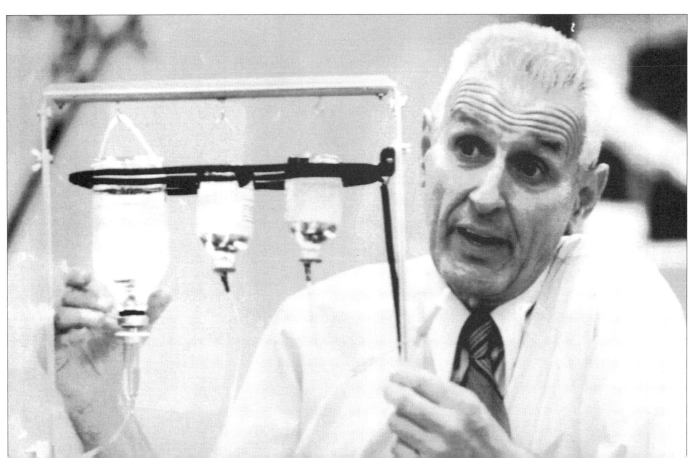

Above: A monster or a saint? Dr Kevorkian argues his point fiercely in court.

Opposite Top: The van that police dubbed 'The Deathmobile'. Inside it Janet Adkins, 54, committed suicide, hooked up to his suicide machine. She was the first to die using it.

Opposite Bottom: Janet Adkins and her husband Neil on their wedding day.

With the aid of his controversial 'Suicide Machine', the former pathologist has already helped at least 16 chronically ill people take their own lives, and his avid belief in the individual's right to terminate one's own existence has fuelled a legal, ethical and medical debate across the entire country.

The device, made from salvaged parts he picked up here and there at flea markets and garage sales, intravenously feeds death-inducing drugs or poisonous gas to a patient, after the victim has pushed the machine's button. The white-haired doctor claims he is 'dedicated to the honourable and ethical practice of alleviating hopelessly irremediable physical suffering'. But his many critics claim he is trying to play God.

Kevorkian, who began practising medicine in 1952, has had a long – and many would also say morbid – fascination with death and other macabre subjects. In the mid-1950s, while working at the University of Michigan Medical Centre, he admits he 'used to take what I called death rounds. I would go around to all of the people (in the hospital) who were about to die and watch. I wanted to see at what point they could no longer be resuscitated. But I don't like to watch someone die. It is a traumatic, wrenching experience'.

THE EARLY PLAN

There was also his early plan, first proposed during his medical school days and shunned by his professors, to 'harvest' organs from prison inmates. There were experiments in how best to take blood from corpses, which he first learned about in 1961 from articles based on the Soviet practice in which blood from freshly-dead corpses was used for transfusions on the battlefield where no other bloody supply was handy. Kevorkian did his own experiments, taking 'blood from immediately dead people – from their heart through a special syringe – into the recipient'.

The practice did not gain popularity because, according to a magazine report of the time, 'US doctors have shied away from it because of prejudice against contact with anything from a corpse'.

Kevorkian, of course, disagreed, saying that blood was no different from an organ for transplant, and that 'superstition' had cost many lives. But his professional reputation was damaged by the controversy, and he admits that he found it hard to obtain work after that.

Later, the defiant doctor again raised eyebrows when he advocated giving death-row prisoners the right to commit suicide, with their organs removed while comatose, rather than be executed.

He said he got the idea from his days as a young resident in pathology, when he was dealing with death-row criminals who wanted to make a final gesture of penitence by donating their organs so that they might save a life. Again, the medical community was shocked. 'They told me you've got to drop the idea or leave the university. So I left the university', he recalled.

Above: *Leslie Williams, 81, and wife Susan, 52. Susan chose to die with Kevorkian present at her end.*

Top: *Kevorkian with Marcella Lawrence (left) and Marguerite Tate, who both took their life with 'Doctor Death' present.*

For many years, Kevorkian devoted himself to writing on death and euthanasia, and wrote many books which were just as controversial as his earlier ideas. But most of the leading medical journals and magazines in the US refused his articles, and Kevorkian slipped into relative anonymity within the medical fraternity. Certainly, his name was unfamiliar to the public. But that, of course, would change...and soon. In 1989, he first

began tinkering with the so-called 'Suicide Machine', following a meeting with David Rivlin, who had become a quadriplegic in 1971 following a terrible surfing accident. In 1989, at the age of 38 and having spent half his life without the use of his limbs, he made up his mind that he wanted to die. But no one at the nursing home he lived in would help him so the desperate man made a public appeal to a Detroit newspaper, in which he begged a doctor to help him commit suicide. Only one doctor responded. It was Kevorkian, who stepped into the spotlight and offered to discuss it with him, but the courts immediately said no.

Still, Kevorkian continued tinkering with his machine and by September 1989 he had it ready to use. When a local medical journal refused to take an advertisement from him regarding its availability, a Detroit newspaper ran a story on him. The following year, he got his chance to use it when he performed his first medically-assisted suicide in June, with the death of a 54-year-old Alzheimer's sufferer from Oregon who travelled to Michigan to die. Janet Adkins had come to him in eagerness to end her life before the full ravages of the disease became unbearable. Kevorkian was ready for his first patient – in fact, he was so keen to realise his idea of medically-assisted suicide that he even had business cards printed. On them, he called himself an 'Obitiatrist', from the word 'obituary' – a doctor of death. 'The world's first', he adds quite proudly.

When Adkins, a mother of three, arrived, she climbed into the back of Kevorkian's old Volkswagen van in a rural Michigan park and watched as he connected her to his Suicide Machine. She then pushed a button three times to ensure the machine's death-inducing drugs would pour into her veins. Her last words, said Kevorkian, were: 'Thank you, thank you'. Her husband Ron, who was there when she died, said his wife 'was very happy to exit. She believed in Dr Kevorkian. She looked into his eyes and said "thank you."'

VIDEO EVIDENCE

Also, Adkins left behind a video-tape, which she apparently made just two days before she died. Adkins, a plump, bespectacled woman, is seen being interviewed by Kevorkian:

Q. Janet, are you are of you decision?
A. Yes.
Q. What does it mean?
A. You have to get out with dignity.
Q. Just what is it you want? Put it in simple English.
A. Self-deliverance.
Q. Do you want to go on?
A. No, I don't want to go on.
Q. What does that mean?
A. The end of...my life.
Q. What's the word for it?
A. Euthanasia.
Q. No, what's the word for the end of life?
A. You're dead.
Q. All right, is that what you wish?
A. Yes.

The next day, when the doctor spoke publicly of her death, the debate began. But if the medical community – and many ordinary citizens – were appalled at the thought of a doctor helping a patient to commit suicide, then Kevorkian was equally appalled at the reaction to his behaviour. 'The medical society is stuck in the Dark Ages', he said recently. 'I'm sure if they could, they would burn me at the stake'.

Not quite, but in March 1991 Kevorkian was charged with the murder of Adkins, but the case was later dismissed. A judge ruled that assisted suicide was not illegal in Michigan and therefore the doctor had committed no criminal act. However, the judge warned Kevorkian that he was not to assist in any more suicides. For a while, the doctor heeded that warning. But fifteen months later, he defied the order. Two more women, Sherry Miller, 43, and Marjorie Wantz, 58, killed themselves with the doctor's assistance. Miller, suffering from multiple sclerosis, took a lethal dose of carbon monoxide from a device which released the deadly gas through a mask placed over her head. Wantz, who had a painful pelvic dis-

Above: *Another controversy for Kevorkian, after he learns that he will not stand trial on murder charges.*

ADKINS CLIMBED INTO KEVORKIAN'S VAN AND WATCHED HIM CONNECT HER TO HIS SUICIDE MACHINE

Above: *Kevorkian with his attorney Geoffrey Fieger in 1991 after having assisted in the suicide of two people. He again escaped prosecution.*

'IT'S TOUGH TO FIND PROBABLE CAUSE FOR MURDER... THESE WOMEN COMMITTED SUICIDE. HE PROVIDED THE MEANS

A PROSECUTOR LABELLED KEVORKIAN 'JEFFREY DAHMER IN A LAB COAT', REFERRING TO THE KILLER WHO ATE 17 VICTIMS

ease, took a fatal injection of drugs administered by the machine. Both women died, side by side, in a secluded cabin in rural Michigan.

Before they died, both spoke on a videotape made by Kevorkian, and made plain their reasons for wanting to end their suffering. 'People tell me you should get out and do this, hang in there', said Miller. 'But you're in such misery that you can't wait to pop a sleeping pill and go to bed, just to get out of the pain'.

Again, murder charges were filed against Kevorkian. District Court Judge James Sheehy, while acknowledging the absence of a law preventing the doctor from assisting in suicides, said some serious questions had been raised in the deaths of Wantz and Miller. Although both women had painful ailments neither was considered terminally ill.

PROBABLE CAUSE FOR MURDER

Despite the medical community's antagonism towards Kevorkian, the Hemlock Society, an Oregon-based association which supports doctor-assisted suicides, said it was shocked that he would be tried

in the deaths. 'I had expected they would drop those murder charges', said Hemlock attorney Cheryl Smith. 'I think that it's tough to find probable cause for murder because these women committed suicide. He provided the means'.

But prosecutors believed Wantz and Miller were incapable of making a rational decision. 'Wantz was mentally ill', said state attorney Lawrence Bunting. 'There was nothing wrong with this lady except she needed mental health treatment and now she's dead because Kevorkian decided to take the law into his own hands. People like Kevorkian can do all sorts of damage'.

'What he did is like veterinary medicine', added Dr John Finn, medical director of a Detroit hospital where some terminally ill patients have tried to seek out Kevorkian's services. 'When you take your pet to the vet, he puts the pet to sleep. I think human beings are more complicated than that'.

One local prosecutor, Richard Thompson of Oakland County, Michigan went so far as to label Kevorkian as 'Jeffrey Dahmer in a lab coat', referring to the monstrous serial killer who murdered and ate 17 boys and young men in Milwaukee.

Yet despite all the outrage, none of the charges ever stuck, because Kevorkian had only assisted in the suicides, and had never done the deed himself. So he was again free to carry out his mission as Doctor Death, caring not a fig for the growing furore. However, authorities revoked his medical licence, which cut off his supply of the death-inducing drugs he needed, so he switched to using carbon monoxide. 'We were told in medical school that carbon monoxide was the best way to commit suicide', he told an interviewer, not seeming to care that he could no longer obtain drugs for his work. 'All you do is get a tank of gas and a mask to breathe it through. The gas offers a simple, painless, odourless death. Better than that, it leaves the corpse looking good. You look better dead than alive. Gives your corpse a lovely, rosy glow'.

In all, Kevorkian has now helped a total of 16 people – ten within the past 12 months prior to July 1993 – kill themselves. Among them: Susan Williams, 52, who wrote 'I'm happy to have his assistance, since I am unable to do this myself',

suffered from multiple sclerosis. Lois Hawes, 52, who had lung cancer; Catherine Andreyev, 46, cancer; Marcella Lawrence, 67, heart disease, who once said 'I wish (the law-makers) could have my pain for one night'; Marguerite Tate, 70, Lou Gehrig's disease; Jack Miller, 53, the first male, who had bone cancer. The list continues (the most recent came in May 1993).

DEFIANT DOCTOR

The defiant doctor helped seven of those commit suicide just before a law banning doctor-assisted suicide went into effect in March 1993. 'I don't care about the law', he said. 'I have never cared about anything but the welfare of the patient in front of me. I help people when their time comes. I haven't killed anybody. I haven't abused this, it's legal'.

Indeed, that Michigan law banning assisted-suicide faced an immediate challenge. The American Civil Liberties Union (ACLU) filed suit against the ban on the grounds that the decision to end one's own

'CARBON MONOXIDE LEAVES THE CORPSE LOOKING GOOD, IT GIVES YOUR CORPSE A LOVELY, ROSY GLOW'

Below: *Fieger staves off reporters and Kevorkian manages a smile after being bailed from a police station on a charge of assisting in a suicide.*

life is an individual right and protected by the US constitution. 'The state has no business dictating an intensely private decision', the ACLU argued. In May 1993, an appeals court agreed, and struck down the law, concluding: 'This court cannot envisage a more fundamental right than the right to self-determination.'

One of the assisted suicides Kevorkian conducted just prior to the law's inception was that of Hugh Gale, a 70-year-old with emphysema and heart disease, who died in his living room with his wife by his side after breathing carbon monoxide. Right-to-life advocates claim they found a document in the garbage that may have indicated that Gale changed his mind at the last minute and wanted desperately to live.

ANOTHER DEATH

The document, called a Final Action Form, and reportedly signed by Kevorkian, claims that Gale asked that the mask be taken off after less than one minute, but then changed his mind again and asked that the gas be continued. After about 20 minutes, with nasal oxygen continuing, the mask was replaced over his nose and mouth, and he again pulled the clip off the crimped tubing. 'In about 30-35 seconds, he again flushed, became agitated with moderate hyperpnea (rapid or deep breathing) and immediately after saying "Take it off!" once again, he fell into unconsciousness. The mask was then left in place...Heartbeat was undetectable about three minutes after last breath'.

Originally, Prosecutor Carl Marlinga said if the document proved authentic, it suggested that death was involuntary and that at the last minute the patient changed his mind,' and charges would be filed against Kevorkian. But Gale's wife, Cheryl, says her husband did not want to stop the suicide process, as did their son, Hugh Jnr., who praised Kevorkian. 'He's really gone out on a limb and look what he's going through', said Hugh. 'Either he's a raving lunatic or he's very strongly committed to helping people. I'm thankful my dad's suffering was finally ended'. Kevorkian's attorney, Geoffrey Fieger, angrily claimed the document had been faked by right-to-life activists who staunchly oppose the doctor's work. 'At some

Above: *Publicity-hound Kevorkian gets a last-minute once-over before he goes on air in Detroit.*

KEVORKIAN KNOWS FIRST HAND THE TRAGEDY OF WATCHING A LOVED ONE WASTE AWAY FROM A DEBILITATING DISEASE

point you got to stop responding to this lunacy', said Fieger. 'A bunch of right-wing Christian nuts again called Dr Kevorkian a murderer. It's laughable'. Eventually, the prosecutor declined to press murder charges.

Kevorkian, a tart-tongued, grey-haired man of 64, who grew up in Pontiac, Michigan, knows first hand the tragedy of watching a loved one waste away from a debilitating disease. 'Our mother suffered from cancer', said his sister, Margo Janus. 'I saw the ravages right up to the end. Her mind was sound, but her body was gone. My brother's option would have been more moral than all the Demerol (pain killers) that they poured into her, to the point that her body was all black and blue from the needle marks. She was in a coma, and she weighed only 70 pounds. Even then I said to the doctor, "This isn't right, to keep her on I.V.", but he shrugged his shoulder and said, "I'm bound by my oath to do that".'

Who knows what effect that horrible experience had on the young Kevorkian, but it is known that while he was studying at the University of Michigan Medical School, his morbid fascination with pathology first came to the fore. He was engrossed with the history of autopsies, and says the ancient Greeks performed assisted suicides thousands of years ago. When he became a doctor, he says he didn't set out to be a medical heretic, but one night that all changed when he was doing his late-night rounds. I was making rounds one night and there was this woman who was dying of liver cancer', he recalled many years later. 'It was horrible, her belly was swollen up so much her skin was almost transparent, you could see the veins. She was in horrible, intractable pain. It looked like she was pleading for death with her eyes. But we couldn't give her that. We had to keep her going, prolonging the agony. It was cruel and barbaric'.

Given the long history of assisted suicide in ancient cultures, Kevorkian says 'I'm not early, I'm late'. And he claims that in the not too distant future 'medicide' as he calls it will be legal. 'You cannot fight changing mores'.

Indeed, this is already happening to some extent in the United States, and Kevorkian has found allies within the growing right-to-die movement, which is being fanned by America's mounting opposition to technology that extends lives regardless of the pain involved for the patient, or the suffering for the family. 'If we are free people at all, then we must be free to choose the manner of our death', said Derek Humphry, Executive Director of the Hemlock Society. But even Humphry agrees with euthanasia opponents when he says Kevorkian is not the right man for the job. 'He's a strange bird', he said. 'A zealot' Indeed, during the hearing into Adkins' death, Kevorkian acted as his own lawyer and his frequent arrogant outbursts – including

*Below: **The front page of the New York Post** after the **grim reaper claims another human being.***

numerous swear words – supported those who insist the doctor isn't the right man to play God.

THE GHOUL'S SIDE OF THE STORY

Kevorkian, who says he gets about 200 letters a year from people asking him to help them die, says he is not a ghoul, but a man who is devoted to ending suffering. 'These are not happy moments', he said. 'The ending of a human life can never be a good moment. I will help a suffering human being at the right time when the patient's

AUTO SATURDAY
Special car buyer's bonanza inside

NEW YORK POST
SPORTS EXTRA

SATURDAY, MAY 16/SUNDAY, MAY 17, 1992 / Rain, mid 60s today, cloudy, mid 50s tonight / Details, Page 2 ★   40¢ in New York City 50¢ elsewhere

Another patient kills self with Kevorkian's 'advice'

DR. DEATH AT IT AGAIN

Jack Kevorkian, the "Suicide Doc," did not assist in the "self-administered carbon monoxide" death of a woman yesterday, his lawyer said. PAGE 4

Associated Press

ALEXANDER'S CLOSES
And a piece of New York dies with it: Pages 2 & 3

condition warrants it, despite anything else. That's what a doctor should do. All these silly religious nuts. All these people, they don't care about suffering humanity. They hate what I am doing. They don't talk about suffering patients. If I were Satan and I was helping a suffering person end his life, would that make a difference? Any person who does this is going to have an image problem'.

THE DEPRESSION FACTOR

Some medical experts claim that Kevorkian is killing people because they are depressed, and not because of their disease. 'What he is doing is killing people because they are depressed', said James Boop, an Indiana attorney. 'But depression is curable. He takes absolutely no account of this. He's not qualified to diagnose depression nor is he qualified to treat it'.

Yet Kevorkian remains steadfast, claiming that in some cases, the severe depression

Above: *Kevorkian after his arrest and bail for assisting in the suicide of Thomas Hyde Jnr.*

SOME DOCTORS ADMIT THAT KEVORKIAN IS VIEWED BY MANY AMERICANS AS A REASONABLE ALTERNATIVE TO MODERN MEDICINE

his patients feel can sometimes justify suicide. 'You can't dope up a quadriplegic', he told an interviewer. 'There's no pain to alleviate, but the anguish in the head is immense, especially after five or ten years of lying on your back looking up at the ceiling'. Moreover, he claims many of his critics have no idea of what these people are going through, and would gladly meet them in debate. 'I will argue with them if they will allow themselves to be strapped into a wheelchair for 72 hours so they can't move, and they are catheterised and they are placed on the toilet and fed and bathed. Then they can sit in a chair and debate with me.'

Even some doctors who disagree with his methods reluctantly admit, however, that Kevorkian is viewed by many Americans as a reasonable alternative to modern medicine, which can be cold and uncaring. Professor George Annas, from the prestigious Boston University School of Medicine, told reporters: 'First we don't tell them they are dying. We do tell them their diagnosis and all the alternative treatments available. But we don't tell them their prognosis. We tell them, "You have cancer, and you can have surgery, radiation, chemotherapy, or all three together, or even any two". We don't tell them that no matter what we do, it's almost certain they are going to die soon'. Moreover, Annas says too many doctors simply ignore their patients' pain. 'Up to 90 per cent of patients die in too much pain. Some doctors actually argue that their patients are going to get addicted. But they can't have thought about it for more than two minutes to say something like that. The vast majority simply don't know how to treat pain, and they don't think that it is important. They want to cure the person. Death is still seen as the enemy. And that's what Kevorkian throws in their face. What he says is, "Some people want death, and I am going to give it to them".'

THE MORAL POSITION

Kevorkian is so adamant about his moral position, that even while the ACLU challenge to the Michigan ban against assisted-suicide wended it way through the courts, he was there for his 16th suicide. That came on 16 May 1993, when Ronald Mansur, a real estate man with bone and lung cancer, killed himself using carbon monoxide. Police found the body – after an 'anonymous' call – at the real estate office. 'He was in hell', a long time friend said. 'He would cry on the phone'.

Kevorkian was promptly arrested, but stung by earlier charges and arrests, refused to tell authorities what had happened. He would only allow that he had indeed been present and had watched as Mansur ended his life by inhaling carbon monoxide. However, he offered no details about his role in the death. After he was finger-printed, Kevorkian was released. While local officials contemplated charging him yet again, the Michigan law outlawing assisted suicide was overturned. They have no choice but to drop all charges.

'We think the statute violated people's privacy rights', commented an ACLU spokesman when the decision to overturn the ban was announced.

At the time of writing, Mansur was Kevorkian's last assisted suicide. But now

Below: *Accused of murder in the deaths of two women, the strain appears to be beginning to tell on Kevorkian.*

that the law has been struck down, it is probably only a matter of time before his name again surfaces in connection with the suicide of another gravely ill person.

Whether he is indeed a ghoulish real-life incarnation of Dr Frankenstein or a medical crusader cannot be fully answered at this time. Only history can decide for sure how he will be remembered, or what effect his foray into hitherto forbidden territory will mean for future generations.

THEODOR MORELL
Hitler's Doctor

The Third Reich's leading quack doctor Theodor Morell dispensed an extensive pharmacopeia of comical and sinister medicines to many leading members of the Nazi hierarchy. His main patient was Hitler himself.

In the pantheon of Nazi leaders there were many sycophants and flunkies, each one of them jostling for power at the elbow of their beloved Fuehrer, Adolf Hitler. There was Heinrich Himmler, the former chicken farmer who became the head of the most infamous elite guard of all time, the SS There was fat Hermann Goering, corpulent, flamboyant, but with a heart blacker than coal. There was Martin Bormann, the sinister party secretary who perhaps more than any general or Nazi party official knew the inner workings of Hitler's twisted mind.

But there was one other, less visible member of the Nazi coterie whose power derived not from some high office or exalted title, but from the well-being of the Fuehrer himself. His name was Dr Theodor Morell and he served his leader as personal physician right up until his suicide at the end of the war. Like many other doctors of the Third Reich, Theodor Morell sold out his Hippocratic Oath by keeping alive mankind's vilest tormentor. He pumped the Nazi dictator full with drugs of dubious merit and poisoned his reasoning with tales of semi-mystical quackery. In a way, Morell may well have deserved a medal for his services – from the Allies. For it's widely recognised that he was a hack of the highest order, an unskilled, semi-literate buffoon whose potions probably served to weaken Adolf Hitler rather than strengthen him. Theodor Morell stands alone in the chronicles of wicked doctors as a man who believed what he was doing was right, when everyone else in the gangster milieu

which was Hitler's court saw him as the impostor he was. Only the fear of offending Der Fuehrer stopped them from ever speaking out against such witchcraft as performed by the good 'Herr Doktor'.

A post-war interrogation of a Nazi official produced this very unflattering portrait of the physician that others who were in Hitler's inner circle dubbed Dr Feel Good: 'He was portly, very obese, cringing in his manner to Hitler and others in the immediate circle of the leader.

'He was inarticulate in speech, gross in manner and known by all as a quack. Reichsmarshall Hermann Goering called him "Herr Reich Injection Master" because

Above: *Heinrich Himmler, leader of the SS, who was intensely jealous of Dr Theodor Morell's closeness to Adolf Hitler.*

Opposite: *Dr Theodor Morell, chief physician of Adolf Hitler.*

Above: *Hermann Goering, humbled at Nuremberg. Like all top Nazis, he paid lip service to the powerful Morell.*

Opposite Top Left: *Crown Prince Willy, son of Kaiser Wilhelm, was one of Herr Doktor's first patients.*

Opposite Far Right: *The compulsive, obsessive, maniacally evil Adolf Hitler became entranced by Morell.*

It was in the early 1930s, just at the time that Nazism was beginning to grow like a bacillus in the body politic of German society, that Morell began his medical career. He started as a ship's doctor on cruise liners going to America, but soon decided that going into business for himself was the only sure way to make money – and money was far more important to Morell than any lofty notions about serving his fellow man. He practised medicine in Munich for a time before returning to Berlin where he opened a surgery on the Kurfurstendamm, the central thoroughfare of the old Imperial city that was comparable in status and charm to the Champs Elysees in Paris. Above the door to his practice he hung the sign: 'Dr. T. Morell, Practitioner in Medicine, specialising in Skin and Venereal Diseases'. A short time as an intern had taught him that sexually transmitted diseases were rife and that people – many of them rich and famous – were willing to pay handsome sums to be treated quietly, discreetly – and quickly.

MORELL'S WAY IN

One of his patients was the former German Crown Prince, known to a generation of British servicemen during the Great War as 'Little Willy.' Willy's patronage – he was actually treated for a nervous condition, not for any sexual infection – ensured Morell the entree to society that he craved so much. Soon they were beating a path to his door, the rich and famous, wealthy and influential. And among the patients were the vanguard of the new society that was rapidly taking over all aspects of life in Germany – the Nazis.

Morell, blessed with an innate ability to cast his lot in with those he perceived to be on the winning side, soon built up a clientele of Nazi party officials and functionaries. Word was circulating in the highest echelons of the party that, in Morell, there had come to Berlin a sorcerer capable of performing miracles upon the human body. In actuality, he offered treatment that was available in every public hospital – except, like the huckster he was, he dressed it up as some kind of miracle 'breakthrough.' He routinely bought up the collections of medicine bottles and jars of old pharmaceutical companies and placed them in his office to give himself the aura of an alchemist!

it seemed to all who came into contact with him that he could cure the ills of the world with a few well placed hypodermic syringes'.

Little is known of Morell's early life in Berlin where he was born to merchant parents. But he was a diligent student who passed entrance examinations to the city's medical school where he applied himself for seven long years of study before qualifying as a physician. He then travelled to study at the Pasteur Institute in Paris where the great Russian bacteriologist Ilya Mechnikov mesmerised him in studies about bacterial infection, immunisation and the spread of communicable diseases.

It was in 1935, with the sickness of a photographer called Heinrich Hoffmann, that Morell came to the attention of the nation's Fuehrer. Hoffmann, the court photographer, had caught a chill in the chilly mountain air of the Berghof, Hitler's Bavarian retreat, which had grown into pneumonia. Several highly placed Nazi officials insisted that Hoffman be treated by the miraculous Dr Morell, now ensconced as the toast of Berlin. With Hoffmann when he came for treatment was a young woman called Eva Braun – fresh faced, lively, beautiful even. He could not know then that she would die with her beloved Fuehrer in the ruins of Berlin in just ten years time.

THE ROUTE TO THE TOP

Again using standard medicines of the day, Morell was able to treat Hoffmann successfully. But in him – and in Eva Braun, the friend who accompanied him – Morell had found the person with direct access to the most powerful man on the European continent. Soon would follow the top functionaries of the party – and in their wake, Adolf Hitler himself.

Albert Speer, the party architect and a man recognised as probably the most sane of the clique which surrounded Hitler, fell

under Morell's spell first. He had his reservations, but felt that he ought to go for fear of offending the Fuehrer's top officials. Suffering from intestinal disorders, largely brought on by overwork in designing the new capital 'Germania' which Hitler wanted to call Berlin, he sought Morell out early in 1936. Later he would' write; 'My stomach and circulation rebelled against an irrational working rhythm and adjustment to Hitler's abnormal habits. I called at Morell's private office and after a superficial examination he prescribed for me his intestinal bacteria drugs, dextrose, vitamins and hormone tablets.

A SECOND OPINION

'For safety's sake I afterwards had a thorough examination by Professor von Bergmann, the specialist in internal medicine at Berlin University. I was found not to be suffering from any organic trouble, as Morell had stated, but only from nervous symptoms caused by overwork. I then slowed my pace down as best I could. The symptoms abated. To avoid offending Hitler and the others I carefully pretended that I

*Above: **Heinrich Hoffmann, Hitler's court photographer, with his wife and stepdaughter at Nuremberg.***

*Opposite Top: **At the court of the Fuehrer, Morell (arrowed) stands behind the Nazi elite.***

*Opposite Bottom: **The portly Morell shakes the hand of his Messiah as he receives the hero's award of the Knight's Cross.***

HITLER WAS A CHRONIC HYPOCHONDRIAC THROUGHOUT HIS LIFE, SEEKING DEMONS WHERE NONE EXISTED

---

was following Morell's instructions to the letter. And since my health improved, I became for a time Morell's showpiece'. Speer did not dare write these words until the 1960s when he was freed from a 20-year jail term imposed at Nuremberg. He, an intellectual, remained silent for fear of offending the star-struck Fuehrer.

THE LONG-SUFFERING LEADER

Hitler is believed to have first visited him in the same year as Speer, although such records were lost in the bombing which reduced Berlin to little more than brickdust. Hitler suffered massively from intestinal trouble throughout his life, probably brought on by the mustard and phosgene gassings he suffered as a soldier at the front in the Great War. A company runner charged with getting messages to and from the front line while under fire, he finished the war as a temporarily blinded casualty of the conflict. On top of his stomach ailments, at the time he saw Morell, he was suffering from a foot rash – probably nothing more than athlete's foot – but Morell saw the opportunity to bamboozle the impressionable Fuehrer with nonsensical twaddle. He said the stomach problems and his foot rash were linked, that one was a symptom of the other because Der Fuehrer had lost vital 'intestinal flora' as a result of inhaling gas during the war. As Hitler lay on his examination table, the Gestapo guards situated just feet away, Morell pumped him with a drug he invented called 'Multflor' which consisted of intestinal bacteria gathered from Bulgarian bulls! Then he gave him several more injections of vitamins, hormones, phosphorus, dextrose and a cortisone-type drug.

A CURE FOR HITLER

Within days Hitler found himself cured of both ailments – but it's highly unlikely that Morell's potions had anything to do with his recovery. Hitler was a chronic hypochondriac throughout his life. Psychologists in the post war years have analysed his condition ad infinitum, coming to the conclusion that he sought demons where none existed and then celebrated like a demented child when they were banished. With his foot rash gone and his stomach

pains vanquished, he proclaimed: 'Nobody has ever told me before, in such clear and precise terms, exactly what was wrong with me. His method of cure is so logical that I have the greatest confidence in him. I shall follow his prescriptions to the letter and shall urge all those who are dearest to me to place their health and well-being into his gifted hands.'

Hitler suddenly took on the living habits of a Franciscan monk. Used to eating sausage and drinking beer, and sometimes a little of the Bavarian wine called Frankenwein, he now became a teetotaller and vegetarian. He hired a vegetarian cook, Frau Manzialy, who was to stay with him until the end, even preparing his last meal before suicide in the bunker in 1945. He banished the heavy chocolate cakes and Linzertorte that had graced his tables since his earliest days and cut out the whipped cream which used to drown out his rich coffee. 'How lucky!' he proclaimed to Himmler at a private audience, 'How lucky that I was able to meet Morell. He has saved my life'. The good doctor was well on his way to beatification from the highest priest of Nazism.

*Above: **The portly Morell on the cover of a pro-Nazi medical journal.***

HIS WIFE WATCHED HIM CHANGE INTO A BROODING, SILENT MONSTER. HE WOULD LOOK AT HER WITH THOSE EYES...

Patronage from Hitler opened many more doors and brought the doctor great riches from various Reich ministries, which he was careful to salt away in bank accounts in Zurich and Geneva. He patented a flea powder for use by the Wehrmacht which was ordered by the ton. Examination of it after the war proved it to be 90 percent chalk with a smattering of household insecticide. He marketed pills which promised an increase in potency and they were bought by the bucketful by the S.S., which was in the market for fertile young men to breed blond, blue-eyed babies with Aryan maidens for the 1000 year Reich. There is no evidence to suggest they were any more effective than ground rhinoceros horn. And there were the high and mighty of Nazism, each one keen to be treated –

and to be seen to be treated – by the Fuehrer's favourite.

On 3 September 1939, the day that Britain declared war on Germany over her invasion two days earlier of Poland, a young, infatuated British maiden called Unity Mitford shot herself on a park bench in the middle of Munich's English Garden. Infatuated by Hitler since his early days, she suddenly seemed to have had a massive conversion back to reality when she saw that the end result of the flags and the banners and the massed 'Sieg Heils' translated into conquest and war and death. Hitler was beside himself with anguish – he had great affection for the upper-class English beauty whom he nurtured because of her fawning admiration. He summoned Morell to treat her in a luxury government clinic, to give her the best care possible. Soon Unity Mitford, lying in a coma, resembled a pin cushion due to the myriad drugs and serums he pumped into her. In eight months of continuous care her condition did not change one iota. Finally, in May 1940, Hitler sent her back to England via Switzerland. Doctors who received her back in Britain were appalled by the treatment she had received – they thought that the injections had actually accelerated her ill health rather than helping to cure it. She died in 1948 – a victim of Morell's hocuspocus as much as the bullet that she tried to end her life with.

FEARS OF A POPULATION

It remains a conundrum whether Morell really believed the potions he peddled were effective in fighting illness, or whether he was a true cynic who knew he was merely cashing in on the foibles and fears of a population looking for life's elixir. With hindsight, it is almost certain that it was the latter. As the heady years of victory in the war turned into the bitter years of defeat, Morell was called upon increasingly to administer to Hitler an ever-more baffling cocktail of drugs. Included among them was a serum derived from bulls testicles, mixed with the hormones from young salamander lizards! Others included: Brom-Nervacit, consisting of potassium bromide, sodium barbitone and aminopyrinen, all mixed together and injected into the abdomen to promote rest; camomile enemas, sympatol which included ethanol tartrate to promote an increased heartbeat and Glyconorm, a mixture of enzymes to ease digestion and reduce Hitler's chronic flatulence.

There was septoid, for respiratory infections and hardened arteries, vitamins in a cocktail he called Intelan to stimulate his declining appetite, Eukadol, to stop his spasms and Omnadin, an animal-fat based serum devised to ward off colds. Any doctor examining this shopping list of quackery now would shake his head in astonishment and incredulity.

As the war raged on Hitler's moods and his general health condition deteriorated with each passing defeat. His monstrous rages were – several of his entourage believed – brought on because of the massive amounts of drugs Morell continued to pump into his weakened frame. General Heinz Guderian, his most brilliant Blitzkrieg tactician, saw the Fuehrer after he had received a dozen Morell injections before breakfast. His animal rage knew no bounds when Guderian tried to point out to him the hopelessness on a certain battle front. The general recalled: 'He raised his fist, his cheeks were flushed with rage and his whole body was trembling. He stood in front of me, beside himself with fury and having literally lost all control. After each outburst he would suddenly stride up and down the carpet then suddenly stop before me and hurl his next accusation in my face. He was almost screaming, his eyes popping out of his head, the veins standing out on his temples'.

After July 1944 and the attempt on his life at his Wolf's Lair command centre in Rastenburg, east Prussia, Hitler went on his final downhill. The bomb planted beneath a map table by a German officer involved in the plot to rid Germany of her greatest bane killed several high-ranking officers but spared the life of the Fuehrer. Within hours Morell was flown to Rastenburg where he administered no fewer than 15 injections within 40 minutes of arrival!

POISONOUS PILLS

A physician called Karl Brandt, who had attended to Hitler when Morell was not available, seems to have been one of the few – perhaps the only individual – who had the courage to speak with him about the effects of the 'medicine' being prescribed by Morell. He tested some ear pills that he was giving Hitler for damage sustained in the Rastenburg explosion – and found them to contain harmful levels of poison. Brandt

AS THE WAR RAGED ON, HITLER'S MOODS AND HIS GENERAL HEALTH CONDITION DETERIORATED WITH EACH DEFEAT

MORELL ADMINISTERED NO FEWER THAN 15 INJECTIONS TO HITLER WITHIN 40 MINUTES OF ARRIVING TO TREAT HIM

Below: *One table away from his master, Morell is close by as Hitler entertains the top echelon of the Nazi party.*

attempted to broach the subject with Hitler, backed up with the findings of an independent university researcher who concurred that Morell's potions were indeed harming his life. Hitler would have none of it. He told him: 'You can say what you will about Morell. He is and always will be my personal physician. I have full confidence in him – he is the only man of medicine who has ever fully understood me'. What Morell understood quite clearly was the hypochondria that afflicted Hitler, a condition that turned to massive paranoia and psychosis as the war ground on.

A DIRTY QUACK

Another person close to Hitler, Eva Braun, had initially believed in the quackery but later became repelled by him. She was disgusted by Morell's personal habits, his 'pig-sty' office and dirty fingernails. During quiet moments she too tried to wean the man she loved from dependency on Morell's elixirs. She too failed.

IN THE BERLIN BUNKER MORELL CARRIED OUT HIS LAST DEMENTED PRACTICES ON HITLER'S WRETCHED FRAME

Below: *The doomed Unity Mitford (second right) at an Anglo-German Fellowship Meeting in 1938. With her are her parents (left) and Dr Fitz-Randolph, a German embassy official.*

Late in 1944 Morell drew up an entire diet for the Fuehrer based on mushrooms. He convinced Hitler that mushrooms were rich in the vitamins he needed and even persuaded Hitler to part with millions of Reichsmarks for a greenhouse at Berchtesgarten to grow them in. But Hitler was never to return to his summer eyrie as defeat loomed ever nearer and the glasshouse remained as another folly to yet another madcap scheme in which he indulged the crazy doctor.

It was in the phantasmagorical, troglodyte world of the Berlin bunker, the subterranean bolthole for Hitler and the last remaining acolytes of his crumbling empire, that Morell carried out his last demented practices upon the wretched frame of the now desperately-ill Fuehrer. His left side shook uncontrollably, his right leg, damaged in the Rastenburg blast, dragged uselessly behind him. He frothed at the mouth in terrifying rages that could last up to 30 minutes – and then slumped, drained, in his chair, staring blankly ahead,

oblivious to all around. All, that is, except Morell. In his remaining time left on this earth Hitler requested and received ever larger dosages of the drugs prescribed by his physician. Karl Brandt was in the bunker too, despite his earlier attempts to put Hitler off Morell's kind of care-giving. He treated Hitler in the final weeks while Morell slept, or if he needed something straightforward, like an aspirin or tranquilisers for sleep.

THE END DRAWS NEAR

Brandt was appalled at the human guinea-pig that he believed Morell had turned the national leader into. He confronted him in the surgery of the bunker one afternoon, six weeks before Hitler ended his life. He told him: 'His face is pallid, his eyes are weak, clouded, he cannot stop shaking and he can hardly stand during conference. I put it to you that you are doing the Fuehrer more harm than good'.

But Morell, who was also doling out massive quantities of his moonshine medicine to assorted party officials, soldiers and SS bigwigs sheltering in the bunker before the final 'Gotterdammerung', laughed in his face. He was incredibly wealthy, thanks

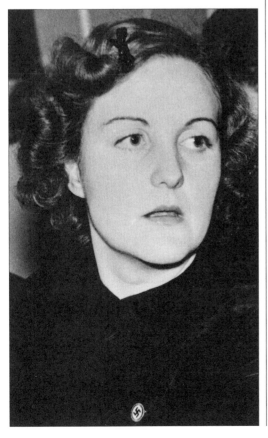

Above: *Dr Karl Brandt, another of Hitler's physicians, appearing before an allied tribunal.*

Left: *Unity Mitford, the English aristocrat who fell under the Nazis' spell. Hitler placed her under the care of Morell.*

HITLER REQUESTED AND RECEIVED EVER LARGER DOSAGES OF THE DRUGS PRESCRIBED BY HIS PHYSICIAN

---

to his secret bank accounts, he enjoyed the patronage of Hitler and he was not guilty of any war crimes. He knew that he, at least, would walk out alive from the mousetrap of Berlin, no matter who arrived to conquer the city first.

But to pay back the insolent doctor he was instrumental in whispering poison into Hitler's ear. Brandt, he told him, had sent his wife and child into an area of Germany that was about to be overrun by allied forces. This was tantamount to treason for the deranged Hitler and he ordered Brandt's summary court martial followed by execution. Brandt was spared only by the direct intervention of S.S. chief Himmler, but the episode proved who remained closest to Hitler right up until the final moments.

Above: *The bed in the Fuhrer's shelter, where Hitler and Eva Braun are alleged to have poisoned themselves.*

Opposite Top: *Morell, grinning behind the Fuehrer, in Poland in 1939.*

Opposite Bottom: *Morell receives a War Work cross for devotion to science from an unsmiling SS aide.*

THE MILLIONS MORELL MADE FROM FLEA POWDER AND FROM TREATING GENERALS AND MOVIE STARS WERE NEVER SPENT

One of his most diabolical acts of the whole war came two days before the Fuehrer and Eva Braun were to commit suicide. Magda Goebbels, unable to live with her beloved Fuehrer gone, asked him for poison to end her life and those of her six children. Morell, who had long ago forgotten the ethics of his Hippocratic Oath, supplied her with the poison. All died in the charnel house, including Goebbels himself, and all were cremated outside the bunker, in shell holes caused by the Russian artillery that ground the once beautiful capital city into ruins.

On 20 April, Hitler's birthday, the leader surfaced one more time above ground to decorate some fanatical Hitler Youths with Iron Crosses. The youngsters, who had grown up only on cinematic and poster images of the Fuehrer, were shocked at his ghostly appearance. Stooped, shaking uncontrollably, he patted them on the cheeks as if they were his own sons, before scurrying back underground with a man clutching a doctor's bag following close behind him. Dr Theodor Morell was about

to give his last consultation for the individual who had caused the deaths of some 50 million people in the global war.

After injecting Hitler with vitamin K and bacterial enzymes for one last time, he was told to flee the city along with an assortment of secretaries and minor officials. Morell, his eyes gleaming with the thought of untouched loot awaiting him in Switzerland, did not need to be told twice to go. While he was certainly cringing to Hitler, scheming in his methods to stay close by him, he was never a Nazi zealot. Dr Morell only ever worked towards one end in his treatment of Hitler and the other Nazi fatcats – the betterment of Dr Morell. Clutching his assorted potions he fled the bunker and headed west, away from the advancing Russians.

But fate played a just trick on the evil old quack. Just when he thought he was safe, having been captured by Americans and placed in an internment camp, he died in May 1948 from TB and heart failure. The millions he earned from flea powder, from treating generals, movie stars, the

Crown Prince and Hitler himself, were never spent.

Dr Peter Masterson, an American historian who has made a study of Morell, said: 'It was a fitting end to a man who betrayed the very ethics of medicine. While he might not have carried out medical experiments like some Nazi doctors, he was, nevertheless, a rogue and a scoundrel who, some believe, deserved to hang for supplying the poison which snuffed out the lives of the Goebbels children.

WEAKENING HITLER

'But in a curious way perhaps it is the allies who should thank Dr. Morell for turning Adolf Hitler into a wretched shell of a creature, someone who was drastically unable to prosecute the conduct of the war due to his weakened state.

'History's judgement is that Morell was nothing more than a confidence man who used a stethoscope and pills to con his patients into believing he was something more than mortal'.

KARL BABOR
Royal Doctor of Death

In World War II, Karl Babor had been an SS doctor at Treblinka and Auschwitz concentration camps, but after the fall of Germany he slipped through Allied hands and made a new life in Ethiopia, where he became a physician at the imperial court. For years he lived well, but his past was determined to catch up with him.

In Addis Ababa, the old colonial-style capital of Ethiopia, they called him Herr Doktor. Herr Doktor had come from the old world to this new frontier where his courtly charm and urbane ways had marked him out as a man of culture and distinction. His manners were not lost on the Emperor Haile Selassie or members of his family who took him under their wing. Soon he was doctor by appointment to the court of

Above: *His Imperial Majesty Haile Selassie, emperor of Ethiopia, who gave sanctuary to Dr Babor.*

Left: *Addis Ababa, which Babor came to call home, was vastly different to the Europe he left behind.*

Opposite: *Karl Babor, camp doctor of the Gross Rosen concentration camp, fled to Africa.*

HERR DOKTOR SPOKE TO
THOSE HE MET ON THE
COCKTAIL CIRCUIT OF HIS
DESIRE TO AID HIS
FELLOW MAN

Left: *Josef Mengele, the camp doctor of Auschwitz, who was supreme arbiter of life and death over millions.*

Below: *The camp gates at Auschwitz bearing the hollow legend, 'Work Brings Freedom'.*

the Emperor. Herr Doktor, German by birth, had come to the east African country in the aftermath of the Second World War. To those he met on the cocktail circuit or in the missions he spoke of his desire to aid his fellow man. Oh yes, he could have stayed in Germany and made a great deal of money in private practice, he frequently said. But his calling was here, where he was most needed. Not only did he look after the health of the Emperor and his brood, he also donated his free time to the Menelik Hospital, a state-of-the-art institution equipped with first-class machinery and medicines given to the nation by the Soviet Union. He was a dark blond man with sad eyes, eyes which were rumoured to have gazed upon much sorrow. Indeed they had – and the sorrow was caused by the brain and hands and heart of their owner. The good doctor was none other

years at the Vienna University medical centre. But six out of seven was good enough for the Nazis. They were always seeking intellectuals, scholars and doctors to their ranks to give credibility to what was an otherwise absurd band of misfits and deadbeats. Babor fitted the mould well.

DEADLY VISITS

When the concentration camp network was assembled throughout Germany – and later in the conquered lands – Babor found himself assigned to many centres as medical officer and later camp doctor. On the side of the living he innoculated a few SS men, stitched a few wounds, punctured a few abscesses. On the side of the dead he moved like a grim blond reaper. A visit from the good doctor to places like Dachau and Buchenwald meant death – usually by an injection through the heart. He killed to collect human tissue for bizarre experiments that had no scientific value. He killed because he wanted to examine brains for mental disorders. Chiefly, though, he killed because he enjoyed it. His most notorious reign was at Treblinka, man for man, child for child, the worst death camp of them all. Treblinka, near Warsaw, was in full service for the Reich for a little over a year and in that time some 700,000 people were executed. There were only 40 survivors at the war's end. Just how many Dr Babor snuffed out with his syringe and his scalpel will never be fully known.

THE HUMAN ABATTOIR

But after Treblinka was closed down in 1943, with the more efficient, and still more deadly, Auschwitz camp going on stream as the premier human abattoir, Babor found himself at the Grossrosen concentration camp near Breslau – later Wroclaw – in Poland. Here there would be a man who could bear witness to what he had done – someone who was to become the conscience, the soul and the avenger for all the victims of Nazism, wherever and however they had died. Simon Wiesenthal was in Grossrosen in 1944, the time of the Third Reich's greatest defeats on the battlefield. But they still had time for their war against the innocent and unarmed, those who could not fight back. Wiesenthal, who

than Karl Babor and his trade in the war was mass murder.

Dr Karl Babor was one of that select band of Nazi war criminals for whom there must undoubtedly be reserved a special place in hell. Like Josef Mengele, the demented medic of Auschwitz who performed bizarre experiments on twins as he sought to produce a master race of blue-eyed, blond supermen for his Fuehrer, Babor conveniently ditched his Hippocratic Oath for the pursuit of pain and suffering. A fervent member of the Nazi Party since the early days of Hitler, he later joined the SS where he knew that his medical training could be put to good use. He was not even a fully qualified doctor when he joined the black order; he had served six of seven

*Above: **Vienna, the Austrian capital, home of the woman who would play a vital part in tracing him.***

MENGELE PERFORMED BIZARRE EXPERIMENTS ON TWINS AS HE SOUGHT TO PRODUCE A MASTER RACE FOR THE FUEHRER

Above: *Scenes from the Warsaw Ghetto uprising. Hitler fuelled the crematoria of his death camps with victims like these.*

'THE FAINT SMELL OF BURNED FLESH IS IN THE AIR. THE YEAR IS 1944. THE TIME MIGHT BE ANY TIME OF DAY OR NIGHT'

THE CREMATORIUM IS SERVED BY A RUSSIAN PRISONER CALLED BLACK IVAN. FEW PRISONERS SEE HIM WHILE THEY ARE ALIVE

has devoted his life to bringing to justice the perpetrators of the Holocaust, said in his memoirs: 'There is a certain scene on the stage of my memory I shall never forget. It is a small room with dark grey walls. The entrance is on the left side. The exit is in the middle of the back wall. The exit leads straight into the crematorium of the Grossrosen concentration camp.

HORRIFIC MEMORIES

'On the otherwise empty stage is a small table with several syringes and a few bottles filled with a colourless liquid. There is one chair. The faint smell of burned flesh is in the air. The year is 1944. The time might be any time of day or night. This is the antechamber of the Grossrosen crematorium. There are no gas chambers in this concentration camp. The crematorium is served by a Russian prisoner called Black Ivan, because constant smoke has blackened his face and his hands. Ivan looks really terrible, but few inmates ever see him while they are still alive. By the time Black Ivan gets to them they no longer know any fear.

He carries their ashes to a nearby field where the camp gardeners plant vegetables for the camp kitchen, for fertilizer. I know all this because I was a prisoner assigned to work in the vegetable garden.

'Now a young man stands in the middle of the room. He wears a white doctor's coat on top of his SS uniform. Most prisoners have seen the young "doctor" before; he is a member of the "selection committee". When the transports arrive, the prisoners are ordered to walk down the ramp and stand at attention at a small table. The "doctor" at the table moves his index finger to the right – life – or to the left, death. An SS man makes a sign on a list. The "doctor" takes a second look at the human wreck before him. "Open your mouth! Wider!" He nods. The prisoner is not entirely worthless. Three gold fillings. The "doctor" marks a big black cross with a thick wet pencil on the prisoner's forehead. "*Abtreten!*" All marked people must register at the camp office. The gold fillings in

Above and Left: *A Russian Orthodox priest and a little boy from the Warsaw Ghetto. Both were enemies in the eyes of the SS and had to be exterminated like vermin.*

THE 'DOCTOR' MOVES HIS INDEX FINGER TO THE RIGHT – LIFE – OR TO THE LEFT, DEATH. AN SS MAN MAKES A SIGN ON A LIST

their mouths are registered in duplicate. They no longer own them but are permitted to use them while they're alive.

'Soon the prisoners directed to the left will stand again in front of the young man in the white medical coat. He is highly skilled at his job. He fills the syringe, tells the patient (who is stripped to his navel) to sit down on the chair. The patient is held by two SS men. The young man quickly steps in front of him, injects the lethal needle into his heart with a sharp thrust. The syringe contains phenolic acid.

DEADLY DOSES

'"Herr Doktor Babor" is well liked by his SS superiors, who call him Herr Doktor. "I always like to give them a little more than the lethal dose, just to be sure", he has told them. The "Doktor" is a very humane man. Sometimes prisoners are frightened when he administers the phenolic coup de grace, but they haven't got much time to think. Other patients are waiting. The bodies of the dead are speedily dragged out through the exit door. A little later people will see smoke come out of the chimney. How often had I seen the smoke come out of the chimney while I was working in the camp garden? It was only the will of God that I had not had to sit down on the chair in front of "Herr Doktor" Karl Babor'.

Babor was caught by the allies at the end of the war. But in the maelstrom of Europe, as the big fish were hunted down, many like him escaped. He spent several months in 1947 at the Landesgericht Prison in Vienna, but the evidence against him was judged 'insufficient' by allied war crimes hunters who were swamped with the monstrous details of what had occurred in occupied Europe during the war. The following year he resumed his studies at Vienna. After having despatched God knows how many souls to meet their maker during the war, he finally made it to being a doctor, swearing 'to serve all humanity' when he accepted his qualifications in the Great Hall of the University.

After an internship at a local hospital he moved to the Alpine town of Gmunden where he settled into the cosy life of a provincial doctor. But his past was already catching up with him. In 1952 allied hunters called on his parents' apartment in Vienna. They had had a special brief to track down personnel who worked at Treblinka. The awful details of the camp were now becoming clearer. His parents tipped him off and he vanished, fleeing to Africa with his wife Bobo and daughter Dagmar. There, in Ethiopia, where westerners and their medicine were always welcome, he inveigled his way into the royal family and became the doctor for other notables. But the memory of the war years and what he had done would never leave him. Slowly, surely, his conscience began to eat away at him like an incurable cancer.

ANIMAL BEHAVIOUR

At night came the nightmares. His daughter Dagmar would later recount how he howled at the moon before sloping off to the jungle to join the animals that he counted more as friends and comrades than any homo sapiens. Chief friend among these 'friends' were the crocodiles; perhaps because, like him, they were cold, calculating killers who had evolved perfectly since the age of the dinosaurs to survive. Unlike him, they had no conscience.

Opposite Top and Bottom: *The now overgrown ground of the Auschwitz extermination camp where three million people perished.*

HE HOWLED AT THE MOON BEFORE SLOPING OFF TO THE JUNGLE TO JOIN THE ANIMALS THAT HE COUNTED AS HIS FRIENDS

Below: *Human cargoes gave men like Babor ample supplies for his grotesque, twisted experiments.*

Wiesenthal, and other Nazi hunters, were desperate to find him but had no idea of his whereabouts. He was spirited out of Germany with the aid of the ODESSA – the organisation of former members of the SS – which set him up with false papers and necessary travel documents. But once in Ethiopia Dr Babor learned three things which made him decide that an alias was no longer necessary by the mid-1950s. One was the fact that Ethiopia was so beautifully remote, far and away safer than other Nazi boltholes like South Africa and Argentina. Two, he enjoyed the patronage of the royal family and was therefore never likely to be sent back to hang at the end of a rope. And three, after ten years Ethiopian law stated that no foreigner could be sent back to face criminal charges in his own land or any other. Dr Babor breathed easy, safe in the knowledge that he would never be called to account for the many thousands he murdered.

But Wiesenthal had a stroke of luck in 1963 when a woman he refers to only as Ruth came to see him in his Vienna office. She had a remarkable tale to tell – one that

BABOR BELIEVED HE COULD NEVER BE BROUGHT TO ACCOUNT FOR THE MANY THOUSANDS HE HAD MURDERED

Below: *Confronting the immediate past, civilians are brought in to see the evil work wrought by the Nazis at the just-liberated Auschwitz death camp.*

would eventually lead to Dr Babor's suicide. It was a fantastic story that Wiesenthal prepared himself to listen to, but then he had heard many fantastic stories before in his never-ending role as the conscience and the avenger for the murdered. Ruth, who was Jewish, had decided to answer an advertisement one day placed by an Austrian overseas who wished to correspond with a woman with a view to marriage. The advertisement was placed by Dr Babor.

LONG-DISTANCE LOVE

The first reply was not from Babor but from an engineer in Vienna who had placed the advertisement on Babor's behalf. It was, in fact, his father, and he wrote seeking a meeting with Ruth so he could better explain the kind of women that his son was looking for and the kind of life she could expect in Ethiopia should she choose to correspond with him and finally travel to meet him. She agreed to write to Dr Karl Babor at Box 1761, Addis Ababa, and see where things might lead from there. The irony of her, a Jewess, writing to this sadist

who had killed so many of her fellow Jews, was, for the moment, lost on her. All she knew was that he was a brilliant doctor to the royal household who had lost his wife and was now feeling lonely. Soon the letters exchanged between them were becoming more intense, more romantic. Dr Babor wrote in a courtly, old-fashioned way that appealed to the soft nature of Ruth. He even sent a picture of himself to her. The eyes, the manic eyes which were the last thing that so many of his wretched victims saw on this earth, appeared 'like whirlpools' to her. She was falling in love with him.

FLYING SOUTH

Soon Dr Babor proposed a trip to Ethiopia and even sent her over a ticket. 'Please come', he wrote. 'My dear Ruth: I so want to see you here and to kiss your hand like I have kissed it a thousand times in my letters. I am sure you will like it here'. She agreed to go and Dagmar, his daughter studying in Paris, flew to Vienna to travel with her as she had not seen her father in two years.

Above: *Israeli prime minister Rabin greets Beate Klarsefeld, the Nazi hunter, who exposed the freedom enjoyed in postwar Paris by a former top Gestapo official.*

> BABOR OFFERED HIS PENPAL NEITHER FOOD NOR DRINK. INSTEAD, HE TOOK HER TO THE JUNGLE TO SEE HIS 'FRIENDS'

Once in Ethiopia any illusions that Ruth may have had about settling down to live happily ever after with the man of her dreams were cruelly shattered. At the airport where Dr Babor met her and Dagmar she judged him cold, calculating, almost sinister. He greeted her with barely a flicker' of warmth. 'It was as if he was thinking of something all the time, something from a very long time ago', said Ruth. 'Something deeply troubled this man to his very soul'.

Upon arriving at his modest home Dr Babor did not offer his penpal either food or drink; instead he took her into the jungle, off to see his 'friends'. They were the crocodiles lying in the fetid, brown water of a river, their red eyes glinting in the setting rays of the sun. On the way back Dr Babor pulled up outside a local police station and stuck his fist into the jaws of a domesticated old lion outside. It bit him, and Ruth noticed with discomfort how he seemed to enjoy watching the blood trickle down his arm. Later he drove back to his home and offered Ruth nothing but a cold can of corned beef for supper while he went to bed. She realised that she was in a for a very strange, a very sinister time.

Above: *The emperor Haile Selassie with his wife. Thanks to Selassie's patronage, Babor became something of a celebrated resident of Ethiopia.*

'I HATE ALL HUMAN BEINGS. PEOPLE OUGHT TO BE GASSED – KILLED AS QUICKLY AS POSSIBLE', SHOUTED BABOR

The next story she recounted to Wiesenthal was an episode which seemed to fly in the face of all his alleged humanitarian instincts and codes as a doctor. The second night she was there a woman knocked on the door of his home clutching a sick child. His daughter Dagmar came for him and told him that he was needed. Babor jumped up and Ruth recalled: 'His eyes were bloodshot and his face was almost distorted with hatred. It was horrible. He shouted at Dagmar that he wouldn't touch the child, that he hated children; let them die. "I've never treated a child and I never will. Out with them!" Dagmar stood transfixed, silently pleading with me, and I said:"Karl, you're a doctor aren't you? That child is sick. Please go and take care of the baby". The good doctor Babor rounded on Ruth, told her she was a dirty fat Jewess, and for good measure added: 'I hate all human beings. People ought to be gassed – killed as quickly as possible. We don't need people. Animals are much better than people – animals must be spared'. He then fled to the Addis Ababa zoo where he spent the night stroking the dangerous wild cats as they slept.

Beate Klarsfeld, the Paris-based Nazi hunter, had already received a tip-off that Babor was in Africa and had, Wiesenthal suspected, found out that the bureaucracy there was interested in protecting a favoured son with connections to the Emperor. When she made enquiries about extraditing the good doctor to the west she was met with red tape, denials and finally official arrogance that, because he had committed no crimes there, he would never be eligible for extradition. After Ruth told her story to Wiesenthal – she fled from the house soon after the incident over the baby – he decided that the best way to get his hands on this most notorious of Nazi murderers might be to shame the government of Ethiopia. Ruth had come to Wiesenthal only on the suspicion of who he might be – she knew nothing of names like Treblinka or Grossrosen. It was Wiesenthal who fitted together the pieces of the jigsaw.

THE PRESS INVESTIGATE

To flush him out Wiesenthal staged a press conference with the Vienna correspondent of the *New York Times* – next to the London *Times*, probably the world's most influential newspaper. He told him the works – who Babor was, who he had been and what his crimes were. The repercussions were instant. From out of the Nazi abyss came forward victims, witnesses, survivors, collaborators – all who deluged the man who saw first-hand the smoke rising from the 'surgery' of this most infamous of Nazi killers. The Ethiopian government scrambled to deny that Babor was a doctor to the court – a denial later proven to be an outright lie. The revisionists argued that Babor had never been in Grossrosen, that Wiesenthal was picking on one minor cog in the whole grotesque machinery of Nazism, purely for personal reasons. And then there was the denial from Dr Babor himself. He set himself up at a press conference in Addis Ababa where he lied: 'I have never been in a concentration camp. I never experimented on prisoners. I was merely a military doctor during the war – a "truppenarzt"'. This was a mistake on his part as the full details of his SS membership, concentration camp service and medical history were available at the time through the Federal Prosecutor's office in Bonn.

FALSE DENIALS

Wiesenthal listened to Babor's denials with patience – the patience which has borne fruit in the pursuit and capture of hundreds of wartime murderers. Then he called his bluff – sending him an airline ticket to Austria together with a promise to pay his libel expenses if he instigated proceedings against him. Wiesenthal, in his book, *The Murderers Among Us*, wrote: 'In my cable I didn't think it tactful to add that room and board would be provided free of charge in the Landesgericht County Jail by the Austrian authorities who still had a warrant out for him. I gave the cable to the local newspapers in Addis Ababa – I didn't want him to be able to claim that he hadn't received it'.

But he received it all right. He just knew in his heart that he could never return to Austria.

Wiesenthal described the 'stage' of his memory upon which the cruel Dr Babor had appeared. It was now left for him to exit the drama of his appalling life for good. He drove into the jungle where he had taken Ruth upon her first night in Addis Ababa – the night when she was still contemplating marriage to this monster with the blood of innocents soaked upon his clothing. At the crocodile-infested river the beasts which earned his undying affection were milling about in the tepid waters, their red eyes glinting above the surface, their movements frightening the few water birds floating on the ripples. They ignored him as he waded out into the depths. When the water almost reached to his shoulders he levelled the hunting rifle he was carrying towards his heart, pulled the trigger, and slipped beneath the waves. Five days later a party of tourists discovered his body – even the crocs, it seemed, were choosy about what they ate.

Thousands of miles and another world

away the flame of remembrance burned at the site of the Treblinka death camp, this most efficient engine of the Nazi extermination programme. The camp buildings are gone, the crematorium destroyed, the gas chambers long vanished. In the ground are the red brick foundations of the original camp and leading to it are the railroad tracks along which 700,000 people were brought to be liquidated – many of them by the needle and scalpel of Dr Karl Babor.

Ruth thought it ironic that she had nearly married him. She had relatives who had died in Treblinka. At least now, with the beast dead, she could say the Jewish holy prayer of Kaddish for their souls.

700,000 PEOPLE WERE LIQUIDATED, MANY OF THEM BY THE NEEDLE AND SCALPEL OF DR KARL BABOR

Below: *It was in a river like this that Babor met his doom at the jaws of crocodiles.*

KLAUS FUCHS
The Traitorous Don

When the US developed the atomic bomb, it had an overwhelming military advantage over every other nation. So secret were the research and experimentation projects on nuclear weaponry that the expertise would have remained the west's sole property – had it not been for traitors like the Rosenbergs and Dr Klaus Fuchs.

Left and Below: *Robert Oppenheimer, architect of America's atom bomb and the result of his brainchild, the aftermath of the Hiroshima bombing. The mushroom cloud rises above the doomed city in which 100,000 people died.*

Opposite: *Klaus Fuchs, the man who gave the secret of the atom bomb to the Russians.*

The world has never been the same since an American scientist called Robert Oppenheimer led a dedicated band of researchers into the nuclear age. When the awesome fireball of nuclear fission exploded over the New Mexico desert on 16 July 1945 it could only be a matter of time before the harnessing of such energy would become the goal of dictators, tyrants and aspiring world-power players. The bomb was called Fat Boy and the mission to develop it The Manhattan Project. Ten miles from the Alamagordo Air Base, a complex of underground tunnels and bunkers, where much of the bomb's construction was carried out, was crammed with military top brass and civilian experts gathered to witness the greatest technological achievement ever reached by man. At 5.30a.m., in the cold morning drizzle, a ball of fire reaching 41,000 feet into the sky 12 feet higher than the tallest mountain, soared above the desert. The sound echoed like rolling thunder and the desert sand turned to glass in the 6,000 degree heat generated at the centre of the blast. Oppenheimer remembered at this incredible moment two verses from Sanskrit, the ancient language of India: 'If the radiance of a thousand suns were to burst into the sky, that would be the splendour of the mighty one. I am become death – that shatterer of worlds'.

Every bomb, every missile, every rocket and explosive charge created since man first fashioned material for his wars was suddenly redundant. Oppenheimer hoped that the nuclear power he had developed would be turned into peaceful uses for the benefit of mankind. He knew that the war against Japan was going to be settled with his creation, but hoped in his heart that it would be so terrible in its destruction that no ruler would ever dream of using it again. For the American government, it was imperative that no government that was hostile to it would ever be given the chance. During wartime the technology for the production of the bomb was denied to the Germans and the Japanese, the Axis powers whose overthrow was imperative to the continuation of the democracies of the free world. After the war it was the Soviet Union that became the ideological enemy of America. At all costs it had to be denied access to both the material and the expertise necessary to construct an atom bomb. But the Soviet Union was to enter the nuclear race — and thus begin the Cold War – thanks to the betrayal of a brilliant scientist called Dr Klaus Fuchs. Fuchs came to Britain before the war from his native Germany, where he was a fugitive from Nazism. His intellect was put to use at Harwell, the government's top research centre where Britain was developing its own atomic programme. Everyone trusted the quiet, bespectacled don, who had signed the Official Secrets Act and who was deemed to be eternally grateful for sanctuary in his adopted country. It was a misplaced trust which gave the blueprints for the bomb to Stalin and set the stage for decades of fear, mistrust and confrontation between the world superpowers.

A MISPLACED TRUST GAVE THE BLUEPRINTS FOR THE BOMB TO STALIN AND SET THE STAGE FOR DECADES OF FEAR

THE SOCIALIST SCHOLAR

Klaus Fuchs came from a long-line of Protestant pastors in Germany, socialist in outlook and beliefs. His father Emil raised his children to believe that the Soviet Union was the future and the salvation of the working man and that Nazism was to be resisted at all costs. In their hometown of Kiel the family were often ridiculed by right-wing newspapers for their convictions. Born in December 1911, he grew up in the shattered remnants of old Germany as first revolution, then inflation and finally the shadow of Nazism stretched over the country. A brilliant scholar, Klaus studied in Berlin, but his classes were soon to take second place to the priority of staying alive. The Gestapo had him and other family members at the top of their wanted lists because of his membership of the communist party and close links with Moscow. The communists smuggled him out of Germany in July 1933, first to Paris and then to London – a destitute refugee carrying everything he owned in a canvas bag.

Communism in pre-war England did not carry the bogeyman tag that it acquired after the conflict had ended. In fact his membership proved to the British government that

Below: *Josef Stalin, Soviet dictator, was determined to harness the technology for the atomic bomb.*

he was a political asset in the resistance to Nazism and Fascism, which were spreading like a cancer across the face of Europe. MI5 and MI6 were aware of his communist past and reports noting it were filed in Whitehall. But he was never considered a security risk when, in 1934, he obtained a student internship under the physics professor Neville Mott at Bristol University. Mott later said of him: 'I had no qualms about him being a communist. Anyone who was against the Nazis probably was anyway. He seemed to know his stuff so I took him on and he produced some excellent work.'

'He was shy and reserved and I can never remember discussing politics with him'. But politics were the engine of Klaus Fuchs. Although he had been given sanctuary in Britain, was learning there, being supported and sheltered there, the reality was that he despised the old order of the British Empire and its colonialism as much as he despised Nazism. From those earliest days there was only one true God that he worshipped, and it lived in the Kremlin and was called Josef Stalin.

Fuchs completed his doctorate at Bristol in 1936 and obtained a post-doctorate position at the laboratory of Max Born in Edinburgh. He never obtained British citizenship and found himself in the position upon the commencement of hostilities of being an enemy alien. He was placed in an internment camp on the Isle of Man, later being sent on to a camp with appallingly primitive conditions for the inmates in Quebec, Canada. Thanks to lobbying in high places by the friends he had made in academia he arrived back in Britain in December 1940, a free man. But there was a price for his freedom extracted by the government – harnessing his knowledge to the A-bomb programme that was underway. The physics community in Britain had a great wealth of talent to draw on as Hitlerism made fugitives of some of the greatest scientific minds of Europe. Klaus Fuchs was to be a cog in the great machine that would work on the greatest scientific project of all history.

Fuchs, with all his avowed history of communism, was allowed to sign the Official Secrets Act to be given clearance to work at the highest levels on the British atomic bomb. He worked on hideously complex mathematical problems for 'Tube Alloys,' one of the code names given to the project, and spent upwards of 16 hours a

Above and Below: *The youthful Klaus Fuchs and the War Office in London, where his security clearance was processed.*

day trying to bring the theories of nuclear fission to reality in a secure laboratory at Birmingham University. In his off time he was a quiet man who rarely spoke unless asked a direct question, one who shunned the convivial company of his colleagues in a drink or a sporting event.

In 1941 he finally obtained British citizenship – just at the time that Hitler's hordes had launched their all-out assault on the Soviet Union. Fuchs was devastated at the news; he sincerely believed that if the communist state should fall it would be the end of civilisation as we knew it. It was after the launch of the invasion of Russia that Klaus Fuchs decided that the only way he could help the country he loved would be to pass on the secrets he had learned of the A-bomb. He had pledged 'to bear true allegiance to the Crown' at the ceremony where he became a British subject, but it was all so much talk to him; he planned to pass on everything he could to his Kremlin idols.

A DANGEROUS MEMORY

As part of his work he was allowed to read classified documents submitted by American scientists working on the development of the bomb. Fuchs was possessed of a phenomenal photographic memory which allowed him to absorb huge quantities of information merely at the glance of a page. It was a talent that would serve him well.

Fuchs' contact with the Soviet Union was Ursula Kuczynski, sister of Jurgen Kuczynski, a German who had been a member of the same anti-Nazi group which Fuchs had belonged to before fleeing the country. She was an agent with the GRU, the forerunner of the KGB, who Fuchs only knew as 'the girl from Banbury.' She was a Mata Hari of considerable skill and cunning, an operative who had served in China, Poland and Switzerland before being assigned to Britain. She and Fuchs were both controlled by a man named 'Alexander' who was a colonel in Red Army military intelligence whose real name was Kremer. Fuchs first hawked the knowledge that he had in his head by visiting the Soviet Embassy in London and offering details of the 'amazing project' that Britain and America were working on.

Sonia lived in Oxford, Fuchs was working in Birmingham so Banbury became the

Above: *He was almost anonymous in his civil service suit and hat, but Fuchs was the Kremlin's puppet.*

Opposite Top: *The Los Alamos administration building in the New Mexico desert, where America's atom bombs were developed.*

Opposite Bottom: *The destruction wrought by the second A-bombing of Japan, this one fell on the industrial city of Nagasaki.*

> FUCHS' PHENOMENAL PHOTOGRAPHIC MEMORY ALLOWED HIM TO ABSORB HUGE QUANTITIES OF SECRET INFORMATION

rendezvous where the secrets of the A-bomb were passed on. Fuchs often gave her written reports and she would transmit them to Moscow using the radio which she hid in one of her children's soft toys. If the reports were mostly mathematical they were sent via the diplomatic pouch between the Soviet Embassy in London and the Kremlin. Fuchs would later say: 'I passed her all the information I had. Since that time I had continuous contact with persons who were completely unknown to me, except that I knew that they would hand whatever information I gave them to the Russian authorities. I used my Marxist philosophy to establish two separate compartments in my mind. The first compartment contained friendships, personal relations, and the behaviour of the kind of man I wanted to be. The second compartment contained the dialectical necessity of correct party behaviour, espionage in the name of historical determinism, which gave me a peculiar sense of being a free man who could be completely independent of the surrounding forces of society. Looking back on it now, the best way of expressing it seems to be to call it a controlled schizophrenia'.

Fuchs had passed on much that was crucial to the Soviet atom programme – but the real treasure trove of information lay in the US. His access to these secrets came in 1943 when he went to America as part of the British mission seconded under conditions of the strictest secrecy to the Manhattan Project, the code name for the development of the bomb. Here Sonia arranged for a man code-named Raymond to become his link with the Kremlin – Raymond later being exposed as the flamboyant and successful spy Harry Gold. Fuchs was assigned to work at the Oak Ridge gaseous diffusion plant for the production of fissionable uranium. Almost immediately he was passing on to his spymasters massive quantities of crucial information.

THE CENTRE OF POWER

On 14 August 1944 he moved to Los Alamos, the desert town in New Mexico which had been completely taken over by the military and sealed to the outside world. This was the inner sanctum, the holiest of holy sites in the charge to develop the atom bomb. Here under the direction of Oppenheimer the greatest physics brains in the world toiled towards their single goal of fissionable nuclear material with the explosive power of thousands of tons of TNT in a bomb no bigger than a refrigerator. In his book Klaus Fuchs: Atom Spy, author Robert Chadwell Williams wrote: 'For Fuchs, the transfer to Los Alamos was a golden opportunity, of which he took full advantage. The British Mission scientists, who were allowed access to many different divisions of the Manhattan Project, often had a better overview of the research than the Americans, who for security reasons were more compartmentalised. The British group made major contributions to the project, particularly in theoretical areas. Everybody knew Fuchs but few knew anything about him. Oppenheimer saw him as a man who seemed to be carrying the world's burdens on his shoulders. No-one seemed to perceive Fuchs as a security risk. To the other scientists he was simply a quiet German bachelor'.

In February 1945 Fuchs visited his sister, who had also escaped to England from Germany, at her home in Cambridge. En route he stopped to meet his contact Raymond in New York where he handed

Below: *The nuclear desert left behind after the Hiroshima detonation.*

over considerable written accounts about the development of the plutonium bomb. At the meeting Fuchs explained he would probably be unable to meet Raymond for another year. The spymaster offered Fuchs $1,500 for expenses, a not inconsiderable sum. But Fuchs, the idealist, turned his nose up at the capitalist offering. 'I do not do this for the money', he told him. 'I do it because it is right. Because the only hope for mankind lies in communism'.

In fact Fuchs was able to get away from the tight security surrounding Los Alamos in June 1945, driving his battered blue Buick car to Santa Fe to meet Raymond as planned. This time the package contained full details of the plutonium bomb that was to be detonated at Alamagordo and the one that was to be dropped last on Nagasaki, the second Japanese city after Hiroshima to be destroyed with a nuclear weapon. He gave Raymond details of the test date and site – and just as importantly, the fact that America was indeed intending to end the war in the Pacific with the use of the weapon against Japan. Fuchs spent the next several months gleaning expert data on the production rate of uranium 235, plutonium and the necessary metal processes needed to keep fission safe before detonation. He handed them over to Raymond in September 1945, after which the two Japanese cities lay in ruins and mankind had awakened to the atomic age.

Fuchs returned to England in the summer of 1946. After spending some time with his family he was absorbed as the leading physicist in the British bomb programme at Harwell, an RAF base on the Berkshire Downs a few miles south of Oxford. The target date for the bomb was set at 1952 and Klaus Fuchs was named as the Head of the Theoretical Physics Division and Deputy Chief Scientific Officer. Fuchs by this time had become an expert on other areas of nuclear power and wrote a landmark paper on fast reactors, predicting that all power stations in Britain would be using nuclear fuel by the 1980s. There was a five-month MI5 check instituted on Fuchs after his communist past resurfaced during a routine security scan, but nothing was ever done to replace him. His clearance by the intelligence community came at a time when new British prime minister Clement Attlee swore that all communist or fascist sympathisers found in a government post involving national security would be sacked.

THE SPYING LIFE

His spying activities continued. He dropped information to couriers at London tube stations and at suburban pubs. He passed on details of the atom bomb tests on the Bikini Atoll and on British plutonium production. But there was something uneasy troubling his compartmentalised mind. As a highly intelligent human being he was having more and more trouble reconciling some of the more grotesque behaviour of the Soviet dictator Stalin with the glories of world communism. He later admitted: 'I knew I disapproved of a great many actions of the Russian government and the communist party'. He missed an appointment with his courier in 1949 and then decided not to keep another rendezvous as he wrestled with the demons of right and wrong. Klaus Fuchs had developed a conscience – but it was too late to stave off the start of the Cold War.

Fuchs was unmasked in December 1949. On the 29th of that month he celebrated his 38th birthday with friends at Harwell, displaying no outward signs of the inner torment which had racked him for the past several months. But those same friends who served him cake and coffee had no idea that just eight days previously Fuchs had been interviewed at Scotland Yard by MI5 intelligence officer William Skardon,

Left: *The Energy Research Station at Harwell where Fuchs worked on the British bomb.*

FUCHS FINALLY CAME CLEAN WITH A CONFESSION THAT HE HAD COOLLY AND CALMLY GIVEN SECRETS TO THE SOVIET UNION

who told him that he was under suspicion as a man who had passed on nuclear secrets to the Russians. Skardon had no evidence and no powers of arrest – the point of the exercise was to try to get him to confess to his crimes. Fuchs denied the accusation while his mind raced as to who might have betrayed him. He also gave Skardon an insight into the way his mind worked when it came to loyalties. Fuchs claimed he was a loyal citizen of Britain, but that he reserved the right to 'act in accordance with my own conscience' if circumstances should arise in Britain similar to those which forced his exodus from Germany in 1933.

On 30 December Skardon arrived at Harwell and spoke with Harwell director Sir John Cockcroft. Cockcroft was told that Fuchs' father Emil had taken a university post in East Germany; that Klaus could be compromised as a major security risk because of it. Cockcroft demanded Fuchs' resignation ten days later and received it. Three days later Fuchs met with Skardon again and finally came clean with a detailed

Below: *Sir Roger Cockroft, seated far right, talks to his research staff at Harwell. Fuchs is standing far left.*

detailed confession that he had coolly and calmly given the nuclear secrets of Britain and America ever since 1942 to the Soviet Union. On 30 January he travelled to the War Office where the statement was formalised and he was placed under arrest for treason. In it Fuchs said: 'At first I thought that all I would do would be to inform the Russian authorities that work upon the atom bomb was going on. They wished to have more details and I agreed to supply them. I concentrated at first mainly on the products of my own work, but in particular in Los Alamos I did what I consider to be the worst I have done, namely to give information about the principles of the design of the plutonium bomb. Before I joined the project most of the British people with whom I had made personal contacts were left wing, and affected, to some degree or other, by the same kind of philosophy. Since coming to Harwell I have met many English people of all kinds, and I have come to see in many of them a deep-rooted firmness which enables them to lead a decent way of life. I don't know where this springs from and I don't think they do, but it is there'. It later transpired that Fuchs had come under suspicion of the spycatchers because of his own actions.

SPYCATCHER SUPREME

Skardon, the government's chief spycatcher, was alerted to Fuchs by one Henry Arnold. In October 1949 Fuchs had gone to Arnold – the security officer at Harwell – and spoken with him about his father's appointment in East Germany, posing the question whether he should resign or not. Arnold, a personal friend, offered no advice but asked Fuchs what he would do in the eventuality of Soviet agents putting pressure on him. Fuchs replied that he really did not know. Such wavering put the seal on his fate as a spy. Arnold put duty above friendship and alerted MI5. The agency was already looking for a mole as spy activity both in Britain and America was suspected due to intelligence leaks from Soviet moles and 'turned' agents from behind the Iron Curtain. Later it was learned that FBI director J. Edgar Hoover took credit for stumbling upon the trail of a British spy, although that has never been precisely proved.

THE NEWSPAPERS EXPLODED WITH WHAT SEEMED THE FORCE OF AN A-BOMB AS THEY TOLD OF HIS TREACHERY

Above: *Security officers from Harwell – Henry Arnold (right) and W.J. Skarden – arrive at the Old Bailey on 1 March 1950 for the start of the Fuchs trial.*

'YOU HAVE BETRAYED BRITISH PROTECTION WITH THE GROSSEST TREACHERY,' SAID LORD CHIEF JUSTICE GODDARD

Signed copies of his confession were sent to the Attorney General who authorised prosecution of Fuchs under the Official Secrets Act. Ironically, if the Soviet Union had been an enemy and not an ally of Britain during World War Two he could have been charged with treason – a capital offence – but as it was the charges would lead him to eventually receiving a long prison term.

It was finally to the Old Bailey that Klaus Fuchs' long spy career ended on 1 March 1950 when he appeared to plead guilty as charged. Before his court appearance the name Professor Fuchs had already become a household name in Britain and the rest of the world. The newspapers exploded with what seemed the force of an A-bomb as they chronicled his treachery over the years, finally asking the question that all free governments were asking themselves: just how much damage had Klaus Fuchs done with his misguided, idealistic, 'compartmentalised' code of ethics which told him that what he was doing was morally acceptable? The answer was, quite simply, enormous damage.

His trial lasted just 90 minutes at the Number One Court – scene of so many trials of heinous criminals stretching back to wife killer Dr Crippen. Some 80 newsmen were present to hear the presiding Judge, Lord Chief Justice Goddard, tell the defendant that what he did bordered on high treason. 'You have betrayed British protection with the grossest treachery', he said, 'fol-

Left: *The Old Bailey, London, where Fuchs was found guilty of spying.*

Below: *The gaunt features of the convict after nine-and-a-half years in jail. He travelled to a hero's welcome in East Germany, his spiritual home.*

was racked by fear that when his sentence was up the British would send him to America for trial, where he may have been sentenced to death as the post-war communist witch hunts were reaching fever pitch. Instead, his father Emil managed to convince the guardians of the East German state that he deserved a place there and it was granted. The British released him early and he was delighted that he was not to be deported to America. He flew to East Berlin as Mr Strauss aboard a Polish Convair plane. At Heathrow Airport he said: 'I bear no resentment whatsoever about Britain. In a way I'm sorry to be leaving'. He lived outside Dresden, becoming director of the country's nuclear physics programme. Apparently, he was rarely troubled that he had sold the nation which had sheltered him from the Gestapo down the river.

lowing the pernicious creed of communism. Your atomic espionage has done irreparable harm to both England and America. You have imperilled the right of asylum and liberty for other refugees from tyranny. Your crime is only thinly differentiated from high treason'. Without further ado he was sentenced to the maximum 14 years in jail and taken down to the cells below.

Evidence supplied in his confession helped the FBI to Harry Gold – Raymond – and a 30 year jail term for his activities. It also helped smash the Rosenberg spy ring, leading to the executions of Ethel and Julius Rosenberg in New York for their trade in nuclear secrets. But the damage had been done with the announcement of the Soviet Union early in the 1950s that it had exploded a nuclear bomb. The reckoning was that it had come seven to ten years before the expected time thanks to the treachery of Klaus Fuchs, the misguided zealot for communism.

A SCHOLARLY PRISONER

He served nine years in jail, sewing mailbags and reading great tomes of Russian literature from the prison library in between organising physics classes for his cellmates. The graduates of the school of armed robbery and burglary suddenly found themselves being taught about neutrons and nuclei by one of the most distinguished minds of the age. While he was inside he

PAUL VICKERS
The Lust Murder

There didn't seem to be a lot lacking in the life of successful surgeon Dr Paul Vickers. He was widely recognised as an expert in his field by his fellow practitioners. However, his relationship with his wife was poor and would end in tragedy.

Dr Paul Vickers was a brilliant surgeon who rose to the very top of his chosen profession. He was also active in the British Medical Association, the governing body for practitioners and their policy, a position which required him to travel to conferences both at home and abroad. The trips were more than just business affairs for Vickers; they became personal escapes from the routine of his home life. At 42, he was locked in an unhappy marriage with his wife Margaret, a woman he had met while studying medicine at Cambridge. During the undergraduate years there Margaret had a reputation of being a social butterfly, a life and soul of the party type who had a ready smile, eager charm and a razor sharp wit. If anything, she was more academically qualified than her suitor, who struggled in his examinations. But they fell in love and married and shortly afterwards she gave birth to their only child, a son they named John. As is often the case in marriage Margaret had to compromise her own career – which looked to be promising – for the sake of her husband and child. But this self-denial seemed to trigger in her a cancer of hatred, of bitterness. When they moved to Gosforth-on-Tyne, to be near his appointment at the Queen Elizabeth Hospital in Gateshead, she went with reluctance. Soon the house was run down, she was moody, the garden was untended and there were constant rows between them. No wonder Vickers relished his trips away, trips where he could meet beautiful women, drink fine

THE HOUSE WAS RUN DOWN, SHE WAS MOODY, THE GARDEN WAS UNTENDED AND THERE WERE CONSTANT ROWS

Opposite: *Respected, comfortable and secure – many men would have envied Dr Paul Vickers his lot in life.*

Below: *Margaret and Paul Vickers on their wedding day. They seemed to be perfectly matched.*

Right: *An anonymous house in an anonymous road. No-one had any idea of the nefarious activities going on inside.*

Below: *The death certificate for Margaret Vickers. Her scheming husband thought that he had got away the perfect murder.*

wine and forget for a few days at least the torment of life with Margaret and her ever-deepening depression.

There was one women he met in 1976, in Brussels, that would change his life forever. She was called Pamela Collison, then, at 29, 13 years his junior, and her sexy allure led him to his doom like a mermaid luring sailors on to the rocks. Pamela was a tall, cool, leggy brunette who liked to wear fishnet stockings and Janet Reger silk underwear beneath slinky, figure-hugging cocktail dresses. She worked by day as a political research assistant – hence her appearance at the medical conference in Belgium – and indeed would go on to work briefly for Mr Michael Heseltine when he was Minister for the Environment. But by night she liked to party. From the moment he saw her, Dr Vickers was hooked. She was sensual, she was beautiful – and,most important-

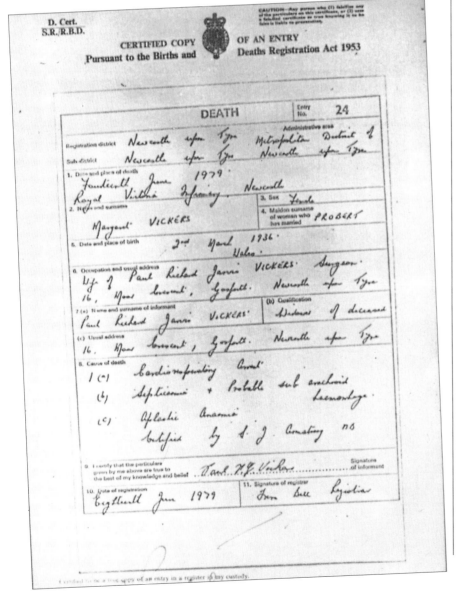

ly, she seemed to be interested in him. He was balding, paunchy around the middle, saggy in the face, and yet seemed to have a magnetism of his own. Later, after his lust for Pamela had destroyed him completely, various friends stepped forward with stories of how he could turn on the charm for the ladies. Alastair MacFarlane, who had known him since their student days, said: 'Paul dressed smartly, was a good talker, but I just can't say why they went out with him or why they stayed with him. He had something I suppose, but I don't quite know what it was'. To someone like Pamela he represented a good 'catch' if he ever chose to leave his wife. He harboured ambitions to become a member of the European Parliament and spoke to her over drinks in Brussels of various money-making schemes he had. They shared conversation and a meal, but the relationship remained platonic. It was when they were both back in England that Vickers realised he was having great difficulty in getting the thought of the alluring Miss Collison out of his head.

THE CHEATING GAME

Dr Vickers was no stranger to the cheating game. When he had first married he had taken a mistress called Julie Heaton, a woman he met on a dance floor at a disco in Newcastle-upon-Tyne when he was a newly-qualified doctor. Schoolteacher Julie went with him to London, Dublin and Paris as his 'wife' as he told her tales of his real wife's mental illness. Another schoolteacher called Mary McNally also became his lover, offering him sex and sympathy as he poured his heart out about being trapped in a loveless marriage. Now Miss Collison became his magnificent obsession and he was determined to do anything to possess her. She lived in London, almost 300 miles from him, so he had to dream up a scheme to get to see her. For the first meeting he attended a medical meeting which in reality held no interest for him at all. But it allowed him to make that all-important first contact with Pamela. They dined at a Mayfair restaurant, sipping fine wine and brandies late into the night before he dropped her off in Knightsbridge. The next night he told her that he loved her and within a fortnight Dr Vickers had become Dr Jekyll and Mr Hyde – the family man in Gosforth during Monday to Friday, the adulterer with his mistress in London on weekends and holidays. Vickers felt elated – not just because he was bedding a beautiful, younger

Former girlfriend Pamela Collison . . . she was once Environment Minister Michael Heseltine's secretary

JURY TOLD OF 'MASS MURDER CONTRACTS'
Page Seven

ACCUSED
Surgeon and girl charged with murder of his wife

SURGEON Paul Vickers and his attractive former girlfriend, Pamela Collison, were charged early today with the murder of his wife.

woman, but because he felt that he was getting what he 'deserved' in life. A cruel streak in him led him to think that he had been cheated of what was rightfully his in his marriage to Margaret. Now he was making up for lost time.

In London there was no attempt at a cover-up – indeed, the newly-liberated surgeon flaunted his mistress like some badge of honour. He even began showing her off in the company of his distinguished med-

Above: The Sun's *glaring headlines say it all.*

Left: *The toll begins to mount on Dr Vickers as evidence piles up against him.*

VICKERS WAS LIKE A LITTLE BOY LOST IN HIS FIRST INFATUATION. HE WORSHIPPED THE GROUND PAMELA WALKED ON

Below: *Mrs Julie Heaton, one of the witnesses called in to give evidence in the case of the twisted surgeon.*

ical colleagues. Dr Gerard Vaughan, one of his associates, later spoke of the embarrassment that he felt when Vickers invited him out to lunch and he saw this unknown woman on his arm. 'He introduced her as someone who was making a study of medical politics', said Dr Vaughan. 'But she contributed nothing to the conversation on that subject. And I was embarrassed by his nod and wink manner of suggesting he had something going with her'. In fact, Pamela was not a woman that Paul Vickers could easily say no to. Forceful and determined in her outlook and temperament, it was she who insisted on going everywhere with him. Someone later commented that Vickers was like a little boy lost in his first infatuation. He worshipped the ground that Pamela walked on and showered her with expensive presents – bought from his not inconsiderable income. Much of the money was spent on her favourite passion – clothes – and she stocked her wardrobe with designer label garments which would one day be aired in a court of law and bring gasps of admiration and envy.

A DEPRESSING PICTURE

Dr Vickers told her that he never made love with his wife, that she was almost a vegetable with her depression. He painted to her a picture of someone who was almost incapable of looking after herself on a routine basis, someone for whom life was not worth living. But this was very far from the truth; although Margaret was a burden to him, she had plenty to live for. With encouragement, kindness, even fondness from her husband who had once pledged to care for her in sickness and in health, she could have made a complete recovery from her fits of depression. Paul Vickers, however, had no intention of ever trying to make a new start of his marriage; his all consuming passion now was Pamela Collison. She was a demanding woman, a woman who told him in no uncertain terms that she would never be content just to play the 'little woman' at home while he was out working. Social respectability and social climbing were the things that interested her and Dr Vickers pondered how best to go about attaining these twin goals for her.

She was thrilled for him when he sought out the patronage of the Tory party to stand as a Euro MP and serve in Brussels – the place where he had first met Pamela. But both he and she were devastated when four separate constituencies turned him down as 'unsuitable'. Tyneside Tory organiser Joan Reeve later said of him: 'From the first time I met him there was something about him which made me shudder. The girls in the office didn't like him either. They said he made their flesh creep'. It dawned on him that Pamela would forever remain 'unsuitable' in the eyes of those who blocked the pathway to promotion and social status while she remained his mistress. He thought about divorce, but was too scared and too much of an emotional coward to put himself and Margaret through such an ordeal. Soon the prospect of the perfect murder began to form in his scientific, calculating mind.

A DEADLY DRUG

Vickers got his mistress – without telling her what it was for – to collect from him on prescription a drug called CCNU. This was a chemotherapeutic cancer drug, used to treat cancerous cells in a body.

But like all cancer-attacking drugs, healthy cells are also killed. Quite simply put, if given to someone who doesn't have cancer, the extremely strong drug would attack the white cells in the bone marrow, killing off the life force which makes up much of the blood in the body. Soon enough white cells would be lost that the patient injected with CCNU would resemble a leukaemia victim.

This is what Paul Vickers, a man hitherto faithful to his Hippocratic Oath if not his marriage vows, was planning for Margaret. At first Margaret felt marvellous when he gave her the first capsule; new energy seemed to return to her and she was up out of bed, spring cleaning the house in a way in which she had not attempted for years. And then as soon as the initial effects of the

drug had worn off she was overcome with a terrible lethargy; every bone in her body ached, she could no longer get up in the mornings, she was frequently sick and she needed naps at all times of the day.

Her 'caring' husband took her to the hospital where he worked and lied to a fellow doctor that she was taking no medication. Four weeks after she had taken the first dose she was sick enough to have all the symptoms of the advanced stages of leukaemia. Consultant Ronald Thompson took his colleague to one side and said: 'She has no chance of survival – you must prepare yourself for the worst'. The drug that he had

Above and Left: *Two studies in how the law takes its toll. Pamela Collison remained breezy, aloof and distant during the trial. The same cannot be said for erstwhile lover.*

been feeding her had literally smashed her body's capability of regenerating white cells. Vickers showed no emotion when the consultant told him this – but his colleagues thought this was merely stoicism on the part of a man who had to mask his feelings in front of numerous relatives over the years when he had to tell them that death was about to claim one of their loved ones.

On the eve of their 17th wedding anniversary in June 1979, Margaret died. The callous Vickers had her buried in an unmarked plot at the local cemetery; he did not even want to shell out for a headstone in her memory. He was now free to marry Pamela Collison. But things didn't work out quite the way either of them had planned. Like thieves falling out over treasure, soon the arguments between Collison and Vickers grew worse. His Oscar-winning performance at faking grief over his wife's death had led her to believe that they would be walking up the aisle as man and wife together within months. But something snapped within Vickers; he realised that the wildcat lover that had aroused him and captivated him so fully was never going to make him happy in the role of a

Above: *Pamela Collison, with the smile of victory on her lips, after being sensationally freed at the end of her trial.*

Below: *Michael Heseltine, for whom she once briefly worked.*

wife. Vickers believed he would be in for a lifetime of misery. Instead he dumped her amid cant, bitterness and hatred – and instead of a lifetime of unhappiness, he is left with a lifetime in prison. For when the affair ended the woman scorned went straight to the police with the tale of a dead wife, dangerous drugs obtained on prescriptions and the story of a torrid affair. But Pamela had walked into a dangerous area – for the police, while believing her

story, charged her with murder too. And for good measure she was charged with obtaining drugs by deception – the one charge she admitted to. Soon the British public were treated to the spectacle of one of the most sensational murder trials this century; only the third in which a doctor has stood accused of murder.

The trial at Teeside Crown Court in 1981 was judicial theatre of the highest order. Day after day the newspapermen in the court struggled to keep up with the machine-gun pace of allegation and counter-allegation in the proceedings. Vickers quickly emerged as a man totally besotted with Pamela Collison – and like thieves who have fallen out, he was quick to paint her as a scarlet woman who was not to be trusted.

DANGEROUS DRUGS

The court heard that Mrs Vickers was fed a total of 52 capsules of the cancer-fighting drug over an eight month period. The defence for Collison was that she knew she was supplying him with dangerous drugs, but that she believed it was for research purposes only. Vickers, a man full of venom, denied murdering his wife and was determined to drag the name of the woman who had shopped him to police through the mud. He claimed that on their first date she had stripped off her clothes in his hotel room and climbed into bed unasked next to him. He claimed that she told him 'of sexual relations with a great number of men, generally two at a time'. He claimed that she talked about whipping and bondage, 'and said that she was a mean hand with a whip'. He claimed that he swore he saw scars on her back caused by a whipping she had received from 'a distinguished academic'. He said that a cigarette burn on her cheek was the souvenir of a way-out bondage session with another man. She said he sent her pornographic pictures of herself which he kept hidden in his home to look at after he had finished work. He said she had been on the contraceptive pill since the age of 12, was raped three times and had contracted a venereal disease once.

He told the court that he had got the powerful drug on forged prescriptions to try to treat his wife not kill her. But soon he said she was using the prescriptions to try to

Above: *Mr Justice Boreham, who tried the Vickers case, sentenced the doctor to life and recommended that he serve a minimum of 17 years behind bars.*

VICKERS CLAIMED THAT COLLISON TALKED ABOUT WHIPPING AND BONDAGE 'AND SAID THAT SHE WAS A MEAN HAND WITH A WHIP'

blackmail him when he wanted to end the affair. He said he paid her £4,000 for work she did which would normally have not exceeded £1000. 'I had to keep seeing her because she was clearly a very disturbed person and I had a feeling of concern for her'. He said his problems were Collison's demands for more money to support her lavish lifestyle and more prescriptions. 'Most of all', he added, 'the CCNU which was arriving at my house in a far greater quantity that I could have wanted'. He then said wistfully: 'I think if two people were not meant to meet it was myself and Miss

'That is total rot. She knew from the first time we had dinner in November 1977 that I was married and I reinforced it when she came into my hotel room'.

PRIVACY DISAPPEARS

Every shred of privacy and intimacy in the relationship was ripped away. The court heard how he called her 'Kitten Eyes' and in one sexy letter said: 'You must realise that I'll master you. If this is not what you want you had better retreat fast'. He saw vivacious Pam as the perfect woman – although a psychiatrist told the court that Vickers was really nothing better than a pathetic little boy. Psychiatrist Dr John Hawkins said: 'He had difficulty in striking up relationships with women. There is no doubt that his relationship with his wife was a disturbed one, probably dictated from childhood. He feels a need to dominate women. He is egocentric and pretends self-confidence to mask his insecurity'. But he said that he was certainly suitable to stand trial on the charge of murder.

Pamela maintained a discreet silence throughout the trial, content to keep the public amused and agog with her stunning array of outfits which she wore day after day. On the 19th day of the trial she held the court's attention completely as she read an 11-minute speech from the dock. She declined to go into the witness box, but exercised her right under British law to make a statement from the dock. Judge Mr Justice Boreham asked her to speak clearly and slowly so that he and a shorthand writer could take a full note of what she was to say. As she spoke her former lover sat slumped against the edge of the dock.

A PREPARED SPEECH

Reading from a large notepad Collison said: 'My lords, I have chosen to make a statement from the dock because there is very little I can add to what I told the police in May 1980. I do not wish to go into the details of the personal and intimate relationship with Mr Vickers. I am not guilty of the murder of Mrs Margaret Vickers. Neither have I been party to any plot to murder her. I cannot say what happened to any CCNU I sent to Mr Vickers. As I told the police, I had prescriptions dispensed for CCNU

Collison'. He went on to tell how he tried to 'ditch' Miss Collison by palming her off on to a friend at the hospital who he thought might like her company. He added: 'I have every considerable sympathy for her, but I think she's an extremely disturbed person, a relentless blackmailer. I was trying to keep the lid on her'. He said his feelings for her began to change after she attacked him with a knife when she saw a picture of him and his wife at a friend's flat in France. Collison's defence counsel Mr Robin Stewart QC said at one point: 'Isn't it true that there was a flaming row between you when she found out you were, and still were, a married man?' Vickers replied:

Above: *Paul Vickers in the trademark pinstriped suit that he wore throughout the trial.*

Opposite Left and Right: *Vickers tried to persuade the court that he had never plotted murder against his wife, but it was all to no avail.*

between September 1978 and December 1978. I have never asked Mr Vickers to provide me with any prescriptions for CCNU and I was never asked to obtain any after I stopped working in Central London since December 1978. Nor did I. No prescriptions were given to me in the name of Mrs Margaret Vickers and I had no idea whatsoever that the drug was for his wife's use. As I told the police, Mr Vickers told me that the drug was unavailable to him in Newcastle-upon-Tyne and he felt that was unfair because he wanted it for research trials. Perhaps I was stupid not to question him further, but I believed him to be acting correctly, being a prominent member of the British Medical Association and the

General Medical Council. I had no idea that the drug was to be used in any way other than was properly, medically directed.

'I have never blackmailed Mr Vickers in cash or kind and resent the attempt to besmirch my name and reputation, and the inference he draws from any relationships. I might have had thrush, which is a common complaint, but I have never had any venereal disease. The contraceptive pill was not available in 1959 when I was 12, as alleged by Mr. Vickers, and I did not take it until my early twenties. I am a pro-

fessional economist and statistician. All my relationships with Members of Parliament have been on a purely political basis. During the time I worked for Mr Michael Heseltine as his political research assistant there were no leaks or unauthorised contact with any member of the Press. I have never made any applications to the Criminal Injuries Compensation Board and have been neither raped nor mugged. I have no scars on my back or elsewhere, nor cigarette burns on my face. I have never threatened to spray paint on Mr Vickers' car or damage his home or property. I have had arguments and fights with him, especially after discovering his marriage. I have never attacked him with any weapon nor terrorised him in any way. The letters I received from Mr Vickers I regarded as nothing more than love letters, and never thought there was anything sinister in them, and still don't. I thought he was seeing his solicitor about his divorce and that is what I assumed many of the references to mean. I only discovered he was married after we had been going out together for five months and I agreed to act as his research assistant for the European Parliamentary Elections. In fact I never met, saw or spoke to Mrs Vickers. Mr Vickers explained to me that his wife was a schizophrenic and had been confined to a mental hospital since the birth of their son. He later told me that divorce proceedings were under way, and I had no idea at the time that he lived with his wife.

COMMUNICATION BREAKDOWN

'Mr Vickers accompanied me to many dinners, conferences and parties. He introduced me to many members of the BMA Executive. In November 1979 I believed I was pregnant and this appeared to be confirmed by my temperature charts. Mr Vickers was in one of his fits of isolationism and I tried to contact his local curate to bring about some form of communication between us. Towards the end of November 1979 we agreed to get married and in early December I made provisional arrangements in London. I then discovered I was not pregnant and so, because of his eccentric behaviour, I cancelled the Register Office Booking. During late November his behaviour became increasingly peculiar. He

Opposite: *The end for Vickers as he is driven away with the judge's life sentence ringing in his ears.*

Left: *Vickers was facing life in jail, but the mistress with whom he had shared good times was free.*

Below: **The Sun's** *headline showed that while Collison was free, she still earned the scorn of many.*

accused me of bizarre things, such as mounting a campaign to remove him from the General Council and he told me on several occasions to commit suicide. I am not guilty of the murder of Mrs Vickers. I have never had any wish to harm her nor have I conspired to bring about her death'.

The trial last for 25 days in all and soon it became clear that Collison had nothing to do with the murder of Mrs Vickers. It had been carried out solely by Vickers, even though Collison had broken the law by cashing in the forged prescriptions he wrote for the drug. The jury took five hours after being sent away by the judge to reach their unanimous verdict of guilty on Vickers. They came back 20 minutes later with acquittal for Collison. Then Vickers was ordered to stand and face the wrath of the judge who told him: 'To judges it is no unfamiliar thing to witness what might be called man's inhumanity to man. But when a medical practitioner, whose vocation is clearly to alleviate pain and suffering, deliberately kills, this – even for a judge – is a new field. And when, as here, the victim was your

wife, and when in particular the killing is achieved not in a moment of passion but by a process which was cruel, insidious and slowly deliberate and then fatal, then in my judgement inhumanity has plunged to the very depths. The case against you is overwhelming'. He sentenced him to life imprisonment with a recommendation that he serve a minimum of 17 years. Collison was given a six month jail sentence, suspended for two years, for obtaining the murder drug illegally for him.

In 1983 his leave to appeal against the conviction was refused as the evidence against him was declared by Law Lords to be 'overwhelming'.

Battling through the mob . . . police escorting Pamela to her car after she was cleared of murder yesterday

Picture by KEITH PERRY

ANGELO/ALLITT
Angels of Death

There are few nightmares that terrorise the entire population more than that of killer nurses. When the image of those who are normally associated with kindness and caring is tarnished by individuals who abuse the trust placed in them, society trembles.

All Richard Angelo wanted to be in life was the good guy – the hero who earned the praise and admiration of his fellow man. Throughout his childhood he was the quiet kid in school who got bullied, the nonentity who could never compensate for lack of friends by winning praise from his teachers. Angelo was an only child who turned to his father for solace and friendship, accompanying him on fishing and hunting expeditions.

As an awkward young man, it was the same story with him. Friends were something that other people had. And respect was a commodity that did not figure highly in his existence. Until the day when he became a nurse and realised that he had the power to give life.

Or death – and it was through the latter that this grey, soulless individual, struggling for recognition in a world that he believed was against him, found the fleeting moments of heroism and respect. As a respected emergency medical technician at a hospital near New York he found the answer to his mediocrity – and four people died because of it. Angelo injected the patients in his care with a muscle relaxant that triggered heart spasms and breathing constrictions. Then, as death seemed about to take his patients, he would rush in, frenzied, authoritative, in control – appearing as a life-giver in a critical situation. The true hero.

But while he pulled off 27 such miracles of medicine, four people died agonising deaths – innocent people who had entrusted themselves to his care, believing that he was a dedicated professional. It was a case that rocked America to its very core and led to more stringent control of such drugs in the hands of nurses like Angelo.

After he was caged for 50 years to life it was left for the relatives of the victims to mourn – and the psychiatrists and mind doctors to debate over where the first seeds of evil were planted in his humdrum life. 'How this God fearing altar boy grew up to become some crazed Frankenstein, performing these macabre and outrageous stunts to satisfy his own perverted ideas of self-worth, must, somewhere hold a salutary lesson for us all', said Dr James Cecilson, who has made a detailed study of the Angel of Death.

He, and others, say that to understand what made him do it it is necessary to look at his roots and comprehend how a desperately lonely boyhood would eventually force him to seek excitement in such a grotesque manner later in life. He was born in 1962 to teacher parents Joseph and Alice Angelo who raised him as a strict Catholic and doted on his every whim. He attended church every Sunday without fail in the small Long Island town of Lindenhurst and became known to one and all as Little Ricky. But Little Ricky didn't stay that way for long – too many sweet pastries eaten from the hand of his doting Italian grandfather turned him into a chubby child by the time he was five. Soon the taunts of 'fatso' and 'lardback' were burning into his psyche, devaluing his own currency of self-esteem like an acid scorching through metal. Instead of being able to taunt children back, he turned in on himself, devoting himself from the age of six onwards to the Our Lady of Perpetual Help Church where he was altar boy.

MUMMY'S BOY

He received a good education at the nearby Perpetual Help Elementary School and later at the St John the Baptist High School, but he was not a stunning pupil. Other children taunted him about his weight, about being a mummy's boy, about being generally stupid. He responded to this by growing closer still to his parents. Only in the goody two-shoes environment of the Boy Scouts did he seem to shine, as troop leader who won

THROUGHOUT HIS CHILDHOOD, ANGELO WAS THE QUIET KID IN SCHOOL WHO GOT BULLIED AND HAD NO FRIENDS

WHEN HE BECAME A NURSE HE REALISED HE COULD GIVE LIFE – IT WAS A WAY OF WINNING RESPECT AND FRIENDS

ANGELO WAS THE GOD-FEARING ALTAR BOY WHO GREW UP TO BECOME A KIND OF CRAZED FRANKENSTEIN

THE TAUNTS OF 'FATSO' AND 'LARDBACK' WERE BURNING INTO HIS PSYCHE, DEVALUING HIS SELF-ESTEEM

Opposite: *Richard Angelo, the boy who craved recognition as a 'lifesaver' and a 'hero'. But his fleeting moments of heroism and respect cost many their lives.*

HE APPEARED TO BE A SERIOUS SCHOLAR, BUT MANY OF THE BOOKS HE STUDIED CONCERNED POISONS AND POTIONS

ANGELO WAS BONING UP ON THE KNOWLEDGE THAT HE WOULD NEED TO TAKE PEOPLE'S LIVES, NOT PRESERVE THEM

HE BECAME UNHAPPY BECAUSE HE DID NOT HAVE ACCESS TO THE DRUGS WITH WHICH HE COULD TAKE LIFE

ANGELO WAS AT THE CENTRE OF ATTENTION, A HERO LIFE-SAVER TO HIS PEERS, BUT ACTUALLY AN ANGEL OF DEATH

many badges. Here he was in his element – someone in charge of people, performing good deeds which he believed raised his worth in their eyes. The young hero.

When he was 17 he left high school and took a course in nursing at the State Agricultural and Technical College at Farmingdale where he seemed to have found his metier. He received good grades and was a diligent student. But while cordial to his classmates, he never joined in the usual high jinks of college, was never present at parties or other social events. Angelo buried himself in his scholar's books and seemed at peace with the world. In reality, the dark side within him was growing. Later, after his appalling crimes were uncovered, it was found that many of the books he took out of the medical library were concerned with poisons and potions – presumably he was boning up on the knowledge he would need to take life, not preserve it.

SOCIAL OUTCAST

After two years he graduated from college and took a job in the Burns Unit at the Nassau County Medical Centre. Here, in a day-to-day environment dealing with both patients and staff, he seemed to revert to his introverted old self and is not remembered fondly by his bosses. Hospital spokesman Edward Smith said: 'He was competent, but no more than that. He was in trouble with his fellow employees. He just couldn't get on with them. He was a social outcast, something of a pariah. He was always in trouble here and always calling in sick. He lasted for six months before resigning for "personal reasons". I understood that the personal reasons were that he wanted to go to Florida'.

In fact he went home and pondered his options for the future. He was unhappy at the hospital for a variety of reasons. Probably, deep down, he was unhappiest of all because he did not have access to drugs with which he could take life.

After working for a year at the Brunswick Hospital in Amityville, he landed the job at the Good Samaritan Hospital in West Islip, Long Island, which would afford him the opportunities he needed for his berserk plan. Here the loner, the outcast, could achieve the attention he needed when he was appointed a member of the

hospital's 'Code Blue' team. Code Blue is hospital argot used to summon the speediest of aid when a patient is dying. The innocent language is used over a hospital's loudspeaker system to avoid frightening relatives or visitors. Doctors, nurses and technicians who are part of the Code Blue team must abandon everything they are doing and rush to the designated spot to begin the battle to save a life.

ANGEL OF DEATH

A Code Blue at the Good Samaritan Hospital was sounded after heart, lung or other monitoring machines issue an alarm – or if a member of staff notices a patient in extreme distress. This was perfect for Angelo – at last he would be at the centre of attention, apparently a hero life-saver to his peers, while in actuality he was an angel of death. District Attorney John Collins, who was later to prosecute him, said: 'I don't think he cared one bit for the people he preyed upon. I think what all this was about was the emergency code and the rush of adrenalin it gave him. His was not the gratification of helping save life – his kick came in the taking of it. In other words, it is analagous to the fireman who sets the fire, and then sits there and watches it burn and then ultimately gets involved in fighting the fire. He doesn't give a damn whether the building ultimately burns down but that he was there to be seen fighting the fire...that he is seen as a hero'.

In the last months of 1987 Richard Angelo treated the emergency rooms at Good Samaritan Hospital as his own personal playground of death. Using the drugs Pavulon and Anectine – paralysing drugs used as muscle relaxants – he could, in the right dosages, induce heart failure. In September of that year he worked in the combined cardiac-intensive care unit as an assistant supervisor, the perfect setting to play the hero – and have access to the drugs which enabled him to do it.

The first to die was John Fisher, aged 75, who was admitted on 4 September with signs of a stroke. By 7 September his condition had stabilised. But the following day he suffered a massive heart attack and died 20 minutes later. The next to die was Milton Poultney, 74, who was recovering from gall bladder surgery when he went into cardiac arrest on 16 September. He died hours later.

Next came Anthony Greene, 57, who suffered from a chronic chest disease. He was doing well until 28 September when he went into a respiratory coma. Although revived, he remained in a coma until he died on 16 October. Then on 9 October Frederick LaGois, aged 60, went into cardiac arrest the night before he was to undergo surgery. He died 12 hours later.

Losing patients in the high-stress, high stakes atmosphere of the emergency ward was nothing new. But no-one had ever had to work with the killer before. It would later transpire that the Code Blue leader – Angelo – had paid a quiet visit to the victims shortly before the alert was issued. And then he would reappear at the head of his team to become a lifesaver.

One man would fight back from the brink of death to give harrowing testimony at Angelo's trial. Gerolamo Kucich, 75, of Yugoslavia, who was visiting his son in America when he began to experience chest pains, found himself in the hospital under the watchful eye of Angelo. Early on the morning of 11 October a man wearing a white coat, who he thought was a doctor, came into his room and asked him how he was feeling before injecting something into his arm. These are the chilling words he related in court about how he felt at the time: 'A female nurse gave me a pill for pain in the morning. Then a man in a white coat appeared. He went right to the monitor and said: "Mr Kucich, how do you feel?" I said: "Not bad".

A NARROW ESCAPE

'The man opened his coat, pulled out what looked like a white fountain pen and said: "Now you are going to feel much, much better". I saw it was a needle. When he struck me I felt cold liquid. I was like dead. My muscles couldn't move. Everything went dead. The female nurse returned and I couldn't open my eyes. I heard her ask someone else in the room what he did and he said: "Nothing". I recognised the voice as that of the man who injected me. The woman was weeping and pleading with him to open my eyes. After a while, seconds or minutes that seemed like eternity, I heard her say: "He's started to breathe"'.

His co-workers began to call him the kiss-of-death because he was always present at so many tragedies. But they did not realise that their sick joke was true in every way. His berserk killing spree was only halted because Kucich made a complaint to police and they followed it up. When he was quizzed Angelo made no attempt at a cover up – even though he would later plead not guilty at his trial. In an 80-minute videotaped confession he said: 'I didn't want to hurt anybody. I did it to create crisis situations so that I would come out looking good'. Unmarked vials containing the drugs he used on his victims were discovered by detectives at his home, along with potassium chloride and hypodermic needles in his locker at work. 'I knew what I was doing and it was intentional',he said. 'The reason I injected it was because the unit was very busy and I felt inadequate in general. I felt I had to prove myself'.

He was found guilty at his trial in 1989 of murder, manslaughter and assault charge on at least six other patients who luckily survived. Superior Court Judge Alfred Tisch, sentencing him to spend 50 years to life in jail, said: 'You had no right to usurp

Above: *A sad, confused childhood undoubtedly had its effect on Angelo's adult life.*

CO-WORKERS BEGAN TO CALL HIM THE KISS-OF-DEATH BECAUSE HE WAS PRESENT AT SO MANY TRAGEDIES

God's function. Each of those patients, in their way, had the right to enjoy every day that was available to them. In my 19 years on the bench I have heard many horror stories but the testimony of Mr Kucich is at the top of the list and gives a new meaning to the term "depraved indifference"'.

Angelo left the court to spend his days in a place where there aren't any heroes – only losers.

BEVERLY ALLITT

If Angelo was the worst nightmare for Americans, then his monstrous British equivalent must without doubt be Beverly Allitt. Her slaughter of the innocents in a hospital ward makes her Britain's worst female serial slayer – the crimes all the more horrifying because they were carried out against children. Allitt, 24, murdered or tried to murder seven babies and toddlers on her ward in a 59-day period. She also attacked six other small victims on Ward Four at Grantham Hospital during the same period, making her a woman more reviled in British society than Moors Murderess Myra Hindley.

A sufferer of the rare syndrome 'Munchausen by Proxy,' Allitt could be a paragon of virtue and love one minute and ruthless killer the next. Munchausen's disease makes sufferers seek to draw attention to themselves by faking heart attacks or desperately injuring themselves. In Allitt's case it was by proxy – the harm was to others. Like Angelo, she craved attention and respect and so played the hero, trying to save the lives of the little ones whose lives she had initially placed in such mortal danger. Because her psychiatric disorder went unnoticed and untreated, she was able to roam about a National Health hospital like the grim reaper, gaining emotional satisfaction at the deaths of children.

DISTURBED CHILDHOOD

The sick hand that rocked the cradle of these doomed children was afflicted almost from birth. One of four children brought up in Corby Glen, a small Lincolnshire village, she was marked out from her earliest days as a child who craved attention. It would manifest itself in displays of tantrums, of dressing up, of talking loudly in class – anything which would ensure her more than a fleeting moment of acknowledgement from those in authority. Soon she took to going to school wearing plasters and bandages – but there were no wounds underneath. When that ruse was discovered she began bruising and cutting herself, proving to her peers and her teachers that she was genuinely hurt.

Her parents, Richard and Lillian, doted on her and believed her extreme methods to draw attention to herself were the product of nothing more than extreme enthusiasm. In fact, her self-esteem barely registered above zero – a precursor for Munchausen's Syndrome. Because she felt lost in the family, even though she was showered with affection, Allitt began to retreat into a make-believe world of wounds and illness-

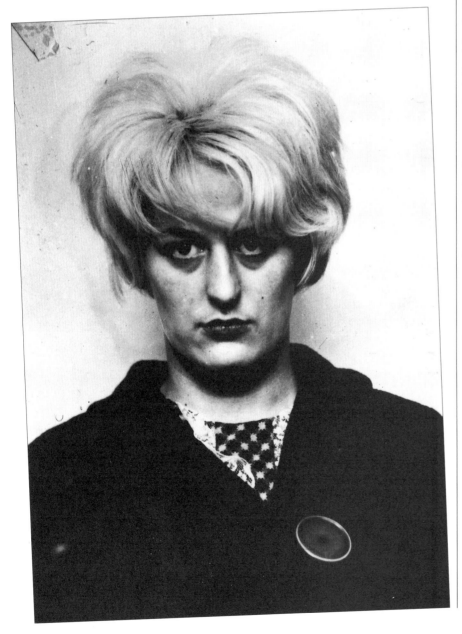

Below: *Myra Hindley, the epitome of female evil – until the Beverly Allitt case.*

es by the time she was five years old, the world which would ensure that she was always the centre of attention. As she got older Beverly Allitt collected maladies the way some young teens collect boyfriends. There were stomach illnesses, urological illnesses, backaches, cramps, headaches and on and on.

A TRUSTED TEENAGER

At school she took CSE examinations and one O-level which she decided to eventually use towards a career in nursing. She had done a great amount of babysitting for friends as a teenager, a practice which earned her the respect and good wishes of all who trusted her. Her schoolfriend Rachel Oliver recalled: 'She did a lot of babysitting because she was very fond of children and seemed to have a knack of handling them. Even when she was very young she was always playing with her little brother, pulling him along in his pushchair. She was just great with kids'.

Allitt enrolled at Grantham College on a preparatory nursing course for two years and from there went to Grantham and Kesteven Hospital as a trainee. But although she passed her exams, she was the only student in her year not offered a full-time job because senior staff were worried about the extent of her sick leave. In one year alone she had 94 days off sick for her imagined illnesses. Between 1987 and 1991 she was treated at the hospital where she was training 24 times for broken bones, bruises, leg, back and head injuries – all of them self-inflicted wounds. In February 1991, however, she landed a six month contract to stay on at the hospital to work in the short-staffed children's ward. One detective would later say: 'It was a make or break period for her. She had been given the chance to shine and show she was a good nurse'. But strange demons in her warped personality were tugging at her. Her obsessive need for success, to be the centre of attention, was pulling at her already. The job which would give her power over life and death would ultimately tip her over the brink.

In 59 days in 1991 there were four deaths and numerous grievously hurt children. The first to die was Liam Taylor, eight weeks old, who suffered a mysterious

heart attack on 23 February 1991. The boy, admitted for a chest infection, was given an insulin injection by Allitt as his parents slept in a hospital cot just feet away. Doctors switched off his life support machine and he died just a few hours later. The following victims are not in chronological order, but in order of the heinousness of the crimes.

Nine-week-old Becky Phillips was killed and her twin sister Katie was permanently brain damaged after two attempts to suffocate her. Peter Phillips and his wife Susan were emotionally devastated after the tragedies – but Allitt's demeanour was such that they believed her story that she had tried desperately to save Becky. They welcomed Allitt into their home and asked her to be godmother to Katie.

Above: *Beverly Allitt is driven away from Grantham Magistrates Court after her first appearance there.*

'SHE DID A LOT OF BABYSITTING BECAUSE SHE WAS VERY FOND OF CHILDREN... SHE WAS JUST GREAT WITH KIDS'

Above: *Superintendent Stuart Clifton of the Lincolnshire police force, who led the investigation into Allitt's crimes.*

WITHIN TEN MINUTES OF BEING LEFT ALONE WITH BEVERLY ALLITT, THE CHILD TURNED BLUE AND COLLAPSED

Katie was declared healthy but doctors decided to run a series of tests on her. The nurse left in charge was – Beverly Allitt. Within ten minutes of being left alone with the child she had turned blue and collapsed. She collapsed again two days later and was rushed to a specialist baby unit at Nottingham City Hospital before being released back on to Ward Four of the Grantham Hospital and once again prey to the tender mercies of Nurse Allitt. As a result the child has cerebral palsy, permanent brain damage, it is unlikely that she will ever be able to walk unaided, she is partially blind and she will never be able to speak properly.

UNEXPLAINED DEATHS

Timothy Hardwicke, 11, was physically and mentally disabled when he was admitted to the hospital. He died three hours later from a heart attack. Kayley Desmond, 14 months old, was admitted with a chest infection. A week later she collapsed after her skin became mottled and breathing became much harder. Luckily she was transferred to a hospital in Nottingham where she recovered. The next victim, Paul Crampton, survived Allitt's unique brand of medicine – but only just. The five-month-old boy received the second highest dose of insulin ever recorded in the British Isles. He was later found to have had 43,147 milli-units of insulin for every litre of his blood when the normal level would have been 12 to 15 milli-units. The only higher reading ever recorded was on an adult doctor who committed suicide by injecting himself with the drug. Ironically, Paul was recovering from his chest infection when he was admitted because Allitt was off, but he deteriorated upon her return. He too was transferred to the hospital in Nottingham where he made good progress away from her ministrations.

Clare Peck was the fourth murder victim. Aged 15 months, she was admitted for treatment for asthma and was briefly alone with Allitt. Later she was found blue and not breathing. She recovered – but collapsed again when Allitt was alone with her again and doctors could not save her.

As a mood of despondency and grief swept the hospital the unexplained collapses continued. People blamed the air condi-

Becky and Katie had been born prematurely and were taken to the hospital for treatment for ailments – in Becky's case, an upset stomach. She was fed by Allitt and released – but her mother recalled the horror that confronted her in the night: 'Her eyes dropped to the bottom of their sockets. I thought I was seeing things but it happened again. Her face was twitching and then she started to cry. It was a pitiful screaming. I have never heard a cry like it before, nor have I heard it since'. The family GP was called but found both heartbeat and temperature normal. The couple took Becky to bed with them but two hours later she stopped breathing. They rushed her to hospital where she was found to be dead upon arrival. Only later was the cause of her death discovered – a massive dose of insulin.

tioning system, believing that Legionnaire's Disease may have broken out. They blamed mysterious viruses and unclean air filters. In fact they blamed everything, except the 13-stone nurse who always seemed to be around when disaster and tragedy struck. No-one as yet believed the children were victims of anything other than cruel fate, except for Paul Crampton, whose insulin reading was triggering alarm bells among hospital management.

The mysterious tragedies continued. Bradley Gibson, five, was admitted with pneumonia and had a heart attack shortly after Allitt started her shift. It took doctors 32 minutes to restore the five-year-old's heartbeat, but he was left disabled. Yik Hung Chan, aged two, fractured his skull in a fall and was admitted on to Ward Four. He was found dark blue and not breathing after Allitt attended to him. He was transferred to Nottingham where he recovered. Michael Davidson, aged seven, was admitted after being shot in an air-gun accident. Allitt was alone with him when his heart stopped. An emergency team saved Michael with seconds to spare.

FIGHTING FOR LIFE

Christopher Peasgood, eight months, was in an oxygen tent with a breathing alarm when it sounded. A nurse found him dark blue and arching his back. Allitt stood nearby. After he recovered she was assigned to look after him again – and he collapsed again. He recovered at Nottingham. Christopher King, nine months, was admitted with severe vomiting. Allitt was again alone with him when he turned a mottled blue colour. Doctors believed he would die but he, too, recovered at the hospital in Nottingham. Patrick Elstone was seven weeks old when he was admitted with an ear infection. He stopped breathing and went blue. His breathing alarm was turned off. Later Beverly Allitt was found guilty of causing him grievous bodily harm. He has been left permanently brain damaged.

In less than two months she had reaped a grim harvest, but it had thankfully come to an end. Police were working on the case when they received information from Dr Derrick Teale, a biochemist at St Luke's Hospital, Guildford, Surrey, about the

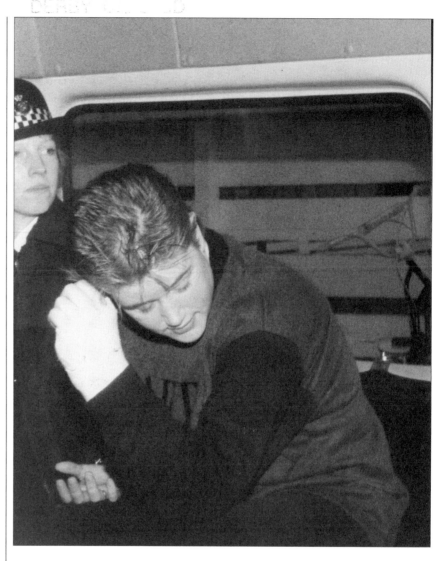

insulin injection upon Paul Crampton. Now Det Supt Stuart Clifton, in charge of the enquiry, knew that whoever was behind the deaths and ailments had access to restricted drugs within the hospital. But the police probe into the tragedies did not begin until 17 days after the attack on Paul Crampton – during which delay there was another murder and three more attacks. It was a lapse which has left many parents feeling bitter towards the authorities.

The police were able to draw certain conclusions in the case almost immediately. Every case had Allitt either treating the victim, or nearby when tragedy struck. She had access to proscribed drugs and in police questioning seemed sometimes overeager to help police out in their enquiries. Her answers were plausible, but Det Supt Clifton said: 'As we collected more and more evidence we discovered that she had been lying. There was a dawning realisation on us that something had gone terribly

Above: *Allitt en route to Grantham Magistrates Court. Parents who hoped for answers to what had happened to their loved ones were met with an arrogant silence.*

EVERY CASE HAD NURSE BEVERLY ALLITT EITHER TREATING THE VICTIM, OR NEARBY WHEN TRAGEDY STRUCK sometimes for five hours at a time. As a result we all had to work longer hours to cover for each other. The stress built up'. During coffee breaks and ward rounds nurses gathered to discuss the crisis on Ward Four. Allitt was always close by, eager and ready to join in the discussion never betraying any of her bestial actions. Another nurse said: 'She was always in the thick of it. It seems unbelievable that the person working so hard in those desperate situations was the one who had caused them in the first place. She was very concerned about the children, it seemed, and she became close to several of the parents'.

It was finally to be good old-fashioned detective work which nailed Allitt. A dozen officers were formed into a squad on 1 May 1991 at Grantham Police Station with sole responsibility to probe the hospital deaths. As detectives searched tirelessly for a common link between the deaths and collapses, a chilling pattern emerged. The first was the obvious fact that no mishaps occurred when she was off duty. The second was a wide probe into the hospital's use of insulin. After the test results on the Crampton boy nineteen other cases were studied more closely. It became apparent that in many of them the insulin, and in some cases

Love on the inside . . . kisses for evil Allitt

THE Sun 25p

GROUP 4 CARTOON SPECIAL PAGE 3

Thursday, May 20, 1993   25p   Today's TV: Pages 36 and 37

Audited daily sale for April 4,081,624 (including Today)

SCANDAL OF ALLITT'S JAIL LOVE

Sun EXCLUSIVE

Fury over gay fling

By MARTYN SHARPE and JOHN ASKILL

ANGEL of death Beverley Allitt is having a lesbian affair inside top security Rampton Hospital, it was revealed yesterday.

The 24-year-old nurse —awaiting sentence for murdering four tots on her ward —has confessed she is besotted with a "macho" arsonist called Sharon.

Parents of her victims were furious after hearing the pair had snatched moments of passion and been pictured kissing and cuddling.

Sue Phillips, whose nine-week-old daughter Becky was murdered by Allitt, said: "It's bloody disgusting that she's having a nice time in there while we're in pieces here.

"They should release her from Rampton, send her home to Grantham, and then the parents will deal with her. She wouldn't be having a nice time then."

Becky's twin sister, Katie, survived a

poison attack by Allitt, and is now brain damaged. Chris Taylor, whose seven-week-old son Liam was murdered, said: "The families will never recover from losing their children, but now we're told Allitt's enjoying herself falling in love inside Rampton.

"All we ask is that she should suffer for what she's done.

"It's disgraceful that we hear about

Continued on Page 13

HERE COMES RENTA SONIC

Deal on games at £2 a night

By NEIL SYSON

TOY giant Sega is to rent out games like Sonic the Hedgehog through a national video chain store.

Kids will be charged £2 a night for computer games from Blockbuster Video's 800 shops.

It will allow children to test them at home before

deciding whether it is worth forking out up to £65 a game.

Arch-rivals Nintendo could now feel forced to hit back with a similar scheme to make their own

games available. The two companies corner the £700million-a-year British market and have been blasted over high prices.

The Consumers' Association claims games cost under £10 to make.

shops to rent out games for a year, but Blockbuster paid more than £300,000 to become the first national outlet.

A spokesman for the Sun Mega Guide said: "It's about time - we have been calling for months for this to happen."

Sega has allowed smaller

amiss'. She was not the only suspect, however, as police had to quiz all nursing and other staff at the hospital. It was a process that took a dreadful emotional toll, leading one totally innocent nurse to kill herself – in lawmen's eyes, another victim of the vile Allitt. Her caring colleagues were haunted by the crimes – night sister Jean Saville, 49, to the point where she took her own life. Police said at her inquest that they were satisfied she had no involvement in the tragedies. A friend of hers said: 'Her feelings of isolation, shock and horror were all too much to bear. We were all under suspicion. We had been quizzed by police,

Above: *News of Allitt's warped love-life in jail was splashed on to the front pages of newspapers.*

ONE TOTALLY INNOCENT NURSE KILLED HERSELF - IN LAWMEN'S EYES, ANOTHER VICTIM OF THE VILE ALLITT

potassium chloride, had been injected without authorisation and in amounts that were too high. In each case they were linked to Nurse Allitt. The third factor was the disappearance of a book recording which patients had been allocated to which nurses – a book which was eventually found in her home. The fourth factor was the disappearance of pages from the report on Paul Crampton's condition – they had been torn out.

Finally she was confronted and charged with mass murderer – and she didn't bat an eyelid. Det Supt Clifton said: 'When she was charged she didn't appear to be surprised at all. I still don't know why she did it.'.

Beverly Allitt was remanded in Rampton top security mental hospital during the months after her arrest before her trial in 1993 which lasted for three months. She lost six stones while on remand, suffering from the slimmer's disease anorexia nervosa, and was placed on a constant suicide watch. At her trial she became the focus of the most intense hatred to grip the British public since Myra Hindley's trial nearly three decades previously. She pleaded not guilty but the evidence stacked against her was enough to condemn her and in May 1993 was found guilty of the four murders, the attempted murders of Katie Phillips, Bradley Gibson and Paul Crampton, and attacks on Kayley Desmond, Yik Hung Chan, Christopher King, Patrick Elstone, Christopher Peasgood and Michael Davidson. Parents who had hoped for some word, some indication from Allitt about why she had committed the heinous crimes were left disappointed. She left court not saying a word about why the murders had been carried out. The judge in the case said there would be counselling available for the jurors who had listened to such a litany of horror during the testimony.

ANGUISHED VICTIMS

A week later, amid the frenzied cries of anguished victims, she stood in court again to be sentenced to four life terms in jail. Again, she said nothing before she was driven away to begin the rest of her miserable life behind the bars and walls of Broadmoor, Britain's most secure establishment for mentally ill criminals.

Mad or bad? That is the question that has confronted experts when trying to come to terms with horror perpetrated on the scale of Allitt or Angelo. Allitt, it was heard at her trial, once exploded: 'I am not competent, far from it. I am one of the bloody crappiest nurses out. I am the lowest of the low'. This self-depreciation, evident also in Angelo, is common among Munchausen syndrome sufferers. And yet Dr David Enoch, a specialist in rare psychiatric disorders at the Royal Liverpool Hospital, said that it is not madness that afflicts the sufferer. He says: 'She is not mad, she is psychotic. When you are psychotic you lose insight and delude yourself. You do not know what you are doing.

ALLITT BECAME THE FOCUS OF THE MOST INTENSE HATRED SINCE MYRA HINDLEY'S TRIAL THREE DECADES BEFORE

Below: *The grim edifice of Broadmoor, home to Beverly Allitt for the rest of her days.*

Those who suffer from Munchausen's know that they are not really ill and have insight into their actions. In Allitt's case, she would have known what she was doing with the children'.

Brian Masters, who wrote an authoritative account of serial murderer Dennis Nielsen, said all of us have the potential within to kill. In people like Angelo and Allitt it is the destructive power which has gained control. 'It's there', he said, 'and we spend most of our lives keeping it at bay. Sometimes people don't succeed and sometimes they become serial killers'.

Such serious fault lines as existed in the personalities of Angelo and Allitt finally split asunder – and the innocents died to glorify what they perceive as their own, miserable lives.

CECIL JACOBSON
The Sperminator

At his trial, Dr Cecil Jacobson claimed that 'I haven't slept with anyone but my wife in 30 years of marriage'. Yet he stood accused of fathering at least 70 children. He had abused his position at his fertility clinic to live out a mad dream of fatherhood.

Twisted medical minds have long nurtured the idea of becoming creators of life. From Dr Frankenstein of gothic-horror fantasy to the grim work undertaken by Dr Josef Mengele in the death camp of Auschwitz – where his mission was to create a race of blonde-blue eyed children for his beloved Fuehrer – the medical fraternity has often been tainted by evil geniuses who twisted the moral of their Hippocratic Oath to suit their own ends. But rarely in modern times has a medical practitioner actually had the opportunity to live out his fantasy in such a warped fashion as one Dr Cecil Jacobson – the man who will forever go down in criminal history as 'The Sperminator'.

Dr Jacobson has every chance to reflect upon his unique 'work' in furthering the human race – sadly for him, however, it may be remembrance of things past from behind the bars of a prison cell. In March 1992 he was found guilty on 52 counts of fraud and perjury – charges which blandly masked his real crime of fathering 70 children, perhaps more, with his sperm artificially inseminated into clients of his fertility clinic. Dr Jacobson's perverted quest to build what he hoped would be an intelligent race of children was finally thwarted after he had fooled medical authorities for years.

At the end of a three-week trial in Alexandria, Virginia, in which Jacobson was both pilloried as an unmerciful con man and saluted as a scientific pioneer who sought only to relieve the suffering of childless women, the verdict left the doctor reeling in an exhausted state of resignation. 'I was astounded I was found guilty on any of these counts', said Jacobson, 55, once a highly respected genetic researcher. He said he made many mistakes during his practice but claimed he was convicted for nothing more than 'trying to help these people' – these people being simple, trusting, childless people who wanted more than anything in the world to have babies. But Jean Blair, one of the numerous women who testified against Jacobson, summed it up for all decent human beings when she said the doctor knowingly put his victims through a living hell. 'He will never know the emotional roller-coaster we were on', said Blair, noting that she suffered seven bogus miscarriages under Jacobson's care. 'We mourned every one of those dead babies'. Prosecutors described Jacobson as a swindler who injected women with high concentrations of hormones so that tests would show they were pregnant when they were not – all so he could enhance his reputation as a successful baby doctor and

Above and Opposite: *They called Dr Cecil Jacobson 'The Sperminator'. He had arrogantly breached every moral and ethical code of his calling by artificially inseminating women with his own semen.*

RARELY HAS A DOCTOR HAD THE OPPORTUNITY TO LIVE OUT HIS FANTASY IN SUCH A WARPED FASHION AS DR JACOBSON charge patients for more office visits. They also said that he intentionally misread sonograms, outlining tiny fetuses where none existed - again so that he could string patients along. They said Jacobson led insemination patients to believe that he had an anonymous sperm donor programme and that they could choose certain characteristics for their new children. He used his own semen and frequently pocketed $20

Right: *The perverted 'Angel of Death' Dr Mengele, in South America. Were his experiments at the Nazis' death camps so different from Jacobson's?*

Opposite: *'I have done nothing wrong' was Jacobson's cry until the end.*

Below: *The end result of the Nazis' experiments to create 'perfect children': some of the victims who were deemed 'not fit to live'.*

cash from patients, saying the money was for the donor.

Jacobson's attorneys attempted to paint quite a different picture, a portrait of a scientist who helped women who had been abandoned by other doctors, either because they were fast approaching menopause or had physiological obstacles to conception. 'I knew my semen was safe', said Jacobson, 'because I haven't slept with anyone but my wife in 30 years of marriage'. They conceded, however, that he misread many test results and was probably better suited to a lab than a clinic. The defence attorneys said that, on occasion, Jacobson used his own sperm, but only because he feared that semen available from sperm banks might be tainted with HIV virus or other diseases. The result, they say, is that many patients who had been told they might never conceive now have healthy, happy children.

PLEA OF INNOCENCE

'We think this doctor is innocent, that he was a pioneer in his field', said James R. Tate, one of Jacobson's attorneys. 'He was so far ahead of his time that back at the time of civil cases several years previously he couldn't find much support. We'll have a lot of support this time'.

The jury of eight women and four men struggled for 22 hours over four days to reach its decision, meticulously examining the case count by count. 'Some of us had over 400 pages of notes', said jury foreman Daniel Richard, who said he at first was convinced of Jacobson's innocence. 'We spent four days just reconstructing each patient's history. That's what took so long. It was a matter of complexity'.

Assistant US Attorney Randy Bellows, who worked on the case for more than two years with the help of postal inspectors and the FBI, was clearly pleased with the results. But Bellows focused his comments largely on the victims, whom he thanked for going 'through the difficult process of coming forward and testifying at trial . . . and reliving very difficult and sad moments in their lives'.

Bellows gave special credit to patients who now have children fathered by Jacobson and who risked public exposure 'to contribute to this search for the truth'.

The prosecution noted that the 11 parents testifying against Jacobson had 15 children ranging in age from four to 14, with more than half of them aged nine or older. Many of the children, he argued, were old enough to discover accidentally their true parentage simply by watching television or reading a newspaper.

Jacobson's attorneys charged the government with endangering the psychological welfare of Jacobson's former patients and violating Jacobson's promise to the parents that the donor programme would remain anonymous. 'It is also ironic that what the government seeks to conceal from these children is that their genetic heritage may, in fact, be superior to what they would otherwise have received', Tate said. 'The donor could have been a vagrant who carried the HIV virus and who sold his sperm to a "sperm bank" used by Dr. Jacobson'.

A LENGTHY AFFAIR

The 15-day trial alternated between wrenching accounts by past patients and plodding presentations by scientific experts, capping a case that began four years ago when more than 20 patients brought malpractice suits against Jacobson for leading them to believe they were pregnant when they were not. The women testi-

Above: The beginning of the end: Jacobson seen going to court in February 1992 to answer the charges laid against him.

DESPITE THE SHOCKING EVIDENCE, AMERICAN LAW DOES NOT IN FACT FORBID DOCTORS TO IMPREGNATE THEIR PATIENTS

fied in civil depositions and at a hearing before the State Board of Medicine that Jacobson gave them hormone shots that triggered false pregnancy tests, used phoney sonograms to perpetuate the fraud, and then told them their foetuses were dead and would 'resorb'"into their bodies. But in November 1992 the case gained notoriety when prosecutors brought a massive indictment against Jacobson, charging the man born in the Mormon state of Utah with using his own semen to treat women who came to him for what they thought was an anonymous sperm donor programme. Prosecutors said their evidence showed that Jacobson may have fathered more than 70 children for patients treated at his now-defunct Reproductive Genetics Clinic. The allegation that provoked massive news coverage as far away as Brazil, France, Britain and Australia – and global indignation that

people's basic rights had been so callously violated. That number was pushed even higher during Jacobson's own testimony in which he said he had used his sperm to impregnate some patients he saw at George Washington University Medical Center when he worked there from 1972 to 1976.

Despite the shocking evidence American law does not in fact forbid doctors to impregnate their patients, and Bellows was forced to rely on commonplace mail and wire fraud statutes to prosecute the bulk of his case. Throughout the trial, despite dozens of government witnesses, the question of why Jacobson would lead women to believe they were pregnant and why he would impregnate his own patients remained blurred – although from observers on the outside there were many theories. Bellows and Assistant US Attorney David G. Barger argued that

Jacobson did it for money, saying that if a woman thought she were pregnant she would return for more office visits and refer more patients to Jacobson. They said the donor programme also was for money, explaining that using his own sperm saved him the expense of creating a legitimate donor bank. Jacobson's Reproductive Genetics Center in Virginia thrived in the 1970s after he became the first doctor in the United States to perform amniocentesis, a method of detecting foetal defects. But as other doctors began to offer the procedure, Jacobson lost patients and income, Bellows said during the trial. Richard, the jury foreman said that he and fellow jurors were convinced that it was 'ridiculous' to believe Jacobson acted for money and that, if anything, Jacobson 'undercharged his prices'. Richard said he felt Jacobson impregnated patients out of sheer ego – an overwhelming desire to play the role of creator, a Jesus Christ figure in his own mind whereby he was making a race of intelligent children in his own image. Psychiatrist James Anderson, who examined the case in close detail, concurred, saying: 'It is obvious that neither fame nor money nor any perverted sexual lusts were behind what he was doing. He was getting his kicks from playing Mother Nature. He saw himself as some kind of superman, the father of the human race. And he got away with it for a long time. There are probably 70 of his offspring walking around in society – perhaps even more – and how do we know how many of them may have inherited his berserk view of life? What kind of problems will these children have in the future? Will it be the sins of the fathers visiting them? These are the most disturbing aspects of this entire sordid affair – the possibility that he has spawned nothing but deviants into society who may yet wreak misery on the parents who will lovingly and tenderly bring them up.

CHARACTER EXAMINATION

'Examining his character, I believe that he was dreadfully frightened of failure and longing to create something more permanent on this earth other than mortgage payments, a home for his family and an impressive work record. He wanted to be recognised as a great man, even if it was only

ever to be savoured in his own mind'. Juror Ronald Mattingly also chalked up Jacobson's misdeeds to a stubborn refusal to accept failure. 'He couldn't stop – he was trying something that didn't work and when he realised it didn't work, he didn't stop', Mattingly said. Deborah Gregory, a key government witness who had three bogus pregnancies, believed money may have

Above: *How many had he fathered? The Sperminator didn't know, but he disputed figures put forward by the prosecution.*

Above: *The Sperminator finds support in his wife Joyce (left) and his father Cecil Snr as he arrives at court.*

played a small part in Jacobson's thinking, but added that he also might have been pursuing the glory he knew when he brought amniocentesis to America two decades ago. 'Research and science is his first love and I believe he saw a way to make money, but also saw a way to experiment with something that might bring fame as well as fortune. He was looking for a new amniocentesis to discover', she said. 'But I resented him taking my money and using me as his guinea pig', Gregory added. 'Don't use me as your experiment and add insult to injury by taking my money and lying to me while you're doing it'.

Because of the quirks in the law which did not specifically forbid the good doctor from using his own sperm, the authorities had to get him primarily on fraud and perjury raps. As a result, prosecutors had to push aside questions of medical ethics and tailor a white-collar mail fraud case to accommodate a host of allegations that were anything but conventional.

Jack H. Olender, one of Washington's most experienced malpractice lawyers,

> LIKE GANGSTER AL CAPONE, JACOBSON WAS CONVICTED OF A LESSER CRIME THAN THE PUBLIC BELIEVED HIM GUILTY OF

compared the U.S. attorney's strategy of using multi-purpose fraud statutes against Jacobson to the prosecutions of old-time gangsters. 'The great gangsters like Al Capone were prosecuted for tax fraud or wire fraud because they couldn't get them on anything else – even though the things they had done to earn the money were much worse', Olender said. In 30 years of practice, Olender can remember only one other case in which a doctor was criminally prosecuted – a case in which a surgeon performed partial abortions and patients had to return for additional treatments. 'It really takes something very bad to transcend civil law into criminal law – something really outrageous', he said.

For America, that really outrageous thing was personified by Dr. Cecil Jacobson.

Gripped by the possibility that dozens of Jacobson's genetic offspring were enrolled in Washington and Virginian schools, newspapers, television companies and Hollywood production companies deluged the usually sedate Alexandria courthouse with requests for information, documents and front-row seats during the trial. He was eventually found guilty of travel fraud, convicted of mail and wire fraud for lying to patients, using the US Postal Service to order supplies and collect bills and using telephones to discuss treatment. The six perjury counts were based on lies Jacobson told during civil actions against him several years ago.

A CRUEL LIAR

When the sentencing came down on Jacobson a month later, it came down with a vengeance. US District Judge James C. Cacheris said he 'cruelly lied to women at the most vital and traumatic point in their lives'. He sentenced him to five years in jail – although he could technically have

JUDGE CACHERIS SAID JACOBSON 'CRUELLY LIED TO WOMEN AT THE MOST VITAL AND TRAUMATIC POINT IN THEIR LIVES'

Below: *Guilty! But Jacobson still finds time to explain himself to the media after his trial.*

given him a maximum term of 280 years inside – but added the rider that it must be served without the possibility of parole or early release. He also ordered Jacobson to pay $116,000 in fines – around £85,000 – saying he had 'not seen a case where there has been this degree of emotional anguish and psychological trauma'. Before sentencing, which came several weeks after Jacobson was found guilty, he repeated claims he made before and during his trial that he never intended to dupe his patients and that he had dedicated his life to helping couples desperate for children.

'I was totally unaware of the anger, anguish and hate I have caused – until these proceedings', Jacobson told Judge Cacheris. 'I ask for their forgiveness so that the healing process can start. But I helped a great deal of other people'. But Dr Richard

Falk, head of the infertility programme at Columbia Hospital for Women in Washington, appeared for the prosecution and ridiculed the notion that Jacobson had done no harm by sowing his seed so energetically. Falk says that at most sperm banks it is standard practice to limit the number of times a donor is used to prevent the possibility of half-siblings unwittingly marrying someday, thus risking retardation and birth defects among their own offspring. To Falk, the suggestion that Jacobson had used his sperm to father so many children was shocking. 'That's unconscionable in and of itself – to have a bunch of families in one area whereby it's almost sure that there'll be several children in a school who are half-siblings', he testified. 'If I was a parent of one of those chil-

JACOBSON DEFENDED HIS ACTIONS BY PROTESTING 'I DID NOT WISH TO HURT THESE PEOPLE. I WISHED TO HELP'

Opposite: *Jacobson talks to reporters while facing the prospect of numerous years in jail.*

Below: *Jacobson's wife Joyce was one of the few people who stood by him during his trial.*

dren I would move right away from the area'. Jacobson, who was released on bond pending his appeal, concluded: 'I did not wish to hurt these people. I wished to help'.

TEARFUL TESTIMONY

Fighting back tears, a woman who testified during the 12-day trial that Jacobson was the biological father of her daughter said the sentence was 'fair', but added that 'nothing ever will make up for the pain she and her husband suffered. The woman, one of 11 parents who testified under pseudonyms to conceal their own and their children's identities from the media glare, said that 'the satisfaction is he can't practise now. Nobody should ever have to go through this again'.

Daniel M. Clements, chairman of RESOLVE Inc., a non-profit advocacy group on infertility issues, said that Jacobson's case and the subsequent publicity, has caused infertile couples all across America to exercise more caution in choosing treatment and physicians. 'Jacobson is viewed for what he was, which is an aberrant practitioner', Clements said. Cramming the building's largest courtroom, a standing-room only crowd of victims, gawkers, Jacobson supporters and journalists sat in mesmerised silence as Cacheris pronounced sentence and brought the nationally celebrated case to a close.

Throughout the criminal case, Jacobson and his attorneys maintained that he was a pioneer whose fertility medicine was on the cutting edge.

LETTERS OF SUPPORT

'All he did was try to help people', said James R. Tate, his attorney, noting that the judge received 90 letters of support from Jacobson's friends and former patients. 'This is breaking his heart. But he still has his integrity and stood up for what he believed in'. Cecil Jacobson Sr., the doctor's father, denounced the case as a government 'witch hunt' and denigrated those who complained about his son as gold diggers who saw an opportunity to make money through civil suits. 'This has not broken our family apart. It's brought us together', said Jacobson's father. 'This thing is all going to blow apart at some point'. Joyce Jacobson, the doctor's wife, said she was insulted by the suggestion that he was greedy for cash. 'We don't buy fancy clothes, and you should see the cars we drive', she said. She also suggested that her husband's use of his own semen was an obvious and safe alternative to expensive donor banks. 'It's like giving blood to me – what's the difference? It has shock value, but when you think about it, where are you going to get better sperm?' The family also took some pleasure in the fact that Cacheris rejected the government's request to have Jacobson jailed while he pursues his appeal, a process that prosecutors estimated would take a year. Assistant U.S. Attorney Randy I. Bellows, who had asked the court to put Jacobson behind bars for ten years and make him pay more than $1 million in

THE EFFECT THAT
JACOBSON HAD ON THEIR
LIVES IS STILL TOO MUCH
FOR SOME WOMEN TO
COMPREHEND

Below: How Britain's Daily Express *reported a scandal that touched a nerve in every parent.*

fines, nonetheless expressed satisfaction with the five-year term, noting that it is a harsh sentence for a white-collar fraud case. Bellows said that Cacheris's ruling made it clear that 'when a doctor is found guilty of lying to his patients on matters of fundamental importance, there will be a severe sentence meted out'. On Tate's request, Cacheris said he would ask that Jacobson be allowed to serve his time at the minimum-security federal prison at Nellis Air Force Base in Las Vegas. The prison, where inmates live in dormitory-style rooms without bars and may be allowed to work on the base, is one of the closest to Jacobson's Utah home. Cacheris ordered that $39,205 of the $116,000 fine be used to compensate witnesses who testified that they had been wronged by Jacobson and who had not collected money through previous civil suits.

What he did is still too much for some women to comprehend. Carole Franda, another former patient, has a 13-year-old son as a result of insemination at his clinic.

Because of his notoriety now she says; 'There is this shadow and cloud over the paternity of these children. This is tearing families apart. It's hurt the grandparents. Most couples never told their parents about the insemination. You have grandparents who loved and doted on these children'.

MORAL DILEMMAS

At the time of writing, The Sperminator is still free while the legal process grinds inexorably onwards towards a verdict. But whatever his fate, it is left to the parents who relied on him to decide what to tell their own children. For Carole Franda, who presumed she was being impregnated with her own husband's sperm, the choice has been made to keep herself – and him – in the dark. 'I love him for what he is', she said. 'If I had his DNA tested he would know that I was questioning his paternity. The fact is he is a human being I love and I think other families should adopt this frame of mind too'.

Guilty! The Sperminator

Doctor who artificially inseminated women himself faces 280 years in jail

THE BABYMAKER: Jacobson leaving court with wife Joyce yesterday

A FERTILITY doctor was last night found guilty of secretly using his own sperm to make his patients pregnant.

Self-styled "babymaker" Dr Cecil Jacobson fathered up to 75 children.

The 55-year-old specialist pretended he was using anonymous sperm donors.

But he was caught out when some mothers noticed their children looked like the chubby doctor.

One woman testified that she noticed her daughter's resemblance to Jacobson in a photograph when the baby was just three days old.

Another patient said he told her: "God doesn't give you babies — I do."

Jacobson now faces a jail sentence of up to 280 years and about £300,000 in fines. But he showed no emotion when the verdict was read out.

Doctors are not forbid-

From IAN MacGREGOR
in New York

den from using their own sperm, but Jacobson's patients were told the sperm was from medical students.

They were able to choose characteristics like eye colour, religion, and hair colour.

Yet a former lab technician for Jacobson said there was no sperm bank and the doctor often went into a bathroom to fill vials.

Lying

Jury foreman Daniel Richard said outside the court: "We knew he was lying to those patients."

Jacobson, who has seven children by his wife, Joyce, always said he did not hurt anyone.

"I've never knowingly lied to a patient," he claimed. "I have misinformed out of ignorance."

The jury in Alexandria,

Virginia, found him g of 52 counts of frau perjury.

He was also accuse tricking women believing they were nant when they were

Jacobson said last "I spent my life tryi help women have dren. It is a shock found guilty of tryi help people.

"I certainly did no fully or intentionally anyone."

But prosecutor R Bellows told the cou doctor was a "man routinely lies to his patients."

Jacobson admitted sionally using his sperm when donors not available.

But he claimed h not know how many dren he fathered.

He will be sentence May 8.

KILLING
AND CRIME

MURDER ADDICTS
Serial Killers

From Jack the Ripper to the Son of Sam, serial killers have left behind a legacy of monstrous malevolence and the bloody, twisted wreckage of their innocent prey. Nothing in the crimson annals of crime can compare to their heinous evil.

Serial killers are the most terrifying, elusive and depraved murderers in society... fiends who represent the darkest, most despicable side of the human soul. At any one time, say law enforcement officials, there are hundreds of them out there, stalking their innocent quarry from lonely country roads to big-city apartment houses.

According to the American Federal Bureau of Investigation, which has conducted lengthy profile studies of serial killers, one of the most terrifying aspects of these vicious psychopaths is their ability to blend in with their community. And until the overwhelming urge to kill strikes them, they may appear to be completely normal, and could even be your next door neighbour, doctor or butcher.

Yet underneath that cheerful, friendly exterior lurks a walking time bomb, capable of the most sadistic murders imaginable. And once the killing starts, the ghoul will not stop until he or she is caught.

Although America is home to most of the known 'recreational killers' – the FBI estimate their victims in the hundreds each year – one of the most shocking cases of serial killing occurred in the former Soviet Union, in and around the woodlands surrounding the industrial town of Rostov-on-Don, some 25 miles from the Black Sea.

For more than eight years, the citizens of the area were held captive by the grim fiend known only as 'The Lesopolosa Killer', after the Russian word for woodlands. Today, we know him as Andrei Chikatilo, family man, one-time school teacher and Communist Party member. By the time he was arrested in 1990, Chikatilo had savagely slain more than 50 men, women and children. Even hardened members of the Soviet militia were stunned by the barbarity of the crimes. Victims were usually found with their eyes gouged out and their sex organs horribly mutilated.

In a sense, Chikatilo was a textbook example of the serial killer. Born in the Ukraine in 1936, during the famine orchestrated by Joseph Stalin, Chikatilo was the product of intense poverty and a dominant, cruel mother, who repeatedly beat and admonished the young boy. Even more telling, however, was the fact that he was born with a brain abnormality which, among other disorders, made him a chronic bed-wetter and sexually deficient. As a lad, he was ridiculed and bullied by schoolmates, and was often the butt of their cruel jokes. Despite this pathetic childhood, however, he was a good student, and, by the time he was a teenager, had even become a staunch Communist and leader of one of the state-approved student clubs which helped senior citizens.

ONE OF THE MOST TERRIFYING ASPECTS OF THESE PSYCHOPATHS IS THEIR ABILITY TO BLEND IN WITH THEIR COMMUNITY

Opposite and Below:
Andrei Chikatilo, the brooding, depraved monster who killed dozens to fuel his abnormal sex drive.

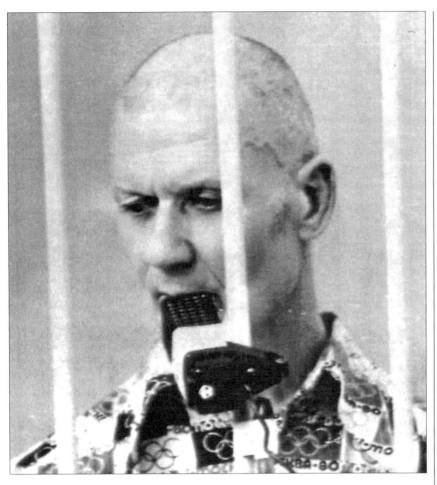

Above: *Chikatilo's shaved head and surly demeanour did little to enhance his appeal as he argued in his own defence in the court at Rostov.*

HIS SEXUAL IMMATURITY MADE HIS EXPERIENCES WITH GIRLS VERY UPSETTING. HE THOUGHT HE WAS A TOTAL FAILURE

But his sexual immaturity made his few experiences with girls very upsetting and, increasingly, Chikatilo began to think of himself as a total failure. That sense of inadequacy was only heightened when he was rejected by the Moscow State University Law School, the most distinguished college in the Soviet Union. After he was turned down, he was drafted, and assigned to a communications unit with the KGB, where he served for three years, and in 1960 he became a member of good standing of the Communist Party.

After his release from service, Chikatilo took a number of minor labouring jobs and settled down in 1963 with his new wife, Feodosia, who would later bear him a son and a daughter, despite his sexual immaturity. For the next 27 years, he would somehow maintain the appearance of a normal family man. A year after he married, he began taking a university course by correspondence and eventually moved to Rostov as a teacher of Russian literature. It was there that his gradual descent into sexual perversion began, and for more than five years, from 1973 to 1978, he sexually abused numerous male and female students. Even though he was fired by several schools, he always found new employment. In those days, the Soviet Union bureaucracy chose to cover up the scandal rather than confront it, and Chikatilo was not even charged, let alone jailed. It was a decision that was to have tragic consequences for dozens of innocents.

By 1981, he had decided to give up his career as a school teacher, and took up a job as a travelling salesman for a government-run steel factory. It gave him the freedom he craved... and soon the killing spree began. The first body, that of bright-eyed 13-year-old Lyubov Biryuk, was found in June 1982, outside her small village of Zaplavskaya. Despite her young age, and the savagery of her death – she had been repeatedly stabbed, sexually abused and had had her eyes gouged out – her murder received little more attention than that of the hundreds of others committed every year in the area. But by October, when two more bodies were found in nearby woodlands – all bearing the same horrible wounds – the militia knew they were not dealing with routine murder.

MORE BODIES

During the course of the following year, seven more bodies were found and, for a while, investigators thought they might have two killers at large because the victims had been both male and female. But in September 1983, the militia believed they had cracked the case when a young man confessed to the hideous crimes after several days of intense interrogation.

Gradually, however, officials concluded he was not the murderer, but had been forced into making a false confession by overzealous underlings eager to get a conviction. Moreover, even while the 'suspect' was being held in jail on another charge, auto theft, the body count grew higher. So much so that by the summer of 1984, bodies were being discovered more quickly than they could be identified.

In all, 23 had been found since little Lyubov had been located and the citizens of Rostov, despite a near-total media blackout by the state-run press and television, began to grow increasingly anxious. The militia were also feeling the strain of long hours and nightly undercover surveillance of bus and train stations where many of the victims had been last seen.

It was at one of those bus stations, in late August, that police noticed a middle-aged businessman chatting with a teenaged girl. Shortly afterwards, the girl walked away and caught a bus. But the man then approached another young woman. The militia on duty identified himself and asked the man for some identification. His name into a nearby park where he spoke to yet more women. Then the officer observed Chikatilo sit down next to a teenager on a park bench. It became evident to the policeman that she was a prostitute when she and Chikatilo engaged in a sex act.

A short while later, after the suspect had left the park and taken a street car towards the city centre, the officer decided to arrest him on the charge of committing a perverted act in public.

Below: *Incongruous in a shirt bearing the Olympic symbol, Chikatilo awaits his fate.*

was Andrei Chikatilo, and he explained to the officer he was merely waiting for his bus to take him home.

The policeman let him go after questioning the young woman, who informed him that Chikatilo had done or said nothing improper. But two weeks later, the officer saw him again at the same station. This time, when Chikatilo boarded a bus, the undercover policeman decided to follow him. For almost three hours, he tagged Chikatilo as he constantly switched buses and started up conversations with lone women. Finally, the bespectacled suspect stopped at a diner, and began talking with a drunk woman. He left, alone, then went

At the station, officers opened Chikatilo's briefcase and discovered a large kitchen knife, a piece of rope, a jar of Vaseline and a soiled towel. The jubilant militia believed they had found their man... they were right, of course, but when a blood test was taken, it was discovered that Chikatilo had type A blood – yet semen samples taken from some of the victims proved the actual killer had blood type AB. Police had no choice but to reluctantly rule him out as a suspect. Tragically, for the more than two dozen victims to follow, the discrepancy in the blood types would later be blamed on flawed laboratory work. The killer did, indeed, have type A blood!

TRAGICALLY FOR TWO DOZEN VICTIMS, CHIKATILO WAS RELEASED BECAUSE OF FLAWED POLICE LABORATORY WORK

*Above: **The sorority house where Margaret Bowman and Lisa Levy were brutally murdered.***

POLICE KNEW OF 36 BODIES BUT CHIKATILO CONFESSED TO 53, AND EVEN LOCATED SOME OF THE REMAINS FOR THEM

The investigation, which was hampered by the crude techniques of Soviet bureaucracy throughout the murderous rampage, was back to square one after Chikatilo's release, and over the course of the next few years, more bodies were discovered and more suspects cleared. The increasing death toll was worrying even the Communist masters of the Kremlin, but the fiend remained at large despite the massive manpower assigned to the case.

It wasn't until the summer of 1990 that police finally got another long-awaited break. Some of the then most recent victims had been found not far from the small railway station of Donleskhoz, set amid a national forest, so officers decided to flood the major stations along the line with uniformed militia, thereby goading the killer into using the smaller one again in his frenzied search for more prey. Undercover officers were assigned to the station, and to

two others along the same route. Names were taken and everyone closely observed. But on 13 November, after the discovery of yet another body, militia officials obtained a list of the names of men who had disembarked from the train at Donleskhoz the day of the woman's disappearance. One name seemed familiar... Andrei Chikatilo.

For the next seven days, the suspect was placed under 24-hour surveillance while police checked his business travel records against the recorded abductions. Yet although they were convinced they had the right man, officials knew they had only circumstantial evidence (in 1990, they were by now aware that the killer had type A blood, not AB). On 20 November, however, they brought him in for questioning, hoping to secure a much-needed confession. It came an exhausting nine days later. But Chikatilo had one last surprise for the police. They knew of just 36 bodies, but he confessed to 53 murders, and even located some of the remains for them. The true total may have even been higher, and he was quickly dubbed 'The Maniac' by the local newspapers.

A DIABOLICAL DEMEANOUR

It was at his trial, which began on 14 April 1992, that the world got its first close look at the Lesopolosa Killer, a bald, middle-aged man with wild, vacant eyes and a diabolical demeanour. During the trial, which lasted six months, Chikatilo would sway back and forth on his bench, often muttering incoherently to himself. He was kept in a cage during his appearances, to keep him safe from the justified wrath of his victims' anguished relatives. On several occasions, his maniacal nature manifested itself in bizarre ways: he would launch into rambling tirades, expose himself, sing, and once even claimed the judge was interested in having oral sex with him.

Some courtroom observers believed his erratic behaviour was a carefully designed ruse to convince the jury he was insane. But in the end, he was ruled sane, and convicted of 52 counts of murder. It was ruled that there was insufficient evidence to find him guilty on one of the counts. The following day, 15 October, Chikatilo was sentenced to death, and in February 1994 he was executed.

Left: *Ted Bundy was the most ruthless sex psychopath America has ever known.*

Below: *The many faces of Bundy, who could either charm his victims or murder them in a blind frenzy.*

A MURDER EXPLOSION

While the monstrous crimes of Chikatilo are believed to be a rarity in the former Soviet Union – remembering, of course, that the old Communist rulers preferred not to wash their dirty laundry in public – the same cannot be said of America. Indeed, in the past 30 years, there has been an explosion in the number of serial killers in the United States, and their legions are growing rapidly. Criminal and social experts say there are many reasons for the dramatic increase, including the widespread use of sexual imagery and graphic violence within the entertainment industry.

Others claim the surge is due in part to an important element of American society – the well-developed interstate highway systems, which means a killer can roam with ease from state to state, leaving police with nothing but a seemingly senseless and unconnected murder on their hands.

Ted Bundy, who hid a fiendish blood lust behind an attractive, almost angelic countenance, was typical of the 'highway killers', murdering at least 28 young women in an orgy of sexual abuse and death across five states. Outwardly, he differed remarkably from the general image of the serial killer: he was devastatingly handsome, popular with women, a brilliant legal scholar and politically ambitious. Yet his inner demons made him a modern-day version of Jekyll and Hyde.

His killing spree began in January 1974, in Seattle, Washington, when a 21-year-old student, Linda Healy, vanished from her lodgings. Police found no clues at the scene, except for her blood-splattered bed sheets. Two weeks earlier, another student,

who lived just blocks away from Linda, had been savagely beaten, but survived. Initially, police had no clues – or reason – to link the two crimes... but a pattern quickly emerged.

On 12 March, 19-year-old Donna Gail Manson left her campus dormitory in nearby Olympia, to drive to a concert. She never arrived. One month later, Susan Rancourt, a pretty blonde student at the Central Washington State College in Ellensburg, arranged to meet a girlfriend at a campus movie house. Like Linda and Donna, she vanished without a trace. Detectives investigating her disappearance made the routine inquiries, checking with fellow students if they had seen any suspicious characters on the campus.

A SLY RUSE

One girl told them she had been approached by a tall, handsome man, who had his arm in a sling. As she walked towards him, he dropped his books, and asked her if she would carry them to his car, a tan Volkswagen parked a few hundred yards away. She agreed, but as they neared the car, she noticed the passenger seat was missing. By some remarkable intuition, she sensed danger, and dumped the books on the car bonnet and fled. As police later discovered, Susan Rancourt's path to the cinema would have taken her through the parking lot.

Less than three weeks after Susan's disappearance, Bundy struck again, abducting Roberta Parks as she strolled through the tree-lined neighbourhood surrounding the State University in Oregon.

Unfortunately, police found no clues this time. But in June, following the disappearance of Brenda Ball from a Seattle bar, investigators got their first real break... she had been seen talking to a handsome man with his arm in a sling. Police had their pattern, and while no bodies had been found, they were certain there was a serial killer on the loose.

Throughout the summer of 1974, seven more women would disappear in Washington and Oregon. Friends of one of the missing girls, Janice Ott, remembered seeing her with a man carrying an arm in a sling, and had overheard him mention his name was Ted. By this time, investigators

Below: Sergeant Robert Hayward, the man who first arrested Bundy.

had a decent description of their man and his car, and when newspapers published the name 'Ted' and the make of the car, police were flooded with tips and possible suspects. The number soon swelled to more than 3,500, among them the name Ted Bundy. In a painstaking search, police officers checked out every Ted, but dismissed Bundy as a possible suspect because of his

clean background and the fact he did some work for the state Crime Commission.

It wasn't until September, more than nine months after the terror began, that a body was found, hidden on a wooded hillside outside Seattle. It would later be identified as Janice Ott. Other bodies, either strangled or bludgeoned to death, were soon located, and police were hopeful that their discovery would soon lead them to the killer. But strangely, there had been no reported disappearances in the area for three months.

They had no reason to know that the mysterious Ted had already left for Utah, until the same pattern quickly emerged: young women disappearing; last seen in the company of a handsome stranger.

Although police in both states kept in contact about the grisly similarities of the

SEVERAL YOUNG WOMEN HAD DISAPPEARED. ALL OF THEM HAD LAST BEEN SEEN IN THE COMPANY OF A HANDSOME STRANGER murders, no-one seemed to have noticed that Bundy was in Utah attending college when that state's terror began. By the winter of 1975, women in neighbouring Colorado also began disappearing. Their bodies continued to turn up for more than eight months. Investigators were stumped. The killer had left a trail of death in four states, yet they were no closer to catching him then they had been 18 months earlier, when the killing spree began.

But on Saturday, 16 August, as the body count rose, Salt Lake City veteran police officer Bob Hayward stopped the driver of a small VW for erratic driving. Upon examination of the vehicle, Hayward booked Bundy on suspicion of burglary. After his arrest, police found credit card receipts and maps that linked him to towns where several of the women had disappeared in Colorado. A woman, who had escaped his clutches, positively identified him, and Bundy was found guilty of attempted kidnapping.

THE ICE-COOL KILLER

In January 1977, he was extradited to Colorado, where he was to go on trial for murder. But the ice cool Bundy had no intentions of facing more prison time. During a hearing that June, he simply strolled into the courtroom library and jumped out of a second floor window. He was caught driving a stolen car just eight days later, and sent back to prison... where he stayed for six months until he escaped yet again by easing his way through a small opening in the ceiling of his cell.

He made it all the way to Tallahassee, Florida, a campus city drenched in tropical sunshine. Within two weeks of his amazing escape, Bundy entered a women's dormitory and raped and bludgeoned to death two students. Less than one hour later, he viciously attacked another woman who lived just blocks away. At the murder scene, police found bite marks in the buttocks of the victims.

Then, on 6 February, he stole a van and drove to Jacksonville, where he murdered 12-year-old Kimberly Leach. Tiny Kimberly was to be his last victim. Police spotted the stolen van and, after a brief scuffle, arrested him. Bundy grimly told the arresting officers: 'I wish you'd killed

Above: *A love of Satan and a loathing for humankind turned Richard Ramirez from Mr Nobody into The Night Stalker, a killer who plunged Los Angeles into fear.*

WITHIN TWO WEEKS OF ESCAPING CUSTODY, BUNDY HAD RAPED AND BLUDGEONED TO DEATH TWO STUDENTS

me'. It was a telling statement that offered a rare peek into the twisted mind of a homicidal maniac.

Once he was positively identified as Ted Bundy, police took impressions of his teeth to compare them with the bite marks on the Tallahassee victims. His killing spree was at an end and, after a lengthy trial, he was sentenced to die in the electric chair for the murders of the two students in Tallahassee and of Kimberly Leach. After an exhaustive, 10-year appeal which went all the way to the Supreme Court, Bundy was finally executed in February 1989.

A BRUTAL SAVAGE

For sheer savagery, however, it would be hard to find a serial killer as evil as Satan-worshipping Richard Ramirez, the so-called Night Stalker who terrorised Los Angeles for 15 months.

His appalling spree of violence hung over the City of Angeles like a death shroud as he slashed, shot and beat his way into infamy.

Pock-marked Ramirez was responsible for as many as 20 murders – the particulars of which are too vile to retell in full detail here – and at least two cases of brutal child rape before he was brought to justice in September 1985. His murder spree began in June 1984, with the slaying of an elderly woman at her home in the suburbs of Los Angeles. For some reason, Ramirez didn't strike again until February the following year, but when he did, he killed at a ferocious pace. His next two victims were mere

> POLICE WERE SICKENED TO FIND THAT THE KILLER HAD CUT OUT HIS VICTIM'S EYES AND HAD TAKEN THEM WITH HIM

children, girls aged six and nine. The six-year-old was snatched from a bus stop as she waited for her morning ride to school, and dragged away in a dirty laundry bag. She was sexually abused, then dumped. The older child was grabbed from her own bedroom, and similarly attacked.

Ramirez, a 25-year-old drifter from Texas with numerous drug offences to his name, struck next in March at the home of Dayle Okazaki and her room mate. Okazaki was gunned down in cold blood, but her friend, Maria Hernandez survived. Fortunately for police, Ms Hernandez gave a remarkably accurate description of the intruder – bulging eyes, rotting teeth and a mass of curly hair.

Unknown to authorities at the time, the Stalker struck again that very same day, shooting to death Tsa Lian Yu, 30, as she drove near her home in Monterey Park. Before the month was through, Ramirez's bloodlust would claim two more lives. On

Above: *Victim Bill Carns' car was covered in Ramirez's fingerprints.*

Above Top: *Richard Ramirez, unrepentant, on trial.*

27 March, he entered the home of Vincent Zazzara, 64, and his 44-year-old wife, Maxine. Mr Zazzara was viciously beaten to death, while his wife was slashed repeatedly. When police arrived on the scene they were sickened to find that the killer had cut out her eyes, and taken them with him.

Other victims followed quickly, and by mid-summer, as reports were leaked to the newspapers, the panic set in. The unknown assailant was dubbed the 'Night Stalker' because many of his victims were surprised in their own homes. At least one of the dead was found with Satanic pentagrams drawn on her body. As Los Angeles sweltered through July and August, police could do little more than count the dead. The madman who struck in the middle of the night vanished after each terrible crime.

By late August, the Stalker had claimed 14 victims, and the city awaited his next move. It came just days later, when he shot and wounded 29-year-old Bill Carns, and raped his young fiancee.

He stole their car, which police found abandoned on 28 August, and fortunately they were able to lift a full set of fingerprints from it. Using a computer search, they discovered the prints matched those of Ramirez. City law enforcement officials broadcast the news, and immediately put his mugshot on television and in newspapers throughout the region.

Just three days after the stolen car was found, Ramirez was spotted and recognised by a group of citizens as he tried to steal another vehicle. Inflamed by the ferocity of his crimes, the mob quickly turned violent, and began beating him. Police arrived in time to save his life, and placed him under strict security while he awaited his trial.

It was after his arrest that a more complete picture began to emerge of the man who had held an entire city in the grip of fear... acquaintances described him as an ardent Devil worshipper, who was obsessed with the Australian rock band AC/DC.

In fact, one of their songs, 'Night Prowler', became his personal anthem. Those who knew him said he would play it repeatedly, often for hours on end, as he sat and stared vacantly at the wall of his run-down apartment.

Yet even after his capture, the man-devil showed neither remorse for his crimes nor pity for those he butchered. During one court appearance, he screamed: 'Hail Satan!', and waved his hand at photographers. He had painted a pentagram on it. In September 1989, he was found guilty of just 13 murders – he is serving life with no possibility of parole – but he bragged to a fellow prison inmate: 'I've killed 20 people... I love all that blood.'

DEBAUCHED DEPRAVITY

If the depravity of Richard Ramirez marked him as the most debauched serial killer in the Los Angeles of the 1980s, then the previous decade belonged to the twisted cousins, Kenneth Bianchi and Angelo Buono, who were known by the single moniker of 'The Hillside Strangler'.

Buono, who was born in 1934, was 17 years older than his cousin. He grew up in Rochester, New York, before his divorced mother took him to L.A., just as World War Two began. Even as a child, he displayed some of the dark characteristics that would later result in the horrible deaths of at least 10 women. He was moody and violent and his teenaged years – in which his morbid fascination with sodomy became apparent – were marked by several run-ins with the law, mainly for car theft. Ominously, his 'hero' during those years was the infamous serial rapist, Caryl Chessman. By the time he had reached manhood, Buono's mood swings had become increasingly violent, but, incredibly, he seemed to attract women and fathered several illegitimate children.

In January 1976, his 25-year-old cousin,

Ken Bianchi, whose mother was a prostitute, decided to leave New York State for the glamourous life in Los Angeles with Buono. Bianchi was a willing participant in the coming reign of terror, having boasted of murdering a man when he was just 20 years old. When he arrived in L.A., he was overawed by his cousin's smooth talk and ability to obtain women – including prostitutes who worked for him. But Buono was a tyrant to his stable of hookers, often raping and torturing them; he derived intense, diabolical pleasure from inflicting pain.

Bianchi, likewise, was a brute, and yet he had the audacity to apply for a job with

Above: *Kenneth Bianchi, one half of the demon pair known as The Hillside Strangler.*

Above: *Angelo Buono, the other half of the partnership brought together under the single moniker of The Hillside Strangler.*

the Los Angeles Police Department. In his twisted thinking, a uniform would allow him to abuse with impunity.

He was crestfallen when he received his rejection notice, but Buono comforted him with an idea – they would impersonate police officers, which would allow them to arrest prostitutes or stop women drivers whenever their sick lust was aroused.

Almost a dozen women would die slow, agonising deaths thanks to cousin Angelo, their sexually battered bodies often left in open display around the city.

The first to die was Yolanda Washington, 19, a prostitute, whose naked body was found on 17 October. By the end of the month, they struck again, this time kidnapping a 15-year-old child. Her body, which was found in a garden, bore the same marks as Washington's. She had been strangled, but not before she had been subjected to the most vicious sexual attacks imaginable. Two more victims were quickly to follow. One, a waitress, was dumped on a highway embankment; the other was found naked beside a motorway.

By 20 November, just four weeks after the attacks began, three more bodies were found. A few days later, the eighth victim, Lauren Wagner, was discovered on a hill overlooking nearby Glendale.

By now, police knew 'The Hillside Strangler' was in fact two men, thanks to an eyewitness account from the daughter of silver screen star Peter Lorre, who had narrowly managed to avoid them. But they still had little to go on and, inevitably, the killing spree continued.

By 9 December, another two women, Kimberly Mann and Cindy Huspeth, were added to the death toll. The murder of

Above: The newspapers reported the Hillside Strangler horror in depth.

Left: Buono, shackled and sullenly quiet at a hearing.

Huspeth, whose body was found in the boot of her sedan, would signal the end of the evil partnership, because Bianchi decided to relocate in Bellingham, in Washington State, fearing that his luck couldn't last.

For more than a year, neither man struck again. They seem to have felt less secure outside their devilish alliance. But that all changed on 11 January 1979, when two young women, Diane Wilder and Karen Mandic, were savagely raped and murdered in Bellingham. Police soon learned they had last been seen making an appointment for a job to house sit a home while the owners were away. Bianchi had been the representative.

He quickly attracted suspicion when, during questioning, he became evasive and gave inconsistent answers. After obtaining a search warrant, detectives went to his home where they found various stolen items. Their suspicions further aroused, they noticed the similarities between the local slayings and those committed earlier in Los Angeles. After contacting the LAPD, Bianchi was also booked on five charges of murder attributed to the Hillside Strangler.

After his indictment, in June 1979, he continued to deny any involvement, but gradually tried to build up an insanity

A WAITRESS WAS DUMPED ON A HIGHWAY EMBANKMENT, ANOTHER VICTIM WAS FOUND NAKED BESIDE A MOTORWAY

Above: *Veronica Lynn Compton, who made a botched attempt at murder to provide an alibi for Bianchi, at her trial with her attorney.*

COMPTON WAS AS SEXUALLY WARPED A BIANCHI, AND POSSESSED A MORBID INTEREST IN MURDER AND NECROPHILIA

defence by claiming he was possessed by several personalities. When his performances convinced no one, he agreed to testify against his cousin in the hope of getting a lighter sentence. Buono was picked up in Los Angeles that October, and charged with 10 counts of murder. After a two-year trial, he was eventually found guilty of nine counts, and sentenced to life, without parole.

Bianchi would also be sentenced to life in prison, but not before he had made one last evil effort to escape justice. In June 1980, an aspiring writer, Veronica Compton, sent him a letter, in which she asked him to comment on her new play, which revolved around a female serial killer. Through subsequent conversations and an exchange of letters, it became apparent that Compton was as sexually warped as Bianchi, and possessed a morbid interest in murder and necrophilia.

Bianchi had found his soul mate and confidently planned his ruse. Compton would go to Bellingham, strangle any woman she could find, then leave traces of Bianchi's sperm at the scene of the crime. That, he believed, would convince Bellingham police that there had been a grave error and that they had apprehended the wrong man. Incredibly, the wicked Compton agreed without hesitation and, on 16 September, she visited Bianchi in his Los Angeles prison. She smuggled out some of his semen in a rubber glove, and flew to Bellingham. Fortunately, she blundered the would-be murder and was herself arrested and sentenced to a minimum of 13 years in prison. Bianchi's final desperate attempt to escape justice had failed.

A SUITABLE SENTENCE

At about the same time as Bianchi was hatching his Machiavellian plot, 2,000 miles away, in Chicago, another serial killer was at last getting his just desserts for the murders of 33 young men and boys.

That man, John Wayne Gacy, who has been dubbed the 'Killer Clown', differs from many serial killers in that he killed only males – some as young as nine years old – and often murdered and buried his victims in his own home.

On the surface, Gacy, an overweight building contractor, seemed a far cry from the portrait of a monster. He was popular with neighbours, entertained sick children at a local hospital by dressing up as a clown, and was deeply involved in politics. He even had a photograph in his home of himself and the then First Lady, Roslyn Carter! But underneath the benevolent exterior beat the black heart of a demon. Like many serial killers, Gacy's upbringing was filled with violence and scorn. His father, an alcoholic, inflicted brutal beatings on him for trivial offences, and, on at least one occasion, threw the young child across the room and hurtling into a wall. His father also ridiculed him relentlessly, deriding him as a useless 'sissy'.

A RESPECTABLE FACADE

After graduating from business school, Gacy became a shoe salesman, and married a woman whose family owned a fast food restaurant in the nearby state of Iowa. They relocated, and Gacy took over the running of the business. He was a natural businessman and, outwardly, he was as normal as any other middle class man, so it came as a shock to those who knew him when he was arrested in May 1968, for coercing a youngster who worked for him at the restaurant into having homosexual sex with him. While the case was wending its way to court, Gacy hired a hoodlum to pummel the boy, and was subsequently hit with more charges. He was given a stiff sentence of 10 years, but was released after serving just 18 months because he was considered a model prisoner.

His wife was granted a divorce while he was incarcerated and, upon his release, he returned to his native Chicago where he established his construction business. He was doing well, and soon remarried. None of his new friends knew of his conviction, and he was quickly accepted into the neighbourhood where he became known for his lavish, laughter-filled parties.

But his lust for forbidden sex remained

Below: *John Wayne Gacy, the clown killer who entertained at children's parties before entertaining himself with mass sex killings at his home.*

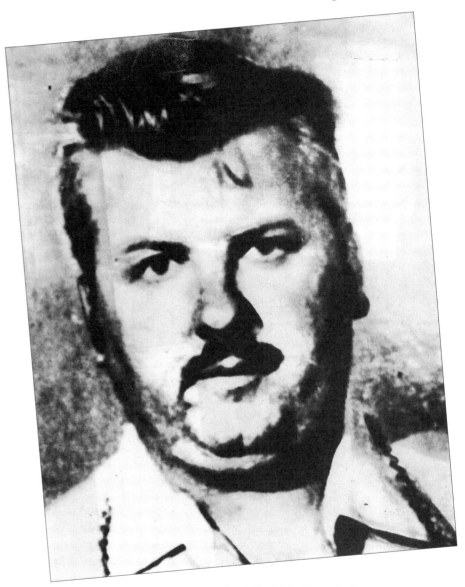

THE 'KILLER CLOWN' KILLED ONLY MALES, AND OFTEN MURDERED AND BURIED HIS VICTIMS IN HIS OWN HOME

and, in February 1971, he was arrested for attempting to rape a young man. However, the victim, a known homosexual, failed to appear at the hearing, and all charges were dropped. Gacy was lucky, and for the next 12 months continued to build his business and reputation. But again, the dark urgings surfaced and, according to his own account, he killed his first victim, a young man he had picked up at a bus station, in January 1972.

His killing spree would last more than six years, and at least 32 more victims would die by his hand. Some of them were employees at his construction business; others were runaways and male prostitutes. Still others were hapless youths he 'arrested' with a fake police badge. Most, however, including employees, runaways and others he met socially, were invited into his house of horrors for a night of drinking, marijuana and pool. As the drink and drugs took their toll, Gacy would playfully suggest that his guest be treated to a magic show, tricks he had perfected entertaining

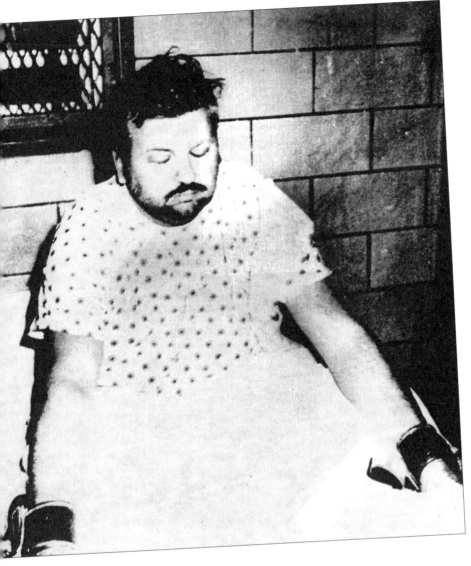

hospitalised children. Usually, he would start off with a few harmless ruses, then bring out his 'magic handcuffs', which he would slip his wrists in and out of with ease. He would then invite his young guest to try them. Gacy's 'trick', of course, was in having a set of keys.

After handcuffing the youngster, he would then manacle him to a macabre rack, and rape him. After his deviant sexual desires were sated, he would flash a twisted grin at his innocent victim and announce he would now do his 'rope trick' – meaning strangulation. Afterwards, he would bury the body in a space underneath his home. By the time he was arrested, in late 1978, police forensic teams would have found 28 bodies. His last five victims were, by

Above: *Bloated and manacled, John Wayne Gacy is restrained on a prison hospital bed. Authorities judged him capable of suicide while awaiting trial.*

AFTER GACY'S DEVIANT SEXUAL DESIRES WERE SATED, HE WOULD FLASH A TWISTED GRIN AT HIS VICTIM

---

necessity, dumped in a local river, because he could simply not fit any more bodies under his house! Incredibly, for four years of his bloody terror, Gacy was married. He was forced to limit his barbarity to times when his wife was out of the house, and explained away the foul odour emanating from beneath the house as sewerage problems. But after they divorced, in 1976, he was free to kill with more assurance and alacrity.

A NASTY SURPRISE

Just after Christmas the following year, one of his victims, who somehow was allowed to live, called police – but it took them months to bring Gacy into court. The lucky man, Jeffrey Rignall, 27, had, like so many others, been having drinks with Gacy at his house. Without warning, the Killer Clown came up behind him, and placed a dirty cloth soaked in chloroform over his mouth. Gacy then took the man upstairs to the rack, where he was raped and lashed for hours. For some reason never explained, Gacy didn't kill Rignall, but dumped his unconscious body by the side of a lake. When Rignall called police, it took seven months for them to bring a charge against Gacy – and the case was still in the courts when he was arrested for multiple murder.

The big break in the case came, tragically enough, when a young student, Robert Piest, was kidnapped in the car park outside a chemist's shop where he worked after school. Witnesses told authorities that Piest had earlier mentioned having to meet a building contractor regarding another job. The trail led police to Gacy, who vehemently denied any involvement in the disappearance. But officers were convinced they had their man and, armed with a search warrant, they returned to the house where they made the shocking discovery of Gacy's burial chamber.

Just as Bianchi would do later in Los Angeles, Gacy tried to fool government psychiatrists into thinking him insane, by blaming his alter ego – 'Jack' – as the real culprit. The doctors were not fooled, and in the subsequent trial, in 1980, Gacy was convicted of all 33 murders. He received the death penalty, and at time of writing remained on death row while the appeal process continued.

In common with the other serial killers mentioned in this chapter, Gacy will never murder again, regardless of the outcome of his petition to escape death. But how many others like him are out there? Who knows when the next one will strike, or who the

Below: *The Killer as Clown: Gacy's mask hid a personality of unfathomable evil.*

victim will be? What grotesque form will his orgy of murder take? No one can know the answers to questions like these, but there is one thing American society can be certain of – he or she is out there, somewhere, and killing at this very moment.

MAFIA BOSSES
Captains of Crime

From the shores of sun-baked Sicily to the mean streets of New York City, the Mafia's head men oversee a vast, seedy empire devoted to crime and corruption. The foul tentacles of their power reach into everything from the drug trade to politics.

Every country in the world unwillingly hosts a violent, criminal element, but only the United States and Italy have the dubious honour of being home to the Mafia.

Behind that vile organisation's complex web of international intrigue, guile and ruthless terror, lie the Godfathers, people of incredible criminal panache whose cunning and brutality make them the true kings of crime. They are among the most vicious men in the annals of law enforcement

Opposite: *Mafia boss Al Capone, the fat-faced crime czar who ran 1930s Chicago as if it were his own personal fiefdom.*

Above and Above Centre: *The close family ties that bind Sicily's Mafiosi stood them in good stead when they emigrated to New York.*

history, and their stories are as fascinating as they are bloody.

No serious discussion of the Mafia godfathers would be comprehensive without first looking at New York City's John Gotti, the so-called 'Dapper Don', whose rise to power was nothing short of mete-

oric. In his heyday of the 1980s, this former high school drop-out was the most feared and most powerful criminal in the United States.

Today, the £1,300 silk suits and monogrammed socks have been swapped for orange overalls and gym boots, and the £300 dinners of pasta and fine wine replaced by watery soups and cold hamburgers. But John Gotti, the 'Capo di Tutti Capi' – the Boss of all Bosses – is still the USA's most powerful Mafia leader despite languishing in prison since his convictions

on numerous crimes in the summer of 1992. That's because Gotti, through his intermediaries, continues to keep his stranglehold on the infamous Gambino Family, America's largest and most ruthless mob clan which pulls in an annual tax-free profit that is estimated in the hundreds of millions of pounds.

Gotti's rise to the top came after a lifetime devoted to crime, which he hid under the veneer of a respectable suburban husband and father. Indeed, the 53-year-old mobster continues to make the preposterous claim that he is nothing more than a salesman for a plumbing firm, although he has spent two terms in prison for hijacking and manslaughter. The first came in 1969, when the 28-year-old street punk was jailed for three years for hijacking a truck-load of goods. He served his time 'honourably' – by not squealing to authorities, and by

Above: *The St Valentine's Day Massacre in Chicago, the most notorious example of the way old-time Mafia hoods did business.*

GAMBINO'S NEPHEW EMMANUEL WAS KIDNAPPED AND MURDERED — HIS TONGUE CUT OUT AND HIS BODY MUTILATED

Right: *The new 'corporate' face of the Mafia: John Gotti, boss of bosses of the Gambino family, at one of his many trials.*

standing up to the tough, black inmates that the traditionally-racist mob abhors. Upon his release, in 1972, underboss Aniello Dellacroce rewarded the rising young hood by naming him a capo, or captain, within the family hierarchy. It was a grand honour.

The old mobster had befriended Gotti before he went to prison, and he had been impressed with his coolness, intelligence and with his deep respect for the ways of Cosa Nostra.

Under Dellacroce's guardianship, Gotti concentrated on organising and consolidating the family's white-collar rackets – payoffs from building contractors, waste disposal kickbacks and protection money from the entertainment industry – using whatever muscle was required. But it was Don Carlos Gambino himself who was to mete out the task which became the ultimate test of Gotti's loyalty and bravery. The aging Godfather, whose name the family still bears, was stricken with grief when his beloved nephew, Emmanuel, was kidnapped and murdered – his tongue cut out and his body mutilated. Once his grief subsided, Gambino was enraged, and pledged

'great things' for Gotti if he could track down and kill the man responsible for Emmanuel's sadistic murder.

Using their widespread street sources, Gotti and his hardened crew soon identified

contract killer James McBratney as the hit man. A few nights later, on 22 May 1973, Gotti and his accomplices located McBratney at Staten Island's Snoopes Bar and Grill. Witnesses recalled that Gotti swaggered up to the killer, pulled out a snub-nosed revolver and opened fire. His associates followed suit and, by the time McBratney hit the floor, his body had been riddled with 12 bullets. But the murder had been too brazen, too public, and within 72 hours, Gotti and longtime friend Angelo Ruggiero, had been identified and arrested in connection with the slaying.

A LUCKY DEAL

Still, Gambino was grateful that his nephew's killer was dead, and he hired one of the city's top lawyers – the late Roy Cohn – to defend his two henchmen. In a remarkable deal, Cohn managed to get officials to accept a manslaughter plea from Gotti and Ruggiero and in return they were given a slap-on-the-wrist sentence of just four years. During his stay at the Greenhaven Correctional Facility in upstate New York, Gotti displayed all the traits which would eventually take him to the pinnacle of organised crime: he fought and savagely beat anyone who dared get in his way; remained loyal to the code of 'Omerta', or silence; and smooth-talked and bribed his guards into letting him enjoy several out-of-prison meetings with his wife, Victoria.

In all, he served just two years for the murder, but when he came out it was to a changed order. Before his death in 1976, Gambino broke with Mafia tradition by appointing his brother-in-law, Paul Castellano, and not Dellacroce, as his successor. It was a slight Gotti would never forgive, or forget. Biding his time, the young capo devoted himself to the business of making money, and his brutality was legendary among the crew he commanded. By the early 1980s, he was targeted as a rising mob star by federal authorities.

A devoted family man – living with his wife and three children in a modest house complete with a white picket fence – he was particularly fond of his 12-year-old son, Frank. Tragically, however, Frankie was killed in an traffic accident when a next-door neighbour ran over him. It didn't

matter to Gotti that the accident was the child's fault – Frank had ridden straight into the path of the car driven by John Favara. A police investigation completely exonerated the terrified neighbour, but Gotti would not be denied his 'justice'. Soon, Favara began receiving anonymous death threats... and, four months later, while Gotti was conveniently away on vacation, Favara disappeared forever.

Rumour has it that the 51-year-old furniture salesman was kidnapped, bundled into the back of a van, and executed. Although his body has never been found, there was much speculation that the hapless victim was shot, then frozen, until Gotti returned

Above: Paul 'Big Paulie' Castellano, shown leaving court in New York with a mob associate. The court had named him head of a crime commission that ruled the other Mafia families.

Below: Castellano was soon to end up like Joey Gallo, pictured here after being blasted to death by rivals in Umberto's Clam House in Little Italy in 1972.

from his holiday. It's believed Gotti then personally cut it to pieces with a chain saw. Gotti never got over the death of 'young Frankie', and he turned the front room of his house into a shrine for his dead son; and, until his most recent incarceration, he paid monthly visits to Frankie's grave site.

Although he was never implicated in Favara's disappearance, Gotti was hauled into the courts three times in the 1980s, yet three times he was found not guilty of charges ranging from racketeering to murder. But as Gotti's power increased, so did his bravado, and he decided that no one, not even current Godfather Paul 'Big Paulie' Castellano, would stand in the way of his ultimate domination of the Gambino Family. According to the federal government, there was never any love lost between Castellano and Gotti. Big Paulie

---

FOUR GUNMEN IN LONG RAINCOATS APPEARED FROM OUT OF THE CROWD AND BLASTED BOTH MEN IN THE HEAD AND BODY

Below: *New Orleans underworld king Carlos Marcello, another of the Mafia's most dangerous men.*

had become increasingly preoccupied with the mob's white-collar criminal enterprises, and despised the street-tough Gotti's continued reliance on muscle and intimidation.

Also, Castellano was a throwback to a more 'innocent' Mafia. He despised the sale of drugs, and ordered his associates to stay away from the trade, fearing the long prison terms for drug-related offences might convince associates to squeal against the family. But Gotti, described by federal agents as one of the most ambitious and ruthless capos within the Mafia, found the massive, easy profits made from drug trafficking too much to resist, and actively encouraged his crew members to get in on a piece of the action. Eventually, Castellano's worst nightmare came true – an FBI informer turned state's evidence, and soon several members of the family, including Big Paulie, were hauled into court facing drug-related indictments.

Not surprisingly, Castellano was furious, and broke Mafia protocol to name his bodyguard/adviser Thomas Biloti as his successor, instead of underboss Dellacroce, Gotti's friend and mentor, who had already been passed over for the top job several years earlier. Gotti saw the move as an outright insult to his old friend (who has since died of cancer), and a clear sign that his own days were numbered. He decided to strike first and, on 16 December 1985, he made his daring move.

A PUBLIC EXECUTION

Castellano and Biloti had just stepped out of their limousine in front of Sparks Steak House on busy East 46th Street in midtown Manhattan for a business meeting, when four gunmen in long raincoats appeared from out of the crowd and blasted both men several times in the head and body. Both died instantly, while the killers, believed to be members of the infamous Irish gang, the Westies, calmly disappeared into a waiting car. The execution, say prosecutors, paved the way for Gotti to become Godfather and, since his bloody ascendancy to power, he has made his family even more profitable.

'In terms of profits, the Gotti organisation is a Fortune 500 company, no question of that,' said Jules Bonavolonta, head of the FBI's organised crime squad in New

York. Gotti, who worked his way through the family as an apprentice bookie's-runner, hijacker, thug, bodyguard and hit man to eventually become the Godfather, repeatedly denied the government's claims that he was connected with Castellano's sensational killing.

But in his dramatic 1992 trial, Gotti was dismayed to learn that his second-in-command, Salvatore 'Sammy the Bull' Gravano, had turned state's witness. He was the highest-ranking mobster to ever inform against his boss, and his testimony, together with wiretapped evidence that had been gathered by the FBI, helped put Gotti behind bars for life. The Dapper Don had finally been bloodied.

THE SOCIETY MOBSTER

If Gotti was the most flamboyant of mobsters – he delighted in having his picture taken for the newspapers and reading about his movements in the gossip columns – then Vincent 'Vinnie the Chin' Gigante is the most reclusive – and enigmatic. Several times every week, the old man can be seen shuffling slowly along the busy streets of Greenwich Village, past the small bakeries and ristorantes that dot the downtown Manhattan landscape. Clad only in his bathrobe and slippers, he mumbles to himself as he heads up Sullivan Street, in the heart of Little Italy. He sees no-one, and hears nothing. To the casual observer, he would appear to be just another crazy New Yorker, benignly making his way to nowhere. But the grocers and bakers who live and work in the area know better. So does the FBI.

The stubble-faced loner is no misguided innocent. He is Vincent Gigante – the man dubbed 'America's Last Godfather' and the most powerful mobster in the country. Yet even law enforcement officials concede that Gigante looks as though he couldn't run a dishwasher, let alone the vast billion-dollar holdings of the Genovese crime syndicate which he has allegedly controlled since 1981.

But that, they say, is all part of his act. Just as it was several years back, when FBI agents paid him a call at his apartment, only to find him in the shower – clad in his pajamas and holding up an umbrella! His lawyers and defenders like brother Louis, a

Catholic priest from the Bronx, claim that was an example of his pathetic mental state. There are many others.

'Sometimes he talks to inanimate objects, like trees, and sometimes he talks to animals that aren't there,' said lawyer Michael Shapiro. Indeed, Vinnie, who still lives with his 90-year-old mother, has been hospitalised more than 20 times for schizophrenia in the past 25 years. But federal officials, who have put four of New York's five crime family leaders behind bars, believe his seemingly bizarre behaviour is just an elaborate ruse designed to avoid arrest and prosecution.

'Once, in 1985, I saw Gigante walking around the streets in a bathrobe,' said a former New York policeman. 'He climbed into a car, and several blocks later the robe came off and he was wearing a suit and tie.' No-one denies that the Chin was a Mafioso. His list of convictions is too long for anyone to reasonably dispute that. The government maintains he is still a Mafioso, but even law enforcement officials acknowledge that proving it is another matter entirely. 'It won't be easy,' one official

*Above: **Gotti became known as the Teflon Don, because no charges ever stuck.***

FBI AGENTS FOUND MOBSTER GIGANTE IN THE SHOWER, CLAD ONLY IN HIS PYJAMAS AND HOLDING UP AN UMBRELLA allowed recently. 'Gigante is one of the most astute crime bosses you'll ever encounter. But the idea is to show that he's sane and then link him to a few murders he approved of as the family's boss.'

Gigante's act, says the FBI, dates back to 1969, when he faced charges of literally trying to bribe the entire police force of a New Jersey town! He never stood trial, successfully convincing a judge that he was mentally unfit.

Officials say the Chin's long-running ploy stems from his paranoia about going to prison... and he is nothing if not an expert at avoiding jail time. Although he has a police record dating back to the 1940s, including charges of gambling, receiving stolen goods and handgun pos-

> GIGANTE IS SO SECRETIVE THAT FOR THE FIRST YEARS OF HIS REIGN FAMILY MEMBERS DIDN'T KNOW HE WAS THE BOSS

replacement contract with the city. But, true to form, he was found incompetent to stand trial and released.

Yet Gigante's knack of staying out of prison is based on more than just his ability to carry out an intricate, two-decades-old mental ruse, say officials. He is, by all accounts, a throwback to the more secretive days of the Mafia, before leaders like the ambitious John Gotti moved the mob to the gossip columns and society pages. In fact, in 1987, Gigante became so angry about all the attention Gotti was bringing to the once-secretive Cosa Nostra that he allegedly put a contract out on his fellow Godfather. Ironically, the hit was called off after Gotti was tipped off by the FBI. Gotti believed the story. He knew Gigante wasn't one to make veiled threats.

According to the FBI, the task of bringing the Chin to justice is made all the more difficult because he never discusses the family's business on the phone or at any of the Genovese clan's 'social clubs'. In fact, Gigante is so secretive that officials say that for the first several years of his reign as Godfather, even his family members didn't realise he was the boss. Certainly, authorities didn't. In 1985, when the U.S. Government successfully prosecuted the members of the 'Commission' – the Mafia's version of a board of directors – front man Anthony 'Fat Tony' Salerno was found guilty of running the Genovese clan. Even today, the 1,500-odd family soldiers do not dare mutter Gigante's name to each other, let alone in public. Instead, they refer to him by simply rubbing their chins.

session, Gigante has served little time behind bars. Even his alleged role in the attempted murder of flamboyant mobster Frank Costello in 1957 failed to land him in prison. In fact, his only sentence came in the early 1960s when he served five years on drugs charges.

He's been on a lucky streak ever since. As recently as 1992, Gigante again successfully outfoxed the law. Along with several members of his syndicate, he was indicted in the so-called 'Windows Case' on racketeering and extortion charges. Officials alleged that he was the mastermind behind the Genoveses' scheme to rig the bids on a £100,000,000 window

Above: Anthony 'Fat Tony' Salerno, head of the Genovese crime syndicate in New York, leaves a court while smoking his trademark fat cigar.

QUIETLY POWERFUL

The veil of secrecy has certainly worked. While Gotti and the Gambino clan have been the focus of all the media attention in recent years, the Genovese family has quietly gone about its lucrative and extensive business. 'It was always Gotti, Gotti, Gotti,' said one official, 'but the Genovese family has always been the country's most powerful. They more or less invented

ers – not one has ever been rubbed out – including Vito Genovese, whose name the family adopted, gradually decentralised control and gave senior members greater freedom and authority to make decisions. One federal agent calls the Genoveses 'the Ivy League' of the Mafia, because many of the members are high school, sometimes college, graduates. 'Most other families have the IQ of an ashtray,' he said.

The Genoveses are also very careful about recruiting: two 'made' members have to personally vouch for every newcomer's trustworthiness and loyalty with their own lives. Which goes a long way towards explaining why, despite the convictions of Gotti and a host of other top mobsters, even government officials have been forced to admit: 'We haven't really made a dent with the Genoveses.'

But officials say they are making minor inroads. They claim they have secret surveillance tapes proving Gigante is fit to stand trial. It is not known exactly what is on the tapes, but one reportedly shows the Chin – sans bathrobe – making regular visits to his girlfriend, who lives on Manhattan's upper east side. Always accompanied by a phalanx of bodyguards, Gigante waits outside in a car until one of his henchmen gives him the all-clear to enter. Like clockwork, he returns home by midnight... where he slips back into his bathrobe, ready for the next day's walk!

SICILIAN TERROR

Despite the omnipresence of the American mob, it pales by comparison to the stranglehold the Cosa Nostra has on Italy, and specifically the island of Sicily, the birth-

labour racketeering. And they have infiltrated scores of legitimate businesses and labour union.'

Two years ago, a New York City police report called the Genovese family the 'most stable,' the 'best counselled' and the most diversified business-crime syndicate in America. Through its union connections, the family has immense power in industries like construction, food distribution and garbage hauling. They also have a stranglehold on the ports of New York, New Jersey and Miami. Experts also contend that some of the biggest stars in the entertainment world can't perform in Atlantic City or Las Vegas without the Genovese family first getting its cut. 'With the unions behind us, we could shut down the city, or the country for that matter, if we needed to, to get our way,' former member Vincent 'The Fish' Cafaro testified before a Senate hearing four years ago.

It was not an idle boast. The Genovese family, which can trace its criminal roots back to the early 1930s and its founder Lucky Luciano – the Mafia equivalent of a patron saint – has always enjoyed the reputation of being a quiet, secretive clan with a knack for business. Its succession of lead-

Above: *Charles 'Lucky' Luciano, the classic mob chief who modelled himself on Al Capone.*

Right: *Sicilian mobster Salvatore 'Toto' Riina after his capture.*

place of the Mafia. Even with the ongoing crack down on organised crime throughout Italian society, the Sicilian mob is virtually a state within the state, with its own territory, citizens, laws and soldiers. And it infects whatever it touches. Recently, Italian authorities had to dismiss 30 city councils because they had been corrupted by the Cosa Nostra, and there is widespread Mafia penetration of the national government.

Below: *Toto Riina on trial in the underground bunker courtroom of the Palermo jail.*

THE SICILIAN MOB IS VIRTUALLY A STATE WITHIN A STATE, WITH ITS OWN TERRITORY, CITIZENS, LAWS AND SOLDIERS

The man responsible for much of the organised crime and corruption is 62-year-old Salvatore (Toto) Riina, the alleged leader of the Mafia for the past 10 years. He was finally nabbed by police in January 1993, but somehow spent years at the top of Italy's 'most wanted' list and lived openly in Sicily for more than 20 years.

Even though he was a fugitive – he had already been found guilty of two murders – he lived an open life, filled with luxuries commensurate with his position as Godfather. He was even married openly in church to his childhood sweetheart, the service being conducted by a priest sympathetic to Mafia causes, who was later defrocked by the Vatican for his involvement in a kidnapping. Between 1974 and 1980, he also fathered four children, all of whom were delivered in the same clinic

under their real names. And for years he freely walked on the streets of Palermo. Yet when he was finally nabbed he was linked to more than 150 murders – including the vicious 1989 killing of three women, the mother, sister and aunt of a turncoat mobster – and other crimes ranging from extortion to drug smuggling.

Yet why was the 62-year-old Godfather, known by police as La Belva, or The Beast, free for so long? To understand the answer, one must understand the Mafia and its place within Italian society. In Italy, the Mafia is, indeed, a state within a state. It has infiltrated government, and even those officials not tainted by corruption were nervous at the thought of taking on the nation's number one crime figure.

MONSTROUS KILLINGS

But all that began to change in 1992, when Riina, who came from the small Sicilian town of Corleone, made famous in the *Godfather* movie trilogy by Francis Ford Coppola, was implicated in the brazen murders of two national heroes, Giovanni Falcone and Paolo Borsellino, both of whom had courageously led the fight against organised crime. Public outrage at their brutal deaths forced authorities to act. Even youths in Palermo, once a breeding ground for future Mafia recruits, took to the streets in protest. As a result, police officials stepped up the pressure and, with the aid of informants, zeroed in on Riina.

On the morning of 15 January 1993, a contingent of heavily armed carabinieri surrounded his modest car as he drove through the downtown section of Palermo. His sudden arrest stunned the whole of Italy. So, too, did his appearance. He was a short, overweight diabetic, dressed in cheap, badly-fitting clothes – a far cry from the more glamourised version of gangsters.

Until his arrest, Zu Toto (or Uncle Toto), had been the undisputed kingpin of Sicilian organised crime, yet there were only three known photographs of him: one of him as a young man, one a composite photo made by the FBI, and the other, taken 10 years ago as he posed, like a million other tourists, among the pigeons in Venice's famous St Mark's Square.

It was at about that same time that Riina had just finished building one of the most successful criminal empires in the world, the result of years of bloody infighting with fellow hoods. He commanded an army of hired thugs who helped him run his billion-pound drug trafficking conglomerate – which stretched from the cocaine farms of South America to the opium fields of South East Asia. The hundreds of bodies found in the streets of Palermo during the early part of the 1980s was testimony to his vicious control. Even some fellow Mafia members, who broke the Cosa Nostra code of Omerta to talk to police, described him as ruthless, vicious and cunning. His philosophy, it was said, was 'if someone's finger is hurt, it is better to be safe and cut off his arm'.

Yet once he was hauled into court, he played the role of a poor, simple man who knew nothing about the Mafia or the insidious drug trade. He was quietly-spoken, gentle, and courteous to a fault, always jumping to his feet whenever he was introduced to prosecutors and senior police officials. Those who knew him claim he also was a devoted father and intensely loyal to his long-time wife, Ninetta.

His arrest was a stunning blow to the

HIS PHILOSOPHY WAS 'IF SOMEBODY'S FINGER IS HURT, IT IS BETTER TO BE SAFE AND CUT OFF HIS ARM'

Below: *Judge Giovanni Falcone pours out wine for a friend. It was to be one of his last drinks – he was murdered shortly afterwards in a massive car bombing.*

Mafia, which had been seriously wounded by a series of sensational indictments and convictions brought by crusading crime-busters Falcone and Borsellino, two good friends of incredible bravery who were completely incorruptible. Together they had spearheaded the biggest and most successful Mafia trial in history, the so-called 'Maxi-Trial', in which more than 450 defendants were hauled into the courts.

The trial, which began in 1985, lasted almost two years, and ended in almost total victory for the prosecution. More than 350 Mafiosi were convicted, and, for the first time, the state proved the existence of a 'commission' – a group of high-level gangsters which oversaw the operations of the Cosa Nostra – and was able to hand out life sentences to 19 of the most powerful crime leaders in Sicily, including Riina, who was tried and sentenced *in absentia*.

But on 23 May 1992, the Mafia struck back, and hard. Falcone, a native of Palermo, his wife and their three bodyguards were driving into the city from the airport, when a massive bomb ripped through the highway. The massive explo-

Above: *Falcone's car after his assassination in May 1992. He was killed, along with his wife Francesca, because of his fearless crusade against the mob.*

THERE WAS WHOLESALE SLAUGHTER ON PALERMO'S STREETS. BROTHERS KILLED BROTHERS. COUSINS KILLED COUSINS

sion killed all the occupants immediately. Then, just two months later, on 19 July, Borsellino and five of his bodyguards were killed by a bomb in downtown Palermo. Their murders – which ripped through the heart of the Italian populace – led to Riina's apprehension.

The shell-shocked Italian government, which had too often ignored many Mafia operations, couldn't overlook such blatant atrocities, the most frightful political assassinations in Italy since former Prime Minister Aldo Moro had been murdered by Red Brigade terrorists more than 20 years earlier. Firstly, a law was passed granting protection to Mafia turncoats and their families; then, organised crime bosses were sent to maximum security prisons, and not to the 'country club' institutions in which they had so often been incarcerated; army troops were ordered into Sicily to help the overworked local police; lastly, and perhaps most importantly, a special, highly-trained task force of elite policemen was set up with just one goal – to get Riina. As Justice Minister Claudio Martelli put it, the murders of the crusading prosecutors would 'prove the Mafia's worst mistake'.

As the unrelenting official crack down continued throughout the second half of 1992, scores of informants and Mafia turncoats came forward. To understand why, one only has to look at the way Riina ruled his huge empire. Unlike in the American mob – or indeed, in the Sicilian mob prior to Riina's takeover – Mafia 'soldiers' had certain rights within the structure of their own 'family'. Members were forbidden to cheat their fellow mobsters, all shared in the ill-gotten gains, and each man was treated with the 'respect' due a comrade.

But under Riina's tyrannical rule, all that changed. He encouraged rivalry within his family and others, and, through cunning and guile, helped soldiers to confront their own bosses. Once those soldiers reached elevated positions in the hierarchy, they then repaid their benefactor with allegiance and the loyalty of their own outfits. Those rival Godfathers who were too powerful or too smart to fall into Riina's trap, were simply murdered. There was wholesale slaughter on the streets of Palermo, because not only were the old guard slain, but also their wives, entire families, friends and other relatives. Brothers killed brothers. Cousins killed cousins. There was wholesale slaughter. By the time Riina was finished and held sway over the whole of the Sicilian Cosa Nostra, more than 1,000 people had been murdered.

But his savage butchery has fostered deep resentment within some elements of the Mafia, and those lucky enough to survive his purge sometimes sought safety in the hands of the authorities. Moreover, because Riina had killed off so many of the old bosses, most of the Mafia's political connections were severed. In the future, there would be no more light sentences for mobsters. But Riina didn't seem to care... if a prosecutor got too close, he was killed. In all, almost 30 officials have been slain by the Riina clan since 1978, including Salvatore Lima, the most powerful politician in Sicily.

REBELLIOUS MOBSTERS

But the growing resentment within the Cosa Nostra could not be silenced even by a hail of bullets. Riina had simply made far too many enemies, even within his own immediate clan. They, too, began to talk of insurrection. Furthermore, many mobsters blamed Riina for not fixing the Maxi-Trial, which he had sworn to do. To deflect their wrath, he decided to murder the officials largely responsible for the stunning convictions: Falcone and Borsellino.

That was his grave mistake, as the Italian people rose up and demanded long overdue justice. Gradually, with the help of informants, the police closed in ever closer to Riina. But every time they prepared to strike, he somehow disappeared. On Christmas Eve 1992, with the arrest of Bruno Contrada, the former deputy police commander in Palermo and a top official with the Italian Secret Service, it became apparent why. According to authorities, Contrada was owned by the Mafia, and would tip them off whenever the police were organising a major strike.

A few days later, with literally hundreds of former Mafiosi now coming forward, authorities finally knew they were within reach of La Belva. Then, just a few days

into the new year, in a stunning victory for the crime-busters, police arrested Baldassarre Di Maggio, who had been Riina's personal chauffeur and henchman. Di Maggio, who was by then on the run himself from Riina and knew it was only a matter of time before he, too, was murdered, decided to co-operate with the authorities. Using his information, police staked out two previously unknown addresses: a luxurious villa in Palermo, and a sprawling farm just outside the city. When Riina moved from the villa, the police were waiting, taking him without gunfire in downtown Palermo.

He was handcuffed and led away, and eventually taken to a jail in Rome. His arrest, however, was only the beginning. Since then, the Italian political sphere has been turned upside down, resulting in the downfall of some of the most powerful politicians in the country. Among them, Giulio Andreotti, the seven-time former prime minister who had hoped to end his career in the president's palace; and Bettino Craxi, who was widely tipped to become the next prime minister. The huge probe into the evil marriage of mobsters and government officials revealed a conspiracy on a massive scale, and the fall-out is still reverberating across the Italian political landscape today.

BY THE TIME RIINA HELD SWAY OVER THE WHOLE OF THE COSA NOSTRA, MORE THAN 1,000 PEOPLE HAD BEEN MURDERED

Below: *The funeral of Falcone, which triggered nationwide resentment against the Mafia not seen in decades.*

KILLERS IN KHAKI
Military Monsters

For most of this century, Latin Americans have been subjected to the autocratic rule of a cadre of tinpot dictators and fascist tyrants. From the steamy jungles of Panama, to the frozen tips of Argentina, jackbooted despots and their military cohorts have ruled supreme.

O f all the tyrants who rose to absolute power in this Third World enclave, few were matched for sheer bravado and evil as Generalissimo Manuel Antonio Noriega. He was known on the decrepit streets of his capital, Panama City, as 'Cara Pina' – or 'Pineapple Face' – because his face was so scarred and pitted. But his authority was so total that anyone calling him that faced two years in one of his stinking, blood-stained prisons. And until he was finally over-thrown by U.S. military might, in December 1989, Noriega, the pariah of Panama, had long defied the strength of his northern neighbour and the will of the Vatican by turning his tiny nation into a personal drug fiefdom.

His greed knew no bounds and, by the time of his downfall, he was said to be worth more than £600,000,000. He owned palatial homes all around the world, includ-ing a chateau in France – which he some-how managed to 'buy' with his officer's pay of less than £800 a month – ate the finest of imported foods, owned a fleet of luxury cars, and had fat bank accounts said to contain tens of millions of pounds.

He also owned radio and TV stations, a casino and a hotel. During his reign, the General maintained that he was not a crook, and that he had never stolen a penny. But what else could one expect of a

man whose entire life was devoted to lies and chicanery?

The pock-marked, pint-sized tyrant, who fancied himself a ladies' man and wanted to be played in a movie by the tall, dashing Clint Eastwood, was a brutal example of

the old rags-to-riches story. He was born into overwhelming poverty in 1934 to an unmarried woman, and, when he was five, given over to a foster home in the tough Panama City district of San Felipe. But those humble beginnings couldn't quell his already-burgeoning ambition. According to his high school year book, he listed his aim in life to be 'president of the republic'.

Originally, he had planned to become a psychiatrist, but after working at odd jobs for several years, he won a scholarship to attend El Chorrillo Military Academy in Peru, where he combined his studies with supplying information on suspected leftist cadets to the Central Intelligence Agency. In 1964, after completing a course in army

Opposite: *Old Pineapple Face, the unaffectionate name given to Panamanian dictator Manuel Noriega by the people he ruled by fear.*

Above: *He called himself the Maximum Leader and liked to cock a snook at the 'damned yankees' who had turned against him.*

THE PARIAH OF PANAMA DEFIED THE AMERICANS AND TURNED HIS TINY NATION INTO A PERSONAL DRUG FIEFDOM

engineering, the 97-pound weakling joined the Panamanian National Guard as a lieutenant, and was posted to Colon Province, where he came to the attention of another ambitious young officer, Omar Torrijos. It was Torrijos, who would later rule Panama, who kept Noriega from being punished when he allegedly raped a prostitute in Colon.

Instead, the young lieutenant was sent to another province, Chiriqui, where he allegedly raped a 13-year-old girl and viciously bashed the child's sister. Again, Torrijos intervened on his behalf. After all, Noriega was doing his job 'well' in battling the guerrillas in the province. It is said that he ordered his men to bring him proof of their success – with a dead guerrilla's ear, for instance. On other occasions, he personally supervised the torture of a young man caught writing anti-military slogans, and was said to shout with perverted delight while a woman was sexually abused in one of his dank dungeons. After his stint in Chiriqui, Noriega spent the next few years undergoing further training at the Panama-based U.S. Army School of the Americas and at Fort Bragg in the U.S., where he studied psychological warfare.

When Torrijos seized power in 1968, Noriega was known for being 'an enthusiastic torturer of prisoners', and was quickly elevated through the ranks by his mentor. Noriega soon repaid him by thwarting an attempted coup in 1969, when Torrijos was out of the country, by securing an airport

Above: Manuel Noriega with some of his female fighters, who he called his 'Black Widows'.

BESIDES HIS ALL-CONSUMING GREED, NORIEGA HAD A PROPENSITY FOR BRUTALITY AND MURDER

Right: Even Noriega's tigresses were no match for the American airborne invasion that ousted him from power.

and allowing the embattled leader to return safely and put down the revolt. In turn, Noriega, then a little-known major, was promoted to colonel and placed in charge of the dreaded G-2, the military intelligence branch.

For a man as evil as Noriega, it was like being handed the keys to the sweets store, and he immediately began compiling dossiers on everyone he suspected of being a leftist or a possible threat. His new power also brought him into close contact with United States intelligence agencies, and he formed powerful alliances both inside and outside Panama.

It was during his long tenure as the head of G-2 that he began taking huge payments from both the CIA and the drug barons of the Columbian cartels. He also is said to have become an agent for communist Cuba, helping Fidel Castro secure intelligence as well as high-tech equipment. Noriega would do anything for money.

But besides his all-consuming greed, his tenure at G-2 was also marked by his alarming propensity for brutality and murder. Leaders of the radical Panamanian Liberation Movement were executed, while others were arrested and tortured. In 1971, for example, he was personally responsible for the sadistic murder of Catholic priest Hector Gallegos, who had opposed the military regime. Father Gallegos was thrown

alive from a helicopter, and lived for five agonising days. Noriega, who had been aboard the chopper, later bragged about the incident, but claimed he had learned a crucial lesson – to always kill a man before throwing him from a helicopter.

In 1981, Torrijos was killed in a mysterious plane crash, and the army decided to rotate the job of commander-in-chief. The first man selected was Col. Ruben Dario Paredes, followed by Noriega in 1983. In 1984, when a general election was held, it was expected that Noriega would throw the support of the armed forces behind Paredes, who was then running for president. But instead, Noriega double-crossed his former comrade by supporting Nicolas Barletta, a Noriega puppet. He won amid an outcry of voter fraud, and lasted just 12 months before Noriega had him pushed from power, after Barletta promised an independent inquiry into the grisly slaying of an opposition leader, Dr Hugo Spadafora, who had accused the general of drug trafficking.

A BRUTAL ACT

U.S. officials say Noriega literally called for Spadafora's head – and, after five hours of horrible torture, he was beheaded. On his body his tormentors had carved 'F-8', the identification of the squad within the Panamanian Defence Forces which had been responsible for his murder. Numerous other atrocities were inflicted on him. Conveniently, Noriega was away in France at the time.

With his iron fist now in total control of Panama, Noriega unleashed a wave of vicious oppression and made a bid for personal wealth. With the millions he made playing all sides against the other, he bought up property in five countries, and filled his Panama City estate with fine art and priceless antique furniture. His greed was matched only by his ego.

He began to wear high-peaked caps to make him appear taller than his diminutive 65 inches, and revelled in surrounding himself with attractive women, even though he had been married for many years to wife Felicidad, who herself was described as highly possessive.

The general fathered at least one illegitimate child, and had a string of lovers.

Right: *A US personnel carrier in the streets of Panama City after the invasion.*

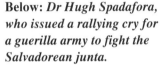
NORIEGA HAD A STRING OF LOVERS, BUT AMONG PANAMA CITY'S SOCIAL SET HE WAS ASSUMED TO BE BISEXUAL

Below: *Dr Hugh Spadafora, who issued a rallying cry for a guerilla army to fight the Salvadorean junta.*

However, among the social set in Panama City, he was assumed to be bisexual.

Although the United States Government had long known of Noriega's litany of crimes and corruption, it tolerated his presence because he made Panama a bastion of anti-communism, helped collect intelli-

Above: *General Alfredo Stroessner at his eighth swearing in as president of Paraguay. He ruled the country with an iron fist.*

COMPARED WITH THE POOR CITIZENS OF PARAGUAY, THE PANAMANIANS' SUFFERING WAS MERCIFULLY SHORT

gence information on Castro and allowed Nicaraguan contras to train in his camps. He also allowed the U.S. Drug Enforcement Agency to seize small boats trafficking in cocaine off the coast of Panama... all the while collecting huge pay-offs from the Colombian cartels for the big hauls which went untouched.

Eventually, his greed led to his downfall. The American government, fed up with his continual involvement in the drug trade, decided to act. Using evidence accrued over several years, the U.S. indicted 'Cara Pina' in February 1988, marking the first time Washington had formally charged the leader of an important allied country with felony offences. Authorities charged him with money laundering, racketeering and drug trafficking. As one government lawyer said at the time, he basically sold his country to the highest bidder.

Despite the indictment, however, there was little the U.S. could do. Noriega was not stupid enough to enter the U.S., and so for the next 20 months thumbed his nose at the 'gringos' to the north.

But the tinpot tyrant pushed and shoved Washington too far. Fearful of growing

government antagonism towards U.S. citizens living in Panama and the future of the vital Panama Canal, President Bush launched a military strike just a few days before Christmas 1989.

Opposition to the invading force was quickly mopped up, and Noriega, knowing his time was up, soon fled to the Vatican embassy in Panama City, where he tried to make one least deal to save himself. However, after a brief stand-off, Noriega surrendered and was flown back to the U.S. in handcuffs. More than two years later, on 9 April 1992, a Miami jury found him guilty on eight counts of drug and racketeering charges. President Bush called it 'a major victory against the drug lords'.

Today, the little general sits in a maximum security prison in Florida. He will be there for the rest of his life... which for the people he oppressed for so many years, is not a day too long.

AN OPPRESSED GENERATION

And yet, compared with the poor citizens of Paraguay, the Panamanians' suffering was mercifully short. For in Paraguay, the odious figure of General Alfredo Stroessner spanned more than a generation.

Stroessner, who seized power in 1954 and held sway for nearly 35 years until his own ouster, was the longest-ruling leader in the Western Hemisphere. During his cruel reign, seven American presidents came and went, while he towered over his landlocked nation like an evil Colossus. So repulsive was his reign that he openly welcomed Nazi war criminals like the 'Angel of Death' Dr Josef Mengele and Edward Rochmann, the 'Butcher of Riga', fallen despots like Juan Peron of Argentina and Anastasio Somoza of Nicaragua, as well as a sordid array of drug traffickers and professional contract killers, to his nation.

To his people, who knew him as 'El Rubio' – the fair-haired one – and later as 'El Viejo' – the old man – he was a brutal oppressor, a tyrant who tolerated no opposition or cries for mercy. Many of his foes, real and imaginary, were horribly tortured and murdered by his bands of roving thugs, and the mutilated bodies were often seen floating down the Parana River.

Like Noriega and others of his ilk, Stroessner was a military man, but his upbringing was a far cry from the destitution which surrounded the Panamanian strongman. Indeed, Stroessner's mother, Heriberta, was a descendent of one of Paraguay's founding fathers, while his father, Hugo, was a successful immigrant businessman from Bavaria. He made a fortune in the timber industry and, like so many other wealthy Paraguayans, sent his son to military school at a young age.

Indeed, Alfredo was just eight when he was sent away to the Mariscal Solano Lopez Military Academy in 1920. Following his years of study there, he then attended a military college in Brazil. In October 1932, he was commissioned into the Paraguayan armed services as a second lieutenant. That year also marked the outbreak of the so-called 'Cacho War' with Bolivia, and the young lieutenant proved himself a courageous soldier. According to army records, he was a natural leader, and was decorated for bravery and promoted to first lieutenant. Shortly after the end of hostilities, in 1935, he was again promoted, to the rank of captain.

His meteoric rise through the ranks continued, and in 1947 he commanded an artillery battery that played a vital role in putting down a bloody revolt against the military government of General Higninio Morinigo. However, soon after the violent civil war was over, Stroessner was sent into exile in Brazil for his Machiavellian manoeuvrings behind the scenes. A year later, in 1949, he quietly slipped back into Paraguay, and helped to lead a successful coup d'etat against the provisional president, General Raimundo Rolon.

Two years later, at the age of just 38, Stroessner was made commander-in-chief of the armed forces. He was now powerful

Below: *Stroessner was one of the last old-time hard-man dictators of South America.*

Below: *One of the world's worst murderers during the postwar years was General Pinochet of Chile.*

enough to plot his next move, but he patiently waited until 1954, when he led the successful revolt against President Federico Chaves.

Three months later, he was president... a position he would hold at great cost to his nation for 35 years. Opponents were quick-

downfall, Stroessner, a workaholic who neither smoked nor drank, had secreted more than £600,000,000 in banks and property around the world.

But after the 1989 coup, there were no discoveries of fabulous art collections, luxurious estates, or wardrobes filled with furs

STROESSNER'S AMENDMENT TO THE CONSTITUTION LET HIM BE RE-ELECTED FOR AS MANY TERMS AS HE WISHED

ly wiped out or sent into exile; what was left of the free press was stifled; loyal aides and cohorts rewarded with plush jobs and a share in the nation's biggest commercial enterprise – smuggling – which accounted for more than half the country's gross national product!

According to numerous reports, Stroessner's Paraguay was the only country in the world where American cigarettes were cheaper than in the United States. And the market in stolen cars was also the best in the world. It's estimated that 50 per cent of the cars on the road were stolen in neighbouring Brazil. Everything could be bought on the black market in Paraguay, and the General heartily encouraged such trade to help fill his personal coffers. It is estimated that by the time of his eventual

and jewels like those that came after the flights to exile of people like Ferdinand Marcos of the Philippines or Jean-Claude Duvalier of Haiti.

'Stroessner was much more intelligent than Somoza, who had businesses in his name', said Paraguayan journalist Ricardo Canese. 'Stroessner received commissions and dividends without ever becoming part of the business itself, without any documents bearing his name.'

With absolute power, the General had no need for pieces of paper to mark his wealth. Indeed, after putting down a series of minor revolts in the first years of his reign, Stroessner ordered a constitutional amendment in 1967 which permitted him to be re-elected for as many terms as he wished. He also ruled under a virtually permanent state of siege, and gave himself emergency powers even when the country was stable. All these measures were ostensibly passed so that he could defend democracy against unnamed insurgents, yet there was no democracy left to safeguard.

But even his critics concede that Stroessner did modernise Paraguay, which before him had been a backward, rural nation. Still, even his grandiose construction plans were motivated by avarice and ego. Kickbacks were of the order of millions of pounds.

One such reported scam involved a local oil conglomerate to charge the government as much as double the world price for oil from 1974 to 1979, giving it an £550,000,000 profit. It's unknown what Stroessner's cut was, but it would have amounted to millions. As his aides liked to boast: 'Not a leaf falls in Paraguay without Stroessner knowing it.'

Ego, too, played a huge part in his make-up, and he saw to it that dozens of schools, even towns, were named in his honour. Indeed, one of the biggest cities in Paraguay was known as Ciudad Presidente Stroessner; the airport in Asuncion also bore his name. In a central plaza in the capital, a huge neon sign blinked interminably with the slogan: 'Stroessner: Peace, Work and Well-being.'

AN ENORMOUS EGO

His ego, like that of all dictators, verged on the maniacal. He loved nothing more than giving speeches, which often lasted for several hours, while loyal supporters fought to keep their eyes open. Most of his long, rambling discourses centred on all the public works he had ordered. Indeed, he attended hundreds of ground-breaking ceremonies every year, even in the most remote villages, and often served as a witness at weddings where he didn't know either the bride or the groom! He just wanted to be seen as a benevolent father figure to his oppressed people.

Still, outside Paraguay he was feted by a succession of American leaders for his staunch anti-communist zeal. Asuncion was one of the few capitals that did not have diplomatic relations with the Soviet Union or China, and even something as trite as a Christmas card from President

STROESSNER SAW TO IT THAT DOZENS OF SCHOOLS, EVEN TOWNS, WERE NAMED IN HIS HONOUR

Below: *Salvador Allende was elected democratically in Chile but reactionary military elements engineered his downfall.*

Reagan to Stroessner was made into front page news. But in the early 1980s, public resentment of his totalitarian regime became increasingly evident, and protesters and police often clashed violently on the streets of Asuncion and in other major towns across the land.

The powerful Catholic Church, and even some members of his own Colorado political party, began to question his rule and accused him of using repressive tactics to keep sway. Inevitably, not even his rabid anti-Communism was able to stave off a reproach from Washington for his constant abuses of human rights. Indeed, in 1985 President Reagan went so far as to lump Paraguay with Chile, Cuba and Nicaragua as the only dictatorships left in the Western

Hemisphere. Reagan backed his words by removing some key trading privileges.

Ironically, when the end came for Stroessner, it was by the hand of the military, which had brought him to power so many years before. The ageing general, who was 77-years-old when he was toppled, had tried to force his most powerful military leader, General Andres Rodriguez into retirement, fearing that he was becoming too much of a threat. That, together with his decision to install his own son as his successor and his ill-advised major shake-up of the armed forces, led to the violent coup of February 1989.

'Stroessner tried to take away some of the regiments controlled by Rodriguez and thus reduce his power – a technique Stroessner had used for many years', said Edgar Insfran, a one-time interior minister in Paraguay. 'But this time he committed a very big indiscretion.'

The coup, short but violent, took about eight hours, and was marked by heated exchanges of fire by soldiers from both camps. Finally, Stroessner conceded defeat, and was placed under house arrest. Twelve hours later, he, his family and a few loyal aides, were bundled onto a military plane and sent into exile in Brazil, to spend the rest of his days as a dictator without a country, a general without an army. El Viejo had fought and lost his last battle.

BLOODY DOMINANCE

Meanwhile, as Stroessner went into exile, events in nearby Chile were also pointing to the end of that Andean nation's despot, General Augusto Pinochet Ugarte, who had come to power in one of the bloodiest coups in South American history. Like Stroessner and Noriega, the cunning, vicious Pinochet took over the Presidential palace without a vote being cast. Like his evil contemporaries, the power of the bullet, not the ballot, was his launching pad to total dominance of the political and social make-up of his country.

Pinochet, who was named after a Roman emperor, was born in 1915 in Valparaiso, a coastal city about 100 miles to the west of Santiago, the capital. His father, also called Augusto, was a customs officer, who hoped his young son would become a doctor. Unfortunately for future generations of

Above: *Stroessner, dressed in all his finery, pays homage to the military on Army Day.*

THE POWER OF THE BULLET, NOT THE BALLOT, WAS PINOCHET'S LAUNCHING PAD TO TOTAL POLITICAL POWER

---

oppressed Chileans, the young boy's mother, Avelina, strongly encouraged him to fulfill his dream of becoming a soldier. Eventually, in 1932, at the age of 16, Pinochet was accepted by the National Military Academy for a four-year officers' training course. Twice before, he had been rejected – the first time because he was too small; the second because he was too thin.

Although his instructors listed Pinochet as an average student academically, he more than made up for it with his rigid sense of duty and his love for the hard regime of the army. In 1936 he graduated as a second lieutenant, and immediately enrolled in the infantry school, where his deep pride in the armed forces was further manifested. It was during this time that he also began to read the works of Marx and Engels, which would foster his lifelong hatred of Communism.

At the outbreak of World War Two, Pinochet, now a full lieutenant, watched in fascination from a distance at the historic battles being played out in Europe, Africa and the South Pacific. Like many of his ilk, he supported the Nazi cause, and held the 'Desert Fox', General Ernst Rommel, in total awe. Still, the events of World War Two were many thousands of miles away, and Pinochet had to content himself with more local problems. In the same year Europe erupted in flames, Pinochet was sent to Concepcion, where he helped the relief operations following a devastating earthquake. It was there he met some Socialist militiamen, whom he would later describe as 'two-bit thieves'.

MILITARY EXPERIENCE

While the war was raging in Europe, Pinochet was sent to a number of posts throughout Chile, and eventually met and married Lucia Hiriart, the daughter of a future Interior Minister. In 1945, he returned to the military academy, where he began teaching. Three years later, when the communist Party was outlawed, he was sent to command the Pisagua concentration camp, where more than 400 leftists had been confined.

His rapid climb up the military hierarchy continued, and he was given various postings, including ones in Ecuador and the United States. He was never singled out as a remarkable officer, but he was praised by his superiors for his loyalty and discipline. Still, by 1971, he had remained discreet enough not to raise any red flags, and was placed in charge of the military garrison in Santiago – the most important in Chile – the year after Socialist president Salvadore Allende Gossens had come to power.

Despite his promotion, Pinochet, in common with many old-guard soldiers, cared little for the new president or his leftist policies, despite his victory at the polls. 'With great bitterness', he was later to write in his autobiography, 'we men of arms watched the road Chile had taken, and we felt the desperation of impotence. As a soldier sworn to protect the fatherland, I felt inhibited from acting, because the instigator of chaos was the very government to which I owed obedience.'

But rightist agitators, backed by the Nixon Administration in Washington, soon brought Chile to its knees. By September 1973, there were widespread strikes, protests and running street battles. Pinochet and his fellow officers knew the status quo

could not be maintained and waited for their chance to act. While he continued to vow his support for Allende – who had selected him just three weeks earlier as the commander in chief of the army after Pinochet vowed not to get involved in poli-

*Below: **Chilean leader Salvador Allende (left) meets his Argentinian opposite number General Alejandro Lanusse in 1971.***

tics – the general was quietly working behind the scenes, preparing for the inevitable coup d'etat. It came on 11 September, amid bloody fighting between the plotters' forces and those loyal to Allende. By the time it was over, an estimated 3,000 people were dead, including Allende, and the presidential palace was a smoking ruin.

Immediately following the takeover, Pinochet was selected as one of four military leaders of the post-coup junta, though within a year he had become so dominant that he declared himself president. Two of his major opponents, generals Oscar Bonilla and Augusto Lutz, both met with mysterious deaths. Lutz, who became violently ill at a party in October 1974, died in a military hospital after several botched

*Above: **Allende in the early 1960s, when he was his nation's foreign minister, on a visit to Cuba.***

Above: *President Allende in a motorcade with a visiting dignitary, shortly before he was overthrown.*

THOUSANDS OF LEFTISTS WERE ROUNDED UP TO BE INTERROGATED, TORTURED, IMPRISONED OR BANISHED

operations. Bonilla died in a suspicious helicopter crash in the January of the following year. Pinochet's efforts to consolidate power knew no boundaries – nor did he have respect for other nations' borders. In September 1974, former Chilean army leader General Prats and his wife were killed in a massive car bomb explosion outside their Argentine apartment.

Pinochet took power with an ambitious vision of forging a complete political and economic transformation of the country. Vowing to eradicate Marxism from Chile, he used the old carrot-and-stick approach, by extending wide social benefits to Chile's legions of the extremely poor and by exiling and torturing those who continued to advocate socialist change. Indeed, thousands of leftists were rounded up to be interrogated, tortured, imprisoned or banished. Many were executed. The press was stifled and Congress was dismantled. Chile became synonymous with Nazi Germany:

books were burned, troops marched in the goosestep style, citizens were roused in the middle of the night by the dreaded DINA, or secret police, never to be seen again.

In 1977, after the United Nations had sharply condemned him for his human rights abuses, Pinochet ordered a national referendum on his rule in order to gag his critics. But the vote was taken under state-of-siege conditions, with no press coverage apart from that given by newspapers in the government's pockets, and no voter registration. Needless to say, Pinochet 'won' the referendum handsomely.

Following the vote, his rule became more oppressive. Military men were placed in charge of universities to stamp out any opposition, while distinguished citizens were promptly exiled. He also oversaw the writing of a new constitution, that all but turned Chile into a military camp with military rule and military law. Pinochet also saw to it that the constitution allowed him to serve an eight-year term, then be eligible for another term after a popular 'vote'.

In 1980, following a few years of economic stability, he held a national vote for an authoritarian constitution that would allow him to stay in power until 1989. After a campaign marked by severe restrictions on the opposition, he won a 60 per cent 'yes' vote. To celebrate, Pinochet ordered a six-hour extravaganza of parades and ceremonies. They were largely designed to keep the people happy, because Pinochet had no great love of such hedonistic celebrations. He was a dour, austere man, who ate simply and never touched alcohol. He would rise every morning at 5.30, and his day was filled with meetings, speeches and briefings from his intelligence officials. And although he shared the same lust for power as other dictators, he did not line his own pockets from the nation's treasury. In fact, one of his first decrees after coming to power was to offer a public accounting of his financial status.

A FEEBLE EXCUSE

But his human rights record was atrocious. And whenever world leaders called on him to ease his repressive tactics, he replied with the old chestnut that he was merely trying to stamp out communists. And not even America could make him budge. When Jimmy Carter came to power in 1976, he slashed Chile's foreign aid to less than £15,000,000. Pinochet reacted by publicly refusing it, proclaiming that Chile had been slighted. Ten years later, when Senator Edward Kennedy came to Santiago, Pinochet and senior officials snubbed him as an enemy of Chile, and government-sponsored protesters attacked his motorcade with eggs and stones while police and militiamen looked on.

That same year, 1986, opposition to Pinochet's despotic regime, which had been festering for more than a decade, resulted in an assassination attempt. His motorcade was ambushed by a group of freedom fighters on a lonely country highway. Five of Pinochet's bodyguards were killed, but the 71-year-old leader was unharmed. He was enraged, and a state of siege was re-introduced. Hundreds of people were arrested and several communists murdered by right-wing death squads in

retaliation for the assassination attempt. Ironically, the attempt on his life actually helped his cause, with many Chileans rallying around the leader who for years had warned them of communist terror.

In 1989, Pinochet again went to the

polls, warning the country that its choice was simple: nine more years of his leadership or, by way of open presidential elections next year, Marxist rule. This time, however, nothing could stop the groundswell of democracy. He lost, and, early the following year, the old man bade farewell – ending more than 16 years of military rule – and gave way to President Patricio Aylwin. Chile's nightmare years had finally come to an end.

But in his final presidential address to the nation, Pinochet clung to the idea that his rule had saved Chile from chaos: 'I want to express our satisfaction and legiti-

Above: *The last picture of President Allende before he committed suicide. He is seen waving from the presidential palace as armed police begin to surround the building during the early part of the coup.*

known as the Watergate of South America. The scandal was a double blow to the long-suffering people of Brazil, a land of immense resources and natural beauty, who had for years been subjected to the whims of dictators and corrupt politicians. Not only did they lose a charismatic leader in Collor de Mello, but many of them also lost their faith in politics, just as the Americans of the post-Watergate era had done. And like Richard Nixon, Collor de Mello resigned in disgrace, just minutes after the Brazilian Senate began to try him on corruption charges.

A PROMISING YOUNGSTER

But exactly three years earlier, he had been the toast of South America when, as the little-known governor of Alagoas, one of Brazil's smallest and poorest states, he won the presidency by assuring voters he would wage a non-stop war against government corruption. At just 40 years of age, he was the youngest – and certainly the most handsome – president ever to lead Brazil.

True to his campaign promises, he began his term with a flurry of energy and changes. He named young men like himself to run the various ministries, and everywhere Brazilians braced themselves for better days, and awaited this enthusiastic new generation of leaders tackling the massive problems of inflation, unemployment and corruption.

Collor de Mello was everywhere, and his flashing smile and swarthy looks made him immensely popular. One day he might be flying a jet fighter; the next, driving a tank; the day after that, practising karate, in which he held a black belt. He was so dynamic, so daring, that even President George Bush dubbed him 'Indiana Jones'. But the real Collor de Mello was soon unmasked, when his own brother, Pedro, turned on him and went public with sordid tales of the President's corruption. Pedro, who owned interests in various media holdings, was prompted to speak out when the President invested in a radio and newspaper company that threatened to compete with his own group.

Pedro took his damning story to the news-magazine *Veja* in Sao Paolo and, despite official pressure – including a presidential decree ordering the Bank of Brazil

mate pride,' he said, 'in having worked unceasingly to save our freedom and to build democracy, and make of Chile a country increasingly prosperous and just. I was disposed always to confront the enemies of freedom and democracy, with neither fear nor oscillations.'

Even in defeat, Pinochet thought himself a national hero.

A NEW APPROACH

If Pinochet, Noriega and Stroessner typified the old style of Latin American leaders with their generals' stars and strutting goose steps, then Brazil's Fernando Collor de Mello represented the new. He was a civilian, who was handsome, well-dressed and appeared to be enamoured by the ideals of democracy and what it could do for his people. Indeed, with his beautiful young wife, Rosane, by his side, he was viewed as the Brazilian Kennedy, a man of honour, looks and boyish charm.

And yet, behind this handsome exterior was a conniving, greedy bureaucrat, whose downfall in December 1992, came to be

Above: *President Carter tried to steer a fine line between opposing communism in Latin America and befriending dictators of the right who had appalling human rights records.*

BEHIND COLLOR DE MELLO'S HANDSOME EXTERIOR WAS A CONNIVING, GREEDY BUREAUCRAT to investigate the publisher's finances – to back away from the revelations, the magazine continued to uncover the president's wrongdoings, just as the *Washington Post* had during the Watergate cover-up. Pedro implied that the graft and corruption endemic to the Collor de Mello presidency was being arranged by Paulo Cesar Farias, the president's campaign manager and close friend. According to Pedro, millions of pounds in kickbacks were funnelled to Farias, who then passed on a substantial percentage to the president, whom he called 'the front man' in the ring. In one episode, for instance, 24 hours before Collor de Mello signed an edict which excused some sugarcane plantation owners from paying a certain tax, they gave Cesar Farias more than £200,000.

Eventually, others in the media began their own investigations, investigations that produced a wealth of evidence and allegations about Collor de Mello's opulent lifestyle, his throng of servants, an apartment in Paris, European shopping sprees for his 27-year-old wife and the more than £1,500,000 spent on landscaping his private garden!

The public clamour for an explanation grew, as did calls in the Brazilian congress. Eventually, in August 1992, as overwhelming evidence poured in, a congressional commission accused Cesar Farias of running a huge kickback ring that involved the President. Collor de Mello denied all the accusations, but there was too much evidence to the contrary. Still, he battled on, but with thousands protesting in the streets, the National Congress voted in September to impeach him.

THE TRUTH IS REVEALED

The final nail in his coffin had been the revelations about his opulent garden. Collor de Mello had defended himself on national TV, claiming the work was done only to build barracks for the presidential bodyguards and to 'reconstruct' some areas damaged by the building crew. But the landscaper, Jose Roberto Nehring, then came forward to say nothing had been 'reconstructed'. He said the massive project had taken him more than two years, and included the installation of waterfalls and fish ponds which were filled with 100

Below: Brazilian president-elect Fernando Collor de Mello when he visited Margaret Thatcher at 10 Downing Street.

exotic fish imported from Japan. 'It's one of the most beautiful gardens in the world,' Nehring crowed, much to the President's embarrassment.

Three months later, in December, just as he was about to go on trial, he realised the game was over, and resigned. Nonetheless, the Senate voted overwhelming, 76 to 3, to convict him.

An interesting footnote to the scandal came in April 1993, when the disgraced Collor de Mello was back as the focus of scandal, after being attacked yet again by his brother, Pedro. In a series of front page stories in a Rio de Janeiro newspaper, Pedro claimed the former president abused his wife, enjoyed kinky sex, and was involved in black magic rituals in which animal sacrifices were made.

The final chapter on the Brazilian Watergate is yet to be written.

COLLOR DE MELLO'S BROTHER CLAIMED THE PRESIDENT ENJOYED KINKY SEX AND WAS INVOLVED IN BLACK MAGIC RITUALS

PREACH FOR PROFIT
Television Evangelists

America's television evangelists proclaimed themselves God's messengers on earth and spread His word from their high-tech pulpits. Privately, they were anything but heavenly. Behind their pious veneer lay the devilish truth: scandal, sex, power and money.

The most sensational case of a shamed 'holy man' was dubbed 'Pearlygate' in the American press and revolved around the diminutive Jim Bakker. The boyish TV preacher fleeced his flock of millions of pounds and paid hush money to a former church secretary with whom he had had forbidden sex.

Bakker, together with his make-up laden wife, Tammy Faye, ran the huge PTL Ministry (Praise the Lord), which raked in millions and millions of pounds every year from ordinary Americans who believed in their sanctimonious mission. But away from the TV lights and Bible-bashing sermons, the Bakkers's sought to build their own heavenly kingdom on earth with plush mansions, expensive cars and hundreds of thousands of pounds in annual wages.

For more than two decades, the Bakkers were institutions on the American TV circuit, telling listeners and church faithful that they needed money to carry on God's charitable works. By the time their empire finally collapsed, the PTL Ministry was raking in more than £80,000,000 a year! That was a far cry from their early days when, in 1966, Jim had landed his first TV ministry on the Christian Broadcasting Network. With tears flowing down his chubby, boyish face, Jim gravely spoke into the cameras: 'We need $10,000 a month or we'll be off the air... Christian television will be no more.' The money

poured in, and did so without interruption for the next 20 years. He was a genius at fundraising.

With his wife, whom he met at a Bible college, by his side, Jim embarked on a flamboyant career to the top of the TV ministry. Outwardly, the marriage seemed to be made in heaven. Tammy, who often sang on the program, was everything 'Christian womanhood' was supposed to espouse. She was supportive, loyal, a caring mother and a devoted child of the Lord.

But off the set, the Bakkers, who had married in 1961, had more than their share of problems, both marital and professional. Disgruntled aides claimed Jim ruled PTL like a dictator, and that both had tainted the ministry through their boundless greed. And as Jim became more and more obsessed with his empire, the marriage turned into a sham. According to Charles Sheppard, who wrote a best-selling book on the PTL scandal, Tammy began to find solace in the arms of country music star

BAKKER AND HIS MAKE-UP-LADEN WIFE RAKED IN MILLIONS AND MILLIONS OF POUNDS FROM ORDINARY AMERICANS

Opposite: *Evangelists Jim and Tammy Bakker ran a religious empire worth hundreds of millions of pounds.*

Gary Paxton, and later with a married PTL executive Thurlow Spurr. Bakker is said to have become so angry at her infidelities that he melted down his wedding ring and turned it into a charm.

But Bakker, too, was finding excitement outside the marital bedroom. He had a Jacuzzi installed in his office, where he is said to have often 'entertained' guests. In

Above: *The Bakkers controlled their own theme park, where Christians could go for good clean fun. But everything was not as it seemed in the religious Disneyland.*

fact, shocked senior executives of the ministry dubbed it the 'Floozie Jacuzzi'. And Bakker didn't limit his sexual conquests to women. A fellow minister claimed that he once caught the pint-sized preacher in bed with his closest aide, David Taggart. The minister later admitted that he, too, had had forbidden sex with Bakker.

Below: *Bakker is led away in handcuffs after being charged with ripping off his TV ministry.*

Another PTL aide, Austin Miles, said he once walked into a steam room to find a naked Bakker cavorting with three young men. 'There they were, frolicking about, taking turns placing each other on the massage table,' Miles said. 'The hands started with the knees, working their way up the thighs into the intimate massages – accompanied by schoolgirl giggles and cries of "Whooeee!"' Despite their problems, however, the Bakkers did enjoy an active sex life together. Aides later recalled that Jim often boasted of their sexual shenanigans, including a very public coupling in a park. But Jim's frequent affairs began to take their toll on Tammy, who turned more and

BAKKER'S AFFAIRS BEGAN TO TAKE THEIR TOLL ON TAMMY, WHO TURNED MORE AND MORE TO THE BOTTLE AND PILLS

more to the bottle and prescription pills for comfort.

Still, the Bakkers continued their sham marriage, knowing that if they split it could seriously hurt their ministry and the luxurious lifestyle to which they had grown accustomed. They presided over a 2,300-acre Christian resort in South Carolina and paid themselves £1,000,000 a year from church funds. They owned four homes, including a £400,000 mansion in ritzy Palm Springs, a Rolls Royce and a Mercedes. They also splurged on minks and jewelry and had an extensive wardrobe. Jim became so drunk with money and power that he regularly had an aide buy him £60 worth of cinnamon buns... not to eat, but simply because Jim loved the aroma. He also splashed out thousands of pounds on an air-conditioned dog house for Tammy's pet!

CONFIDENT LIARS

Despite their excesses, the Bakkers were marketing geniuses. 'They were phenomenal, charismatic personalities,' said Miles. 'Even when you knew they were lying through their teeth, there is something folksy and good about them. No one else could have pulled it off.'

They were also cold and uncaring. Miles remembers one fundraising telethon in 1982, when the Bakkers went on the air and lied that if they didn't receive several million dollars by a certain date, they would have to pull their show off the air. 'Tammy was crying, mascara running – "We've sold everything we have. This is a real crisis",' Miles recalled. But later, once the millions had poured in, Miles learned the entire event had been a complete sham. The ministry had sufficient funds, and was in no danger of closing down. But outrageous lies were nothing new to the Bakkers. Over the years, Jim often made up non-existent financial crises to stir the faithful and fatten his coffers. Miles says Jim would often write to followers claiming some make-believe crisis, and timed the letters so that they arrived at the same time as did the trusting souls' meagre social security cheques.

Given their all-consuming greed and Jim's sexual cravings, the road to ruin was inevitable. The end, which came in 1987, was rooted in a 1980 incident, involving Jim and a virginal church secretary from Long Island, Jessica Hahn. No one denies that Bakker and Jessica had sex that afternoon, but Jessica called it rape. But she was frightened and confused – Bakker had been a holy man to her. Richard Dortch, the executive vice president of PTL, told her no-one would believe her story anyway, and her silence was bought by tens of thousands of pounds. 'I remember Richard Dortch told me, "You're just a local church girl. You can't get to us,"' Hahn recalled many years later.

But Hahn did keep her silence until 1987, when revelations emerged that the PTL had paid out almost £180,000 to keep her quiet. The sensational news hit the PTL ministry like a sledgehammer. Within days, the embattled Bakkers called on fellow preacher, Jerry Falwell, to take control of the ministry until they could strengthen their position. But Falwell, a well known political and religious activist in the United States, quickly discovered that the Bakkers had more to hide than just Jim's dalliance with a church secretary. Falwell, who moved quickly to isolate the Bakkers, withholding their salary and firing some of their closest associates, announced that there were numerous financial irregularities within PTL, and that despite raking in more than £80,000,000 every year, it was somehow £30,000,000 in debt!

DESPERATE MEASURES

As Falwell acted, the brazen Bakkers made one last stand to save their ministry – and lifestyle. They organised rallies on their own behalf, and warned Falwell that a 'holy war' would erupt unless he handed the PTL back to their closest associates. But the defiant Falwell refused to yield, and he continued to find glaring problems in the financial books of the PTL. The U.S. Government and other state authorities also began looking into the Bakkers' shoddy practices, and found the PTL owed millions of pounds in back taxes and penalties.

Under the growing onslaught, the Bakkers retreated to their Palm Springs estate. While the whole nation sat glued to

Above: *Tammy looks for divine intervention as her husband goes on trial.*

Left: *Former church secretary Jessica Hahn, who accused Jim Bakker of rape.*

THE TRIAL WAS AS
DRAMATIC AND, AT TIMES,
COMICAL AS ANYTHING THE
BAKKERS HAD EVER DONE
ON THEIR TV SHOW

their TV sets to await the latest allegations, Jim and Tammy dropped out of sight for several days. When they did reappear, they knew the battle was lost. As Tammy sobbed by his side, Jim announced: 'Without a miracle of God, we will never minister again.'

But if the Bakkers thought that was the end of their unholy charade, they were sadly mistaken. For the next two years, the roller coaster continued, with yet more allegations and claims of financial impropriety. Finally, in August 1989, Jim Bakker was ordered to stand trial in North Carolina on 24 counts of fraud and conspiracy.

The charges focussed on the more than £100,000,000 Bakker had raised by selling what he called 'life partnerships' in his religious theme park, called Heritage USA, a smoke-free, drink-free refuge for the faithful and their children. For a minimum contribution of some £650, buyers were entitled to three nights' free accommodation

for life in hotels inside the sprawling complex. According to prosecutors, Bakker sold about 153,000 partnerships between 1983 and 1987. But there were only 258 rooms available at the park, meaning most buyers were never able to stay there.

The trial, which culminated in October that same year, was as dramatic and at times comical as anything the Bakkers had ever done on their TV show. On the third day of the trial, for instance, witness Steve Nelson, a former PTL executive who was testifying for the state, suddenly collapsed in his chair. After Bakker's attorney nudged him and whispered 'Jim! Jim! Jim!', the preacher suddenly darted to Nelson's side, then knelt down next to him and solemnly began to pray! Then, the very next day, while Bakker was attending a meeting at his attorney's office, he crumpled to the floor and hid his head under a couch! He began to sob uncontrollably, and the fed-up judge ordered that he undergo psychiatric evaluation. Later, Bakker claimed he had also been hallucinating, seeing the throngs of news people at the trial as 'giant ants with antennae waving'!

But despite the bizarre atmosphere at the trial, Bakker was eventually found guilty of defrauding his followers of more than £2,500,000 and using the money to indulge his every whim. Indeed, the jury found him guilty on all 24 counts. As the verdict was read, a scattering of still-loyal followers burst into tears. Bakker, of course, was as unrepentant as ever, declaring: 'I went into the courtroom innocent of the charges against me, and I came out innocent of the charges. My faith is still in God.'

Unfortunately for Bakker, his faith, which he had wielded as a shield for so long, was not enough to save him. He was sentenced to more than 20 years behind bars. 'I think the Devil caused a lot of problems,' he said with a straight-face.

A DEVILISH DEFENCE

The belief that the Devil made him do it was also the defence used by the Rev. Jimmy Swaggart, the fire-and-brimstone preacher who would soon follow Bakker down the path to damnation and disgrace.

Swaggart, America's most-watched television evangelist with an average of 8,000,000 viewers a week, was from the

Below: Fellow preacher Jerry Falwell was brought in to help clear up the mess left by the Bakkers.

old school of preaching. Where Bakker was charming and gentle, Swaggart was blustering and fiery, often regaling his attentive flock with the bizarre notions that the Devil had created movies, beer and rock'n'roll... something his cousin, famed rocker Jerry Lee Lewis, would no doubt have found hard to believe. He would prowl the stage, using his deep voice and the raw emotions that had built a £100,000,000 empire from literally nothing.

But Swaggart, who wore an expensive Rolex watch and lived in a 20-acre, £1,600,000 mansion in Louisiana, was also two-faced. When the PTL scandal erupted, Swaggart pounced on the hapless Bakker with unbridled glee, describing him as 'a cancer on the body of Christ'. And yet, the outspoken minister was hiding a dirty secret of his own... a penchant for kinky sex and prostitutes.

Swaggart, like Bakker, was born in the South, a bastion of political conservatism and bible-thumping Christianity. From an early age, he would preach the Gospel to anyone who would listen and, by the time he had grown to manhood, he had taken his powerful performing skills on the road as a travelling evangelist. Slowly, he became popular enough to have his own radio show, which was broadcast weekly to his followers. In the late 1960s, like so many other preachers, he turned to television to reach an even larger audience. His dynamic presence soon catapulted him to national prominence, and he eventually took his teachings to Latin America and Africa. And while other ministers used their pulpits to preach conservative politics, Swaggart focused intently on personal morality. Many times he stressed sexual fidelity, and blasted abortion, homosexuality and extra-marital sex as abominations before God. He also called the Roman Catholic Church 'a false cult', and blasted the United States

Above: *Jimmy Swaggart, one of Bakker's critics, was himself forced to admit less than divine behaviour.*

Below: *Swaggart's famous cousin, Jerry Lee Lewis.*

Congress and the Supreme Court as 'institutions damned by God'.

So it came like a bolt from heaven when, in February 1988, with America's evangelical community still reeling from the Bakker affair, Swaggart was accused of dallying with prostitutes. His accuser, a Louisiana minister named Marvin Gorman, said he had photographs of Swaggart in very compromising positions. The pictures were turned over to the ruling body of the

Below: *Preacher Marvin Gorman caught up with Swaggart as he left a seedy hotel after a tryst with a prostitute.*

Assemblies of God organisation, who dragged Swaggart in for a hastily-called session to explain them.

Gorman, who had, ironically, himself been defrocked after Jimmy Swaggart had accused him of adultery, reportedly had been receiving anonymous phone calls for several months detailing Swaggart's liaison with a prostitute.

Initially, Gorman thought the calls were the work of a hoaxer, but after they continued for several weeks, he decided to put the caller in touch with a private detective. In October 1987, Gorman was tipped off by the undercover specialist, who told him he could 'catch' Swaggart in the act if he

---
IT CAME LIKE A BOLT FROM HEAVEN WHEN JIMMY SWAGGART WAS ACCUSED OF DALLYING WITH PROSTITUTES
---

would hurry over to a hotel in a seedy, run-down section of New Orleans.

What followed was like a plot from a Hollywood detective thriller. The private eye snapped pictures of Swaggart entering the hotel room, then deflated the tyres of his car to give Gorman time to get to the scene of the 'crime'. Eventually, Gorman did arrive, suitably disguised in sunglasses and a cap, and he saw Swaggart hurriedly trying to change his tyres.

Gorman kept the story quiet for several months, reportedly hoping that Swaggart would change his ways himself. When he did hand over the photos, which showed him in the company of convicted prostitute Debra Murphree, to the Assemblies of God, all hell broke loose. Swaggart quickly apologised to the gathered hierarchy, and the nation waited for him to make a public statement. It didn't have to wait long.

A SELF-CONFESSED SINNER

The following week, as 8,000 worshippers crowded his Family Worship Centre in Baton Rouge and TV cameras waited in expectation, the contrite Swaggart took to the stage as he had done so many times in the past. However, this time, the once-fiery preacher did without the screaming and yelling. 'I do not call it a mistake, a mendacity,' he said gravely. 'I call it a sin... I have no-one to blame but myself.'

As the throng listened intently, Swaggart sobbed as he begged for forgiveness, first from his family, then his church, then his devoted followers. Lastly, in an odd, theatrical gesture he lifted his moist eyes to heaven and said: 'I have sinned against you, My Lord, and I would ask that your precious blood would wash and cleanse every stain until it is in the seas of God's forgetfulness, never to be remembered anymore.' He then stepped down from his global TV ministry.

Although Swaggart never actually said what sin he had committed, a hotel owner in New Orleans said that the minister had often frequented the red light area, underneath the shadow of a billboard with Jesus warning 'Your Eternity Is At Stake'. The owner said that Swaggart always used the girls' names when checking in, and always came in wearing a disguise of sunglasses, a hat or a headband.

Indeed, sources inside the Assemblies of God said Swaggart had admitted to a life-long fascination with pornography, and that he had struggled with his darker side for many years. Ironically, in one of his sermons, he blasted pornography as evil because it 'titillates and captivates the sickest of the sick and makes them slaves to their own consuming lusts'.

After the dramatic televised confession, the woman at the centre of the scandal, Debra Murphree, came forward to claim she was the woman in the photos. She claimed Swaggart had been using her services for over a year, but said no intercourse ever took place. Instead, she said, she would pose naked for him, and sometimes performed pornographic acts for him.

SOURCES INSIDE THE ASSEMBLIES OF GOD SAID SWAGGART HAD ADMITTED TO A FASCINATION WITH PORNOGRAPHY

Right: *Swaggart admitted to church elders that he couldn't control his deviant behaviour.*

Below: *Prostitute Debra Murphee came forward and said that Swaggart had been a long-time customer.*

Murphree eventually sold her story to *Penthouse* magazine. A prostitute with a record in two states, she also re-created the poses she had adopted for Swaggart for *Penthouse*. She even went on a national media tour to promote her story of their sexual liaison and the graphic pictures which were so hot that they had to be sealed in each issue.

Murphree said the evangelist, who scoffed at Bakker's travails until he, too, was caught, patronised her for more than a year and she went along with his bizarre sexual requests as long as he paid the going rate, but became enraged when he suggested that her nine-year-old daughter watch them!

In the wake of the scandal, Swaggart's popularity dropped dramatically. His TV show lost millions of viewers, and the once overflowing coffers of his organisation quickly emptied. Still, he wouldn't quit, clinging to his ministry like a drowning man clings to a life jacket, despite a three-month suspension.

For the next few years, he faded into the background, content to preach at his Family Worship Centre. But on 20 October 1991, Swaggart was again forced to tell the worshippers that he had been caught with another prostitute. This time, however, there were fewer than 1,000 people on hand to hear the details. Nine days earlier, a police officer had observed Swaggart swerving through the Californian town of Indio in his Jaguar. He ordered the minister

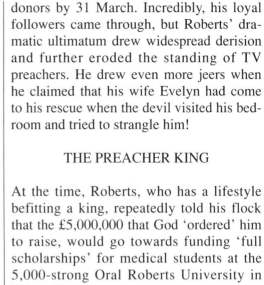

Below: Evangelist Oral Roberts' bizarre calls for money left many followers questioning his motives.

to pull over, and caught him consorting with a prostitute, Rosemary Garcia.

Then the final indignity came when he was ordered to pay Rev. Gorman more than £6,000,000 stemming from a defamation suit brought against him for spreading

rumours of Gorman's alleged philandering.

Although he is now considered a national joke in many quarters, Swaggart continues with his diminished ministry.

ROBERTS CLAIMED HIS WIFE HAD SAVED HIM WHEN THE DEVIL CAME TO HIS BEDROOM AND TRIED TO STRANGLE HIM

BIZARRE STATEMENTS

Oral Roberts, unlike his two fallen brothers, was not caught up in any sex scandal... but he managed to raise just as many eyebrows with a series of bizarre statements from the pulpit. It all began in January 1987, when Roberts, a long-time veteran of TV evangelism, went before the cameras and claimed God would 'call me home' unless he raised some £5,000,000 from

donors by 31 March. Incredibly, his loyal followers came through, but Roberts' dramatic ultimatum drew widespread derision and further eroded the standing of TV preachers. He drew even more jeers when he claimed that his wife Evelyn had come to his rescue when the devil visited his bedroom and tried to strangle him!

THE PREACHER KING

At the time, Roberts, who has a lifestyle befitting a king, repeatedly told his flock that the £5,000,000 that God 'ordered' him to raise, would go towards funding 'full scholarships' for medical students at the 5,000-strong Oral Roberts University in Tulsa, Oklahoma.

However, the following year it was discovered that the scholarships were in fact loans, and that in return for their four years of college, the students would agree to work as medical missionaries for four years after graduation to pay back the money. But the contracts were suddenly changed, and students found themselves facing extra years of post-graduate missionary work, or dropped. The switch angered many students who felt used – and left donors wondering about how their £5,000,000 was actually spent. In fact, delegates representing tens of thousands of people condemned his fundraising as 'offensive, inappropriate and objectionable'.

Roberts insisted that he had never promised the medical students anything beyond one year's help, but University faculty members thought differently. Assistant Dean Milton Olsen 'admitted in front of the whole class that he represented this as a four-year programme because that's what he thought it was,' said Donald Godfrey, a former associate professor. 'That was my understanding too.'

Indeed, Roberts himself had earlier declared in an article: 'God's instructions were for me to raise the $8,000,000 it will take to give full scholarships to each of our young physicians-in-training, including their room and board. This way, when they finish their residencies they will not have to go into practice here in America, where there is already a surplus of doctors, to pay off heavy educational debts before they can go to the mission field. They can go immediately, debt-free.'

'Right in the middle of my dad's sermon, a woman came running up to the platform with her baby in her arms, screaming: "My baby has just died. My baby has just died,"' he claimed. 'The child had died during the service. My dad had to stop in the middle of his sermon and lay hands on that child. And that child came back to life again. There are probably dozens and dozens and dozens of documented instances of people who have been raised from the dead.'

But as the controversy mounted, Oral Roberts began to play down the boast. During a follow-up TV appearance, he said that a baby he had brought back to life 'years ago' appeared to have died during a service. 'Only a doctor could say if the child was clinically dead,' he said, 'but the mother thought it was dead, I thought it was dead, the crowd thought it was dead.'

The eccentric evangelist also once claimed that while he was reading a novel in his bedroom in March, God spoke to him from the doorway and told him his work 'on the other side' is more important than the work he is doing here. Later, he said God told him that he, Roberts, 'will be coming back with my Son to reign'.

'I'm coming back,' Roberts exclaimed. 'I'm going to help bring that world back with me. I'm going to reign. I got a picture in my mind that he's going to position us to rule and reign. Maybe we'll have more power in the second try.'

But suddenly, students discovered that under the new contracts, they had to pay for their own travel and living expenses during their missionary service, which they must accept 'in any domestic or foreign location, without limitation'. And most students learned they would now have to do 15 months of missionary work for each year of scholarship funding! 'They want us to hitchhike to the poorest parts of the world, work for free, and feed our families on our good looks – what a deal!' said one disgruntled student.

Following that furore, Roberts further upset the evangelical community when, just a few months later, he claimed he had been raising people from the dead! Before a congregation of some 6,000 faithful, he said he had to literally 'stop a sermon, go back and raise a dead person'. Although he gave no more details at the time, his son, Richard, 38, said his dad had raised as many as 50 people from the grave! He also remembered the incident concerning the 'dead' infant.

Above: *Roberts begs his faithful to send him millions of pounds.*

Right: *The preacher claimed that he could raise people from the dead!*

ROBERTS UPSET THE EVANGELICAL COMMUNITY WHEN HE CLAIMED HE HAD BEEN RAISING PEOPLE FROM THE DEAD!

WINNIE MANDELA
Wicked Queen of the ANC

The African National Congress's struggle for freedom in South Africa was embodied by Nelson and Winnie Mandela for three decades. When, in 1991, Winnie was revealed as a liar and an accessory to kidnapping and assault it irreparably damaged the couple's image.

Opposite: *Winnie Mandela was considered the mother of her country until her evil ways caught up with her.*

Below: *Winnie was the resistance movement's most visible leader when her husband Nelson was sent to jail.*

To many black South Africans, Winnie Mandela was the 'Mother of the Nation', a stalwart of the natives' determined struggle for equality from the racist regime of Pretoria. She was, in essence, their queen, a woman millions looked upon as the voice and soul of the anti-apartheid movement.

For more than 27 years, beginning in 1963, she was also the most visible and famous symbol of black resistance, struggling to deliver her downtrodden people while she coped with a deep personal tragedy – the imprisonment of her husband, Nelson, at the time the deputy chief of the African National Congress, who had been sent to jail by the South African authorities. Ardent supporters even spoke of the 58-year-old Winnie as a future leader of South Africa and the logical successor to the 74-year-old Nelson. And even her critics lauded her bravery, especially when she was under police restrictions almost continuously from 1963 to 1986 and was held in solitary confinement for 17 months in 1969-70, before undergoing eight years in solitary banishment in a small town in the Orange Free State.

But in recent years Winnie's twin mantles of dignity and defiance have been largely eroded, her reputation irreparably tarnished, and her role in any future government seriously threatened. First, at a rally in 1986, she endorsed the brutal prac-

> TO MANY BLACK SOUTH
> AFRICANS, WINNIE
> MANDELA WAS THE SOUL
> OF THE ANTI-APARTHEID
> MOVEMENT

tice of 'necklace killings', in which a burning tyre is placed over the head of a suspected government collaborator. Her endorsement shocked many people in her homeland, and stunned supporters of the anti-apartheid cause around the world.

Then, in 1987, she flaunted her luxurious lifestyle, while her people remained among the world's most impoverished, by building herself a hillside mansion that was surrounded by tiny, overcrowded houses in the black township of Soweto. There was such a wave of criticism that Winnie, who had been embarrassed into submission, decided not to move in.

Yet the fiery activist, who has been fêted by presidents and royalty, somehow managed to not only survive those problems, but remain a potent force in the ANC. But all that changed when a young activist, 14-year-old James 'Stompie' Moeketsi Seipei was kidnapped along with three of his col-

went and became involved in violent feuds with members of other black gangs.

To her growing list of critics within the ANC and other black organisations, Winnie was a power-hungry, ruthless vixen, and the Stompie affair only reinforced their poor opinion of her. Her arrest on such serious charges not only hurt the image of the ANC around the world, but also opened her husband to ridicule.

After Stompie's disappearance, Soweto community leaders confronted Winnie with the allegations that she was holding the remaining boys to prevent them from accusing members of her own football club, who were also associated with a rash of robberies and other crimes against fellow blacks in Soweto. Stompie, who was last seen alive on 1 January 1989, was found in a field one week later, his throat cut and showing indications of internal bleeding; the result of a vicious beating. Her refusal to cooperate with either the police or with black community leaders resulted in her being immediately ostracised by fellow anti-apartheid activists, and spray-painted graffiti on signboards and walls in the township proclaimed 'Winnie Mandela, the Killer'. Only a call from her husband in prison that the football club be disbanded and his wife

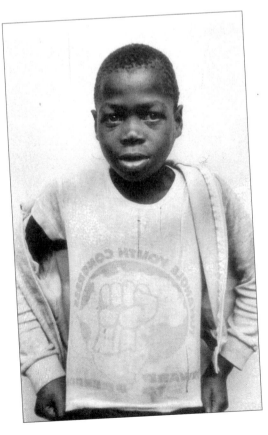

Above: *Winnie poses with the notorious thugs of the 'Mandela United Football Club'.*

Right: *Young Stompie Moeteksi, whose discarded body was found in a field after his throat had been cut.*

leagues assaulted in December 1988. Winnie was convicted in connection with the kidnappings, and of being an accessory after the fact to their beating at her home. Jerry Richardson, her chief bodyguard, was convicted of Stompie's murder in 1990. Richardson was the 'coach' of the so-called Mandela United Football Club – Winnie's strangely-named bodyguard unit, which protected her against harassment by government officials and white extremists. The youths accompanied Mandela wherever she

THE FURORE OVER STOMPIE'S DEATH WAS HEIGHTENED BECAUSE OF HIS OWN STANDING WITHIN THE BLACK COMMUNITY

Left: *Before the killing of Stompie, Winnie Mandela was hailed as a hero and protector in the black townships.*

Below: *Stompie's funeral attracted tens of thousands of mourners.*

'rehabilitated' saved what was left of her tattered reputation.

The furore over Stompie's death was heightened because of his own standing within the black community of South Africa. In 1985, when he was just ten years old, he led a township army of 1,500 children who were known as the Under Fourteens and who battled the black municipal police and their allied conservative black vigilantes during the civil unrest of the period. At the age of 11, he then became the youngest political detainee in the country under the government's state of emergency and spent his 12th birthday in a police cell.

A year later, Stompie addressed a major anti-apartheid meeting at Johannesburg's University of the Witwatersrand and after spellbinding his mostly white audience was taken to lunch by the university's vice

chancellor! Stompie, whose name in Afrikaans means the toughest part of the core of a tree, was also known as 'the Little General' because of his command of the

Under Fourteens, whose youngest member was only eight-years-old. The gang was widely believed to have set the township hall on fire in 1988, after the black councilmen refused to open it to the local civic association. They also boasted that they were protecting the adults from harassment by the white police, and Stompie said in an interview two years before his death that 'we are braver than adults'.

Although Winnie fervently denied any wrongdoing in the kidnappings and murder,

---
ALMOST FROM THE OPENING STATEMENTS, WINNIE'S DEFENCE STRUGGLED TO KEEP PACE WITH THE DAMNING EVIDENCE

she was dragged into the Johannesburg Supreme Court to face trial, which began in March 1991. It was a highly sensitive moment for the government of President F.W. de Klerk, coming at a time when de Klerk needed to maintain good personal relations with Nelson Mandela if the two men were to negotiate a new constitution for South Africa.

But almost from the opening statements, Winnie's defence struggled to keep pace with the damning evidence. Then a key

Above: A defiant Winnie pleaded innocent of all charges when she stood trial in connection with Stompie's murder.

witness in the trial testified that the anti-apartheid leader punched and whipped him and the three other activists, then danced and hummed while her followers continued the vicious assault. He said Stompie begged her to stop beating him.

Kenneth Kgase, who escaped and told church and community leaders that he had been kidnapped and subjected to savage beatings, said Mandela and her ring of followers bashed him and the other black activists to make them confess to having had homosexual relations with a white minister. Kgase said Mandela struck him again and again in the face, then lashed him with a whip at her Soweto home. 'She said we are not fit to be alive', Kgase told the stunned court, adding that she had singled Stompie out for particular abuse by labelling him a police spy.

VICIOUS VIOLENCE

Kgase, 31, testified that he and the three others – Tabiso Mono, Gabriel Mekgwe and Stompie – were then all beaten by a group of Mandela's followers. Stompie fought back fiercely and suffered severe injuries. 'After that there was pandemonium. I was myself punched by too many people', said Kgase. Kgase and Mono initially refused to testify, saying they feared for their lives. But while they eventually changed their minds, Mekgwe disappeared.

Mandela's lawyers, led by George Bizos, who also defended her husband in his 1964 treason trial, claimed that she was not at her home at the time of the incident, and knew nothing at all about it. They argued that the four men were not even kidnapped, but were merely 'removed' from a Methodist Church home because of reports that they were being sexually abused by the white minister, Rev. Paul Verryn, who was subsequently cleared of wrongdoing by the Methodist Church. Winnie steadfastly maintained that the youths had willingly sought refuge in her home to escape Verryn's homosexual advances.

But Winnie changed key aspects of her story as the trial continued and the evidence piled up against her, later admitting that the youths had actually been taken to her home by aides Xoliswa Falati and Johan Morgan, though she still insisted the action was to protect the youths from

Verryn. She also offered an alibi for the assaults, saying that she left for the Orange Free State town of Brandfort, 200 miles from Soweto, before the youths arrived at her house and that she did not return until 31 December.

She denied vehemently that the youths had ever been beaten in her house, saying that they had received only a 'few slappings' from Richardson.

Few people believed her story and, just three months after the sensational trial had begun, Winnie was convicted by Judge Michael Stegmann (South Africa does not have jury trials), who issued a damning statement about her role when he stated that 'to imagine that all this took place without the involvement of Mrs. Mandela as the motivating spirit is like *Hamlet* without the prince'.

Below: *Loyal Nelson Mandela stood by his wife during the trial, but it was clear to his colleagues that he had had enough of Winnie and her ways.*

He found her guilty of kidnapping the youths as part of an evil conspiracy to discredit Rev. Verryn, and ruled that she was an accessory after the fact to the assaults. 'It was a cool bluff', said Judge Stegmann, of Mandela's defence, referring to the alle-

Below: *The Mandelas continued to press the cause for majority rule throughout the murder trial.*

forcing them to testify about Verryn's alleged homosexual activities. Since the plot involved taking the boys to Mandela's home, with the assistance of members of her soccer team, in her green minibus, and driven by her close friend Richardson,

gations of homosexual abuse against the Methodist minister. But in the end, he said, Winnie exposed herself 'on a number of occasions to be a calm, unblushing and deliberate liar'.

He accepted her alibi that she had gone to Brandfort, but said she had been 'evasive, equivocal and conspicuously vague' while on the witness stand. He added that Winnie had gone to 'absurd lengths' to distance herself from the football club. Stegmann insisted that the allegation of homosexual abuse against Verryn was nothing more than a smokescreen, and that the defendants had failed to demonstrate that they actually believed the vile charges.

The plot, Stegmann said in summation, involved abducting the four youths and

POLICE FORENSIC
EVIDENCE TRACED BLOOD
ON WALLS, ON A BLANKET
AND ON WHIPS IN WINNIE
MANDELA'S HOUSE

Stegmann concluded that Mandela must have authorised the kidnappings. Forensic evidence bolstered his assertions. Police found traces of blood on walls, on a blanket and on whips in her house.

Yet after Stegmann's ruling Winnie was somehow strangely jubilant. 'I am delighted', she told the throng of reporters and hundreds of her supporters, who had assembled outside the courtroom. 'As long as you all now know that I didn't assault any child, that is all that matters to me.' It was a bizarre announcement, given the tongue-lashing she had just received from Judge Stegmann.

The following day, 14 May 1991, Stegmann sentenced Winnie to six years in jail, and blasted her for abdicating her responsibilities as a leader of South Africa's liberation movement. Her co-defendant, housekeeper Falati, also received a six-year sentence, while Morgan received a one-year suspended sentence. (Morgan would later tell a newspaper that he had lied at their trial, and claimed that Winnie had indeed been present and began the beatings of the four youths. Morgan, who said he decided to speak out after Winnie Mandela refused to pay the expenses for his appeal, also alleged that it was she who had ordered him to remove Stompie's battered body from her Soweto home and 'dump the dog'.)

A POOR EXAMPLE

As Winnie listened in stunned silence, Judge Stegmann said her actions had made a mockery of her reputation as Mother of the Nation: 'You, Mrs. Mandela, bear a heavy responsibility, for you were a leader called upon to give guidance to those who turned to you. Leadership does not entitle you to play with the liberty of others for your own purposes. One of your worst features was your lack of compassion towards the victims of the assault who you had deprived of their liberty.'

After posting bail of just £50, Winnie was released pending an appeal, which Bizos said would centre on the fact that Stegmann had no direct evidence on which to base his finding that Winnie Mandela had formed a conspiracy to smear Verryn, nor evidence that she had been aware of the severity of the assaults that had been committed in her absence.

While the appeal process dragged its way through the courts, Winnie was beset by yet more personal problems. Less than 12 months later, in April 1992, her husband announced that he and Winnie were separating after 34 years of marriage due to what he described as 'tensions' over unspecified differences. 'My love for her remains undiminished', he said, 'however, in view of the tensions that have arisen owing to differences between ourselves on a number of issues in recent months, we have mutually agreed that a separation would be best for each of us.'

Mandela told reporters when he emerged from prison in February 1990 that he felt guilty for having been unable to do any-thing as a father and husband to defend his wife and their two daughters during their own long ordeals. 'She (Winnie) endured the persecution heaped upon her by the government with exemplary fortitude and never wavered from her commitment to the struggle for freedom', he said. 'Her tenacity reinforced my personal respect, love and growing affection.' To make amends for his long absence, Mandela worked hard to promote his wife's political career inside the ANC, but admitted they were unable to continue as husband and wife. 'Owing to the pressures of our shared commitment to the ANC and the struggle to end apartheid, we were unable to enjoy a normal family life', he said.

The separation announcement capped months of speculation that the Mandelas were no longer living together and that Winnie was having a romantic affair with one of her chief assistants. Moreover, there had been widespread rumours that a large

JUDGE STEGMANN SAID HER ACTIONS HAD MADE A MOCKERY OF HER REPUTATION AS MOTHER OF THE NATION

Below: *In public, Nelson and Winnie looked the picture of marital bliss. But there were deep divisions in private.*

MANDELA AND HER
COMPANION ENJOYED
FIRST-CLASS FLIGHTS AND
ACCOMMODATION ON A
TRIP TO THE US

Right: *A grim-faced Nelson escorts his wife out of court.*

Below: *The Mandelas were an internationally-celebrated couple before their split. Here they are with French president Francois Mitterand and his wife.*

section of the ANC had been urging Mandela to divorce his wife in order to protect the organisation from further scandal and internal rifts.

Indeed, the following month, when new allegations of financial and other misconduct surfaced against Winnie, she lost even more support and was stripped of her position as a regional chairwoman of the ANC's Women's League. Reports alleged that she misused thousands of pounds of the ANC's Department of Social Welfare, which Mandela headed until she was forced to resign in April. The money, according to newspaper reports, was believed to have been used in 1991 on first-class air travel to the United States and expensive accommodation for Mandela and her companion, 25-year-old lawyer Dali Mpofu. Winnie denied that ANC money was used for the 1991 trip, during which she and Mpofu crossed the Atlantic in Concorde, stayed in connecting rooms at a luxury hotel, and shared a cabin at singer Dionne Warwick's Californian estate.

Despite all her problems, however, and the fact that she had become a major embarrassment to the ANC, Winnie did enjoy the support of many black youngsters, who remembered her commitment to their struggle. They celebrated with her in June 1993, when the South African Appeals Court, while upholding her conviction on kidnapping and conspiracy charges, waived the jail term and ordered her to pay fines and compensation totalling some £7,000.

A POLITICAL DECISION

The unanimous judgment of the five-judge Appeals Court was considered by some to be more of a political than legal ruling. 'If they had put her in jail, there would have been an outcry that would have resounded to the heavens', Alf Stadler, the chairman of the political science department at the University of Witwatersrand, told reporters. 'Then she would have come out in a year or two with an even bigger following than she has now. I don't know about the legal side of the decision, but the politics seem pretty adroit.' And the Lawyers for Human Rights, a nationwide anti-apartheid group that usually takes up the cause of the accused, issued a terse statement saying only that Winnie 'was indeed fortunate to have escaped a term of imprisonment'.

In July, however, a warrant was issued for her arrest for failing to pay the fine imposed by the Appeals Court. Winnie faced a year in jail for default of the payment, but the Supreme Court in Johannesburg allowed her a few extra days to pay up, which she did. However, as of writing, Winnie had still not paid the £3,500 in compensation to the three surviving victims of the kidnapping.

That same month, Winnie was back in the political ring, thanks to her standing among young black South Africans, who remained largely loyal to her because of her militancy. She was elected to a top position in the leadership of the South African Civic Organisation (SANCO), which is the umbrella body for several civic associations throughout the sprawling

black townships. Mandela, who runs the Co-ordinated Anti-Poverty Programme within SANCO, is a big favourite with the country's rural and squatter communities, and recently has called for militant responses to attacks on squatters.

Still, even though she is clawing her way back into the arena, there are few people who think Winnie Mandela can ever regain her former status as the soul of the anti-apartheid movement and 'the mother of the nation'. In the end, she was brought down by her own imperious demeanour.

Above: *As the accusations of corruption and infidelity spread, Winnie was stripped of her position within the ANC Women's League.*

FEW PEOPLE THINK WINNIE CAN EVER REGAIN HER FORMER STATUS AS THE SOUL OF THE ANTI-APARTHEID MOVEMENT

Left: *Winnie is now unlikely to play a major political role in the new South Africa.*

JACK RUBY
The Mysterious Assasin

When Jack Ruby shot Lee Harvey Oswald dead his act looked to be fuelled by emotional revenge against the man who had been arrested on suspicion of killing President Kennedy. Later investigations unveiled a much more complicated and sinister explanation for his actions.

On the balmy afternoon of Friday 22 November 1963, a rapid series of shots rang out around Dealy Plaza in downtown Dallas, leaving President John F. Kennedy mortally wounded. The blinding confusion that followed lasted just a few seconds as the presidential limousine bearing the fallen President, his head a shattered, bloody mess, and his blood-splattered wife, Jackie, sped off to the hospital. But in reality, the confusion sur-

rounding those brief few seconds in Dallas remains to this very day.

No-one, with absolute certainty, can say exactly what occurred during that tragic day in Dallas, but nowadays only a few stalwarts still cling to the long-discredited notion that the young, well-loved President was assassinated by a lone gunman – Lee Harvey Oswald, an ex-Marine who had once defected to the Soviet Union and who had some ties with the US Central Intelligence Agency.

Oswald, a thin, boyish-looking man protested his innocence in connection with the Kennedy killing when he was picked up by police just a few hours after the president succumbed to his wounds. Indeed, Oswald maintained that he was 'just a patsy', a fall-guy set up to take the heat away from a secretive, sinister group which was really behind the murder.

Above: *Lee Harvey Oswald was gunned down by Jack Ruby despite having a large police escort.*

Opposite: *Ruby silenced the only man who could have shed light on President Kennedy's murder.*

Left: *Ruby claimed he was an avenging angel.*

The ruse, if it was such, worked perfectly, because Oswald was a dead man from the moment he was taken into custody. Less than 48 hours after Kennedy died, Oswald, too, was gone... the victim of one Jack Rubenstein, alias Jack Ruby, who gunned down the former Marine on national television as he was being led through a basement by Dallas police officials.

Oswald was handcuffed to one policeman, surrounded by others and on the way to a waiting car that was to take him across town to a more 'secure' cell. But suddenly, out of the corner of the basement, Ruby emerged, squeezing off a single round from his .38-calibre revolver. It was all over in a matter of seconds and, with Oswald dead, the groundwork for the single gunman theory had been laid.

That groundwork was later completed by the Warren Commission, set up by the new president, Lyndon Baines Johnson, to investigate Kennedy's death. It concluded that Oswald, acting alone, fired three rapid shots from the Texas Book Depository building which overlooked the presidential motorcade. According to the Commission, Oswald was a loner and a man frequently out of control. He was twice court-martialled – once for having an unauthorised handgun in his locker – during his stint in the Marines.

Below: A stunned America – already reeling from the death of Kennedy – saw the murder of Oswald on live television.

San Francisco Chronicle
THE VOICE OF THE WEST

99th YEAR   No. 329   FINAL HOME EDITION ★   MONDAY, NOVEMBER 25, 1963   10 CENTS   GArfield 1-1111

Oswald Shot Dead By Dallas 'Avenger'

The Killer Strikes

Single Bullet

Fatal Attack As Police Move Accused Man

A.P. & U.P.

Dallas

Lee Harvey Oswald, accused assassin of President Kennedy, was shot and killed while being transferred from one jail to another yesterday, 48 hours after the death of the President.

He had never wavered in his insistence that he was not the President's killer. He died without saying a word.

The man who shot Oswald, Jack Ruby, 52, bachelor owner of two Dallas night clubs, had stepped swiftly through a mass of police and newsmen at a basement garage ramp in city hall.

He rushed up to Oswald and sent a single pistol bullet into his abdomen.

Oswald dropped unconscious at Ruby's feet, within a cordon of escorting police officers.

At least eight police
See Page 1-C, Col. 5

JACK DAVIS DEEPLY MOURNS AND

S. F. Stands Still Today To Mourn

San Francisco's down-

Lee Oswald doubled up as Jack Ruby (with gun) fired the fatal shot

Left: *John F. Kennedy (left) with his brother Bobby who, in 1968, would also become the victim of a political assassination.*

Below: *Just seconds after this picture was taken, President Kennedy was dead.*

He was also a sometime supporter of the Soviet Union and Fidel Castro, and had even lived in Russia for over two years. In 1962, he and his new wife, Russian-born Marina, returned to the United States. The Commission discovered he was also a gun buff and, according to Marina, fired the rifle he had recently purchased through the window of an outspoken conservative in Dallas – the same rifle he would use just seven months later to kill Kennedy.

A few months after the window-shooting incident, he moved to New Orleans, and became active in a pro-Castro organisation, which called for an end to U.S.-backed sanctions against the fledgling dictatorship. Before returning to Dallas on 3 October, he was also reportedly seen by CIA field officers at the Soviet embassy in Mexico City.

On that fateful day in November, Oswald allegedly came to work at the Book Depository carrying his rifle, which he disguised in brown wrapping. Shortly before the president's motorcade was due to arrive, he took up a position at a sixth floor window at the Depository. After allegedly shooting Kennedy, he was spotted, by a policeman and one of his fellow employees, hurriedly leaving the building. A short time later, he was apparently stopped by Officer J.D. Tippitt, who he reportedly shot and killed. He then fled to a cinema, where

he was eventually nabbed. After his arrest, Oswald was held in the Dallas Police and Court Building, where he was grilled by local police and federal agents. He denied any involvement in the Kennedy killing... and was then silenced for good on 24 November.

That same day, half a continent away in Washington, D.C., the flag-draped coffin bearing the body of the dead president was carried on a gun carriage through the streets, drawn by a team of horses. A riderless horse followed, and further back came heads of state from around the world.

Ruby, who would later die of cancer in a prison cell, claimed at the time that he idolised John Kennedy and had acted out of compassion for the beautiful young widow, Jackie, to save her from the anguish of having to testify at Oswald's trial. For some years, people believed he was an avenging

angel, a vigilante who had given Oswald his just desserts.

Immediately after he killed Oswald, Ruby received dozens of congratulatory telegrams, praising him as a hero who had given the assassin exactly what he deserved. Indeed, even the Warren Commission fuelled that idea by concluding that Ruby was a patriot who slew Oswald because of his deep affection for the First Lady and her two young children! No one ever saw fit to explain that when the Kennedys were driving through Dealy Plaza, Ruby was in a nearby newspaper office placing an ad for his strip club rather than being on the streets to see his 'idols'.

The Warren Commission, in fact, was a whitewash. The real story of Ruby and his involvement in the conspiracy surrounding the president's murder, is a far cry from the one he and others tried to sell to the American people. The truth was that Ruby was a violent, sordid man, tied to the Mafia, the CIA and rabid anti-communists who blamed President Kennedy for the failed take-over of Cuba in the infamous Bay of Pigs disaster.

AN UNDERWORLD EXISTENCE

Ruby's formative years were spent as a flunkie for mob bosses in his native Chicago, and, in the early 1940s, he was caught up in the rough-and-tumble world of the streets where politics and crime often blended, associating with rising mob star Sam Giancana and fellow gangsters like 'Needlenose Labriola' and Barney Baker, a close friend of the Teamsters' Union boss Jimmy Hoffa, later the focus of an intensive probe by Kennedy and his crusading Attorney-General and brother, Bobby.

It is interesting to note that just before he shot Oswald, Ruby telephoned Baker and a Teamsters' official. However, when the FBI began probing Kennedy's murder, they officially reported that they could find no links between Ruby and Hoffa, despite the evidence contained in the national archives and briefly outlined above.

It is also interesting to note that in 1947, the year Ruby went to live in Dallas, then congressman Richard Nixon 'intervened on behalf of a Chicago gangster who was about to be called as a witness before a congressional committee'. That memo,

Below: The First Lady and her family grieve as the slain president is lain to rest.

written by an FBI assistant, not only proves that the Bureau knew of Ruby's underworld connections, but also reveals a link between him and the future president.

The memo continues: 'It is my sworn statement that one Jack Rubenstein of Chicago, noted as a potential witness for hearings of the House Committee on Un-American Activities, is performing information functions for the staff of Congressman Richard Nixon, Republican, of California. It is requested that Rubenstein not be called for open testimony in the aforementioned hearings.'

Later that year, Rubenstein changed his name to Ruby and moved to Dallas, joining fellow gangsters Benny Binnion and Paul Jones. Binnion ran an illegal gambling house just outside the city limits called The Top of the Hill. Jones was the mob's 'fixer' in Dallas – meaning he bribed local law enforcement officers.

Together, they sought to expand the Mafia's fledgling network in Texas, and Ruby eventually ended up running a sleazy topless nightclub, the Carousel Club, where local police, sheriff's deputies and gangsters were all frequent guests.

But Ruby had more going for him that just nightclubs and gambling. He was also in the gun-running business, reportedly in cahoots with Carlos Prio, the exiled former

Above: Teamsters' chief Jimmy Hoffa hated the Kennedys and tried to sidetrack their investigation into his union's activities.

Below: Ruby was a well-known mob associate.

Cuban president who originally backed Fidel Castro, only to be later double-crossed by the cigar-chomping revolutionary. Ruby was involved with the approval of Meyer Lansky, the financial wizard behind some of the Mafia's grandest and most lucrative scams. Like many in the mob, Ruby assumed that once Castro came to power, things would return to the days under Prio, when the syndicate all but ran Cuba as an island-casino. Indeed, in 1959, shortly after Castro came to power, Ruby visited Havana. Eventually, however, Castro booted out the Mafia, which infuriated the bosses.

Despite all the evidence to the contrary, the Warren Commission concluded that there was no 'significant link between Ruby and organised crime', nor did it find anything to to substantiate 'rumours linking Ruby with pro- or anti-Castro Cuban activities'! Moreover, in the past few years evidence has surfaced that Oswald, who knew both CIA extremists and elements in the mob, may have actually known Ruby. At least one witness claimed to have seen Ruby talking to a man very similar in description to Oswald at the Carousel Club shortly before the President was killed.

On 4 October 1963, attorney Carroll Jarnagin, who had such a remarkable memory that he once got a perfect score in a dif-

ficult university exam in chemistry that involved very complex formulas, visited Ruby's club. He remembers seeing a young man, whom he later believed was Oswald, walk into the club and take up a seat in a secluded booth with Ruby.

Further, Jarnagin said he overheard parts of the conversation, and clearly remembers Ruby saying: 'You'll get the money when the job is done.'

A MARKED MAN

The attorney claims that Oswald was duped into believing the target of the hit was Texas Governor John Connally, who was riding in the presidential limousine when Kennedy was killed. Ruby said that Connally, who was seriously wounded in the shooting, was a marked man because he would not co-operate with the Mafia and their plans for Texas. When Oswald complained that the killing of Connally would bring law enforcement down on the mob, Ruby replied: 'Not really, they'll think some crackpot or communist did, and it will be written off as some unsolved

Above: Ruby apparently believed he would be given a light sentence for killing the president's assassin.

EVEN BEFORE THE ASSASSINATION, OSWALD WAS MARKED FOR DEATH, AND THE ASSIGNMENT WAS HANDED TO RUBY

crime.' There were other witnesses who linked Ruby and Oswald prior to that dark November day, including a motor mechanic who said he saw Oswald driving the club owner's car.

When Fidel Castro turned on the mob and turned Cuba into a Communist camp, he angered not only the Mafia, but also the CIA, which was patently anti-Marxist. Over the next couple of years, there were several bizarre plots on Castro's life – including exploding pens and poisonous cigars. But in the wake of the Bay of Pigs fiasco, the mob's wrath turned squarely on John Kennedy.

Santo Trafficante, another of Ruby's friends from the old days in Chicago and by now a powerful boss in Florida, even boasted to a Miami businessman that Kennedy 'is going to be hit. Mark my word, this man Kennedy is in trouble, and he will get what is coming to him.'

Even before the assassination, Oswald 'the patsy' was marked for death, and the assignment was handed to Ruby, who his bosses knew could easily gain access to the Dallas police building because of his many

contacts on the force. Ruby dared not dis-
obey. To do so would have meant instant
death. And if he went ahead with it, he had
every reason to believe that his sentence
would be very lenient, given that he had
executed the President's murderer.

It is no secret that the Mafia had the
motive – and the muscle – to kill President
Kennedy. Not only did they feel betrayed
by Kennedy over the Bay of Pigs, but they
also felt they had been 'double-crossed' by
JFK after the 1960 election. The Kennedy
clan had asked for – and received – Mafia
help in winning key electorates during the
campaign... but they had 'rewarded' the
mob with the greatest anti-gangster investigations in U.S. history. According to attorney Frank Ragano, who was close to Hoffa,
the President's murder was organised by
New Orleans crime czar Carlos Marcello
and Trafficante. Trafficante headed the
once-lucrative Cuban operations for the
Mafia, while Marcello had actually been
deported to Guatemala by the crusading
Bobby. Ragano says he met with Hoffa in
early 1963 and 'Jimmy told me to tell
Marcello and Trafficante they had to kill
the president'.

NO LAUGHING MATTER

'Hoffa said to me, "This has to be done,"'
recalled Ragano. Ragano thought Hoffa
was joking, but when he mentioned it to
the two mobsters a few days later, 'they
didn't laugh. They were dead serious'. The
night Kennedy was killed, Ragano added,
Hoffa, Trafficante and Marcello all celebrated as if there was no tomorrow.

But for the conspiracy to leave no loose
ends, Oswald, too, had to be silenced. And
so, on Sunday 24 November, Ruby gained
access to the basement of the Dallas police
station. Initially, officials claimed that
Ruby, who had two prior arrests for carrying concealed weapons, had tricked his
way in by pretending to be a news reporter.
How this could have happened is beyond
logic. Ruby was very well-known to many
of the officers on the force, many of whom
were frequent visitors to his strip club.

Further, Ruby was also a frequent visitor
to police headquarters, and was seen there
on at least three occasions just hours after
Kennedy was killed! Even more disturbing
is that immediately after he shot Oswald,

he was 'suddenly' recognised by the detectives who grabbed him! In later years, it
emerged that he was allegedly escorted
there by none other than the Assistant
Chief of Police, Charles Batchelor! An
attorney, James Neill, claimed that when
someone started to search the basement
before Oswald's transfer, Batchelor told
him not to. When Ruby carried out his
assignment with cool daring, he was immediately bundled off to jail by the same
policemen who had been assigned to protect Oswald.

Three months later, on 17 February
1964, Ruby went on trial for the murder of

Oswald. Was it mere coincidence that the
same prosecutor, Henry Wade, who
announced Oswald was the lone killer of
Kennedy and closed the case as soon as he
(Oswald) was murdered, should be present-
ing the case against Ruby? Courtroom
observers said that Wade tied himself in
knots to keep from having to ask questions
that might have reopened the Oswald case.

This determination not to delve too
much into Oswald's background was also
shared by the defence AND the U.S.
Justice Department! In a letter sent to
Ruby's lawyers, the Justice Department
said it would offer them 'reams of helpful
information... on the condition that they do

*Above: Santo Trafficante
(right) was the Mafia
Godfather of New Orleans.
More than anyone, he wanted President Kennedy dead.
He is shown here with his
lawyer, Henry Gonzalez,
after appearing at a 1977
congressional hearing into
Kennedy's murder.*

Above: Ruby was stunned when he was sentenced to life in jail. He later repeatedly tried to kill himself.

into his prison cell wall. He also ranted and raved that the Jews might be blamed for the assassination plot, and how 'they' were 'putting the Jews in kill machines' and slaughtering them.

At other times, however, he appeared lucid, and begged the Warren Commission to get him out of Dallas and take him to Washington where he promised to tell them everything he knew about the Kennedy killing and the ensuing cover-up. 'If only you knew my motivation', he told investigators. 'You will never understand the reasons for my actions.' Judge Warren and fellow commission member Congressman Gerald Ford, who succeeded Nixon as president and pardoned him for the Watergate scandal, came to Dallas to see Ruby. 'I may not live tomorrow to give any further testimony', he told them. 'I can't say it here... it can't be said here. I want to tell the truth and I can't tell it here.'

NO SAFETY GUARANTEE

Unfortunately for Ruby – and history – his request to be taken to Washington was denied. Incredibly, Judge Warren, the Chief Justice of the United States, said he couldn't guarantee Ruby's safety in Washington! 'We have no place there for you to be safe', the judge claimed, 'and we are not law enforcement officers, and it isn't our responsibility to go into anything of that kind.' Warren is telling this to the man responsible for silencing the president's 'assassin'!

Ruby continued begging to be taken out of Dallas where he thought his life was in danger. When Ford asked him if he could shed any more light on the events if he was taken to Washington, the mobster replied: 'Yes... I am used as a scapegoat.

'But if I am eliminated, there won't be anyway of knowing. Right now... I am the only one that can bring out the truth... I have been used for a purpose, and there will be a certain tragic occurrence happening if you don't take my testimony and somehow vindicate me.'

Amazingly, Chief Justice Warren replied: 'But we have taken your testimony. We have it here. It will be in permanent form for the President of the United States and for the Congress of the United States and for the people of the entire world. It is

not ask for anything at all about Ruby's alleged victim, Lee Harvey Oswald'. It was an incredible decision. Here was the man accused of killing the president's purported assassin, and yet all sides agreed not to touch upon the Kennedy murder!

Ruby's guilty verdict surprised no-one. But the sentence did: Death. Ruby and many others were stunned by the severity of the ruling. For the next few years, while he awaited the endless appeals of his sentence, Ruby seems to have snapped, even trying to kill himself by ramming his head

there. It will be recorded for all to see. That is the purpose of our coming here today. We feel that you are entitled to have your story told.'

Ruby then replied: 'You have lost me... You have lost me, Chief Justice Warren. I won't be around for you to come and question me again.'

He wasn't. Two years later Ruby was dead of lung cancer – which he believed he contracted through injections – without ever officially telling what he knew. However, just before his death, he admitted to his prison psychiatrist, Dr Werner Teuter, that he 'had been part of a plot to kill Kennedy', and that he was 'framed to kill Oswald'.

In the years since those dark days of Dallas, there have been many attempts to lay bare the real story of John F. Kennedy's killing. Through the maze of cover-ups, conspiracies, red herrings and a sinister collection of suspects, it can almost certainly be concluded that President Kennedy

was killed by the Mafia, and with the possible help of the CIA. If only Jack Ruby had been taken to Washington as he so often begged, the real facts behind the most shocking assassination in history may have been uncovered three decades ago.

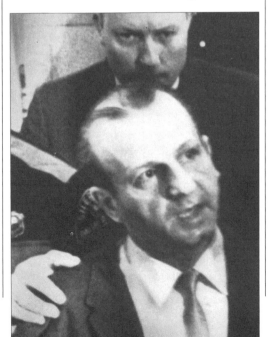

Above: *There was evidence to suggest that Oswald (above) and Ruby knew each other.*

Left: *Ruby took his secrets with him to the grave – he died of cancer a few years after the trial.*

RUBY DIED OF LUNG CANCER WHICH HE BELIEVED HE HAD CONTRACTED THROUGH INJECTIONS WHILE IN JAIL

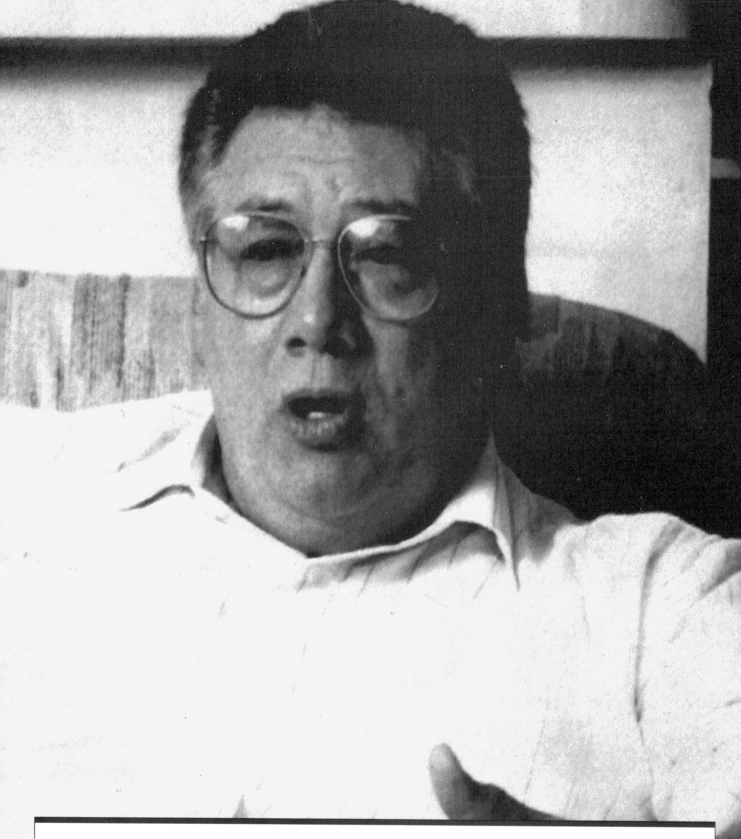

ENEMIES WITHIN
The Spying Game

Spies put their own self-interest before that of their country, and, for a few dollars or pounds or misguided ideals, endanger their own and their fellow citizens' safety. But their greed and folly usually ends in them unwittingly betraying themselves to the forces of law and order.

From its very humble beginnings on 1 July 1935, the Federal Bureau of Investigation has stood as America's bulwark against crime, corruption and enemy agents. For nearly 60 years, the true-blue crime-busters of the Bureau have prided themselves on that amazing achievement, and their daring exploits and hair-raising adventures have captured the hearts of the American public.

From their undercover work against Nazi and Japanese spies during World War Two to their diligence in the fight against organised crime and Communism, to the arrest of savage serial killers, the men and women of the FBI have a proud and heroic heritage. The agents, who pride themselves on a strict ethical code and an imperviousness to corruption, are rightly called the elite of America's law enforcement officers. Indeed, to prevent enemy infiltration, the FBI makes rigorous background checks of every person being considered for an agent's job, while new agents are closely supervised. Moreover, every single agent has to undergo periodic lie-detector tests. It is a stringent requirement, but one that has helped safeguard the Bureau from the corruption which has run rife in so many other law enforcement agencies.

Yet on 2 October 1984, one man single-handedly tarnished the hard-won image of integrity because of his greed and sexual lust. Literally overnight, the FBI was haunted by the nightmare which faces every police and intelligence organisation – a trusted agent had gone over to the other side. And for the first time in an illustrious history, FBI agents had to arrest one of their own kind. Richard Miller, who worked in the Los Angeles office, was taken away in handcuffs on charges of spying for the Soviet Union.

Miller, who joined the FBI in 1964, a few months after graduating from Brigham Young University, said he initially responded negatively when an FBI recruiter came to his parents' home in Lynwood. At the time, Miller said he was 'selling tyres at the Sears Roebuck store in Compton with my college degree'. He said he reluctantly filled out the FBI application to pacify his mother who wanted him to join up.

Twenty years later, he stood in the dock, accused of selling highly classified infor-

THE FBI'S DARING EXPLOITS AND HAIR-RAISING ADVENTURES CAPTURED THE HEARTS OF THE AMERICAN PUBLIC

Opposite: *Richard Miller – the first FBI agent in history to betray his country.*

Below: *Soviet agent Svetlana Ogoridnokova had a torrid affair with Miller and fed his information to her Kremlin masters.*

MILLER SUCCUMBED TO
OGORODNIKOVA'S FEMININE
CHARMS AND EVENTUALLY
BETRAYED THE BUREAU
AND HIS NATION

mation to his Kremlin masters through his intermediary, attractive Svetlana Ogorodnikova, 34, a Soviet émigré with whom he had had a torrid sexual relationship. Miller, a veteran agent, was, at first glance, a far cry from the popular image of the cloak-and-dagger brigade. He was bespectacled, grossly overweight – he had even been reprimanded by the Bureau for his obesity – and had had a rather mundane career. Not surprisingly, then, it was only by accident that the FBI had reason to suspect that he was a mole and had gone over to the Soviets.

While routinely watching Ogorodnikova because of her ties to the Soviet Consulate, agents noticed that she was frequently visited by Miller. He was soon placed under surveillance, and was seen entering the Soviet Consulate in San Francisco. The

FBI also put wiretaps on both of their telephones and placed eavesdropping devices in their cars. In September 1984, the FBI picked up information that KGB plans were being formed to send Miller to Eastern Europe, where the agency suspected Miller was planning to sell secret documents to the KGB. Among information he sold, in the hope of getting some £40,000 in cash and gold, was an FBI manual detailing American objectives and methods of obtaining foreign intelligence secrets.

But after his arrest, it was also revealed that Miller had financial and family problems at the time of his contacts with Ogorodnikova. He had eight children, and had recently been excommunicated from the Church of Jesus Christ of Latter-day Saints for adultery.

Also, his weight problems – he had ballooned to about 300 pounds – were getting worse. Earlier in 1984, his superiors even suspended him for two weeks without pay for not meeting FBI standards.

MONEY AND SEX

According to investigators, Ogorodnikova swayed Miller with money and sex, at a time when she was aware that he was plagued with pressing and immediate problems relating to his personal finances, his weight, pressures at work, a crumbling marriage and his excommunication from the Mormon church. In the battle of wills, Miller easily succumbed to her feminine charms, and while emotionally entangled with Svetlana he eventually betrayed the Bureau and his nation.

Yet throughout the three trials which lasted six years, and resulted in his being sentenced to 20 years in jail, the unrepentant Miller denied he was ever a spy, let alone a traitor. 'I was absolutely not a spy', he said. 'I never was. I never will be.' He said his affair with Ogorodnikova, who was sentenced to 18 years in prison, was simply a stupid mistake, but claimed it never led to betrayal. Instead, the convicted turncoat claims FBI bureaucrats 'without scruples' were out to get him and invented the charges against him.

During his trials, his lawyers even sought to portray him as a bumbling oaf, not unlike the movie character, Inspector Clouseau, immortalised by the late British

actor Peter Sellers. Indeed, during one trial attorney Joel Levine recalled that Miller would often leave the keys to the Bureau's office in the door when he went home at night! His defenders claim the spying incident was all a mistake, and blamed it on his naïvety and a bizarre attempt to revive his sagging FBI career. They – and Miller himself – say he had somehow got it into his head that he could emulate James Bond and single-handedly penetrate Soviet intelligence through Ogorodnikova but the plan had gone horribly wrong!

'I felt I could do what nobody had done before – infiltrate an active Soviet intelligence network', Miller testified in 1986. 'I had a James Bond kind of fantasy. I'd come out a hero.'

But U.S. Government officials say that was just a pathetic ruse, and that Miller had indeed let his personal problems take control of his professional life. 'Miller had no plan of infiltrating anything', said one of the prosecutors. 'He was an intelligent, conniving individual who chose to go down in flames because the prospects offered by Svetlana far outweighed the prospects of serving his country.' Officials

Above: *John Walker ran the most damaging spy ring in American history.*

Below: *Some of Walker's ill-gotten booty goes up for auction.*

claimed that Miller also failed several lie-detector tests. Miller continued trying to get his conviction overturned until January 1993, when he lost his court appeal.

ODIOUS TREACHERY

While the bumbling Miller stunned his FBI colleagues when it became known he had turned informer, his spying did not cause irreparable harm to the American intelligence network, however odious his treachery. But the following year, there emerged another spy, a former Navy man, who achieved what Miller had not, setting up the most damaging espionage ring to ever operate in the United States.

His name was John Walker Jr., a retired U.S. Navy chief warrant officer who not only sold out his country, but also his family, by recruiting them into his operation – much to the delight of his Soviet masters. Intelligence officials described Walker as almost the perfect spy: he was clever, completely without scruples, and daring. By the time he was finally arrested in 1985, he had been handing America's national secrets to the Kremlin for more than 18 years!

His information was so sensitive that U.S. Defence Secretary Caspar Weinberger claimed the KGB considered the Walker case the 'most important' operation in its history. Indeed, the KGB agent who helped develop Walker's spy skills was later declared a 'Hero of The Soviet Union' and awarded his country's highest honour. Vitaly Yurchenko, a high-ranking KGB defector to the West, later said that the Walker spy ring was so valuable that 'if there had been a war, we would have won'.

Walker, the son of an abusive, alcoholic father, was in trouble with the law at an early age. As a teenager, he was arrested for a string of petty burglaries and sentenced to a few months in prison. However, thanks to the pleas of his older brother, Arthur, a naval submariner, the judge granted him probation. The following year, when John was 18, he followed his brother into the service.

At the age of 20, Walker married Barbara Crowly, a 19-year-old whose childhood had been as miserable as his own. They had four children, but John was a pathetic father and husband. Barbara found comfort in a Vodka bottle – and her heavy drinking would play a key role in his eventual arrest. He was a failure as a father – he beat his children viciously – he was a success in the Navy. Almost from the time he signed up, his superiors were impressed by his flair for electronics and his apparent intense loyalty to the service. To all appearances, he was a first-class seaman, and he eventually worked his way up the ranks to become a chief warrant officer.

He held that rank in 1968, by which time he was an expert communications technician with a complete knowledge of naval cipher machines, codes and systems. Yet Walker, who never saved for his retirement, and found himself staring at a bleak future once his naval career was over, decided to

> THE TWO MEN SLIPPED THEIR CONTROLLERS THOUSANDS OF DOCUMENTS VIA ARRANGED DROP-SITES

Right: *Walker's son Michael, who served on board the USS Nimitz, readily joined the spy ring.*

Below: *Arthur Walker, John's brother, being led away after the case had been cracked.*

trade his expertise for cash. One day, he sneaked into the Soviet Embassy in Washington, and handed over some intelligence information for which he was paid some £1500.

He was thrilled, and decided then and there that he would become a full-time spymaster, recruiting his close friend Jerry Whitworth, a fellow Navy communications expert, into the scheme. Together, the two men slipped their controllers thousands of documents via carefully arranged drop-sites around Washington, which enabled the KGB to decipher more than a million of the Navy's most secret communications, and gave the Soviets an intimate view of the Navy's secret underwater warfare tactics and strategy.

Over the next few years, Walker tried to recruit even his own children into his nefarious organisation. First, he tried Margaret, his eldest. He invited her to come and live with him in Norfolk, Virginia, and urged her to join one of the services.

But Margaret simply was not interested in enlisting. Walker's next target was his daughter Cynthia, 19, whom he had once described as 'a retard'. But Cynthia, who had learned from her mother that Walker was a spy, also refused to enter the Navy and join his scheme. But Walker had no intentions of giving up.

Next on his list was youngest daughter Laura who, much to his surprise and excitement, joined the Army in 1978. After learning this, Walker immediately tried to recruit her. He went about it slowly, never mentioning who the buyers were, but Laura refused to co-operate. Later, when she met a fellow army regular, Philip Mark Snyder, she fell pregnant, and they married.

Walker was getting desperate, because Whitworth decided to quit the Navy, and Walker was horrified when Laura said she was leaving the Army because of the pregnancy. He even tried to convince her to lose the baby: 'Why don't you just get an abortion? I mean, you can always have more kids later', Laura quoted him as saying when she spoke to an interviewer several years later.

Walker became very abusive, telling her she would never amount to anything if she did not co-operate with him in betraying their country. But Laura, thankfully, remained steadfast. She would not turn traitor. The following year, in 1980, Walker had some success in his recruitment drive, ensnaring older brother, Arthur, into the ring. A few years later, his son, Michael, also a Navy man, enlisted in the operation.

PERSONAL PROBLEMS

Ironically, it was Walker's personal life that eventually led to his downfall. He and Barbara had divorced in 1976 and yet, despite the hundreds of thousands of pounds he was earning from his trade as a spy, he gave no money to either her or their children. Barbara knew of his traitorous acts almost from the start, but didn't go to the authorities until 1985 – and then only after her drinking problems and the guilt became too much for her to bear any longer. In May that year, after Barbara had tipped off authorities, FBI agents waited for Walker to make his next move. They arrested him, after watching him drop off a bag of Navy secrets at an appointed drop-site in Maryland.

With Walker in custody, the espionage ring was quickly broken up. Today, Walker is serving two life sentences, plus 10 years. Whitworth was sentenced to 365 years in prison. Arthur Walker received three life terms and another 40 years. Michael was given two 25-year terms.

Above: *John Pollard acted not out of greed or lust, but for his love of Israel.*

Top: *Anne Pollard helped her husband sell sensitive documents to the Israelis.*

In contrast to the Walker ring and Miller, Jonathon Pollard, a counter-intelligence analyst for the U.S. Navy, initially carried out his spying not for money or sex, but for his love of Israel. Pollard and his wife, Anne, sold documents to the Israelis from the summer of 1984 until November 1985, when he was arrested after trying to find asylum at the Israeli Embassy in Washington, D.C.

After his arrest, which stunned the United States because the documents were being stolen for a close ally, the Israeli government maintained the spy ring was a 'rogue operation' that was not officially sanctioned by Tel Aviv. But Pollard later admitted several high-ranking Israeli officials knew of and condoned his activities.

But by then, Israeli officials, who were struggling to contain the grave damage done to their country's vital relationship with the United States, had already betrayed Pollard by providing evidence against him! A devoted agent until the end, Pollard had begun by lying about Israel's involvement, and only began co-operating with the United States when he learned that his former masters in Tel Aviv had betrayed him. Still, Israeli intelligence officials admitted that Pollard was originally inspired to spy because of his intense love of Israel. The money they paid him for the stolen data was their way of corrupting him and ensuring that he would not quit the operation, which was providing a wealth of information for Israel. In all, he received more than £30,000 in cash for the documents and was promised at least £200,000 more in a numbered Swiss bank account.

Some of the documents that he stole included information disclosing the location of U.S. warships and the timing and location of training exercises. 'He made a judgment up front of "Israel right or wrong"', said a government prosecutor. 'In combination with the breadth of this man's knowledge, the depth of his memory and

> POLLARD SOLD MORE THAN 1,000 CLASSIFIED DOCUMENTS TO THE ISRAELIS OVER A PERIOD OF 15 MONTHS

*Below: **Anne Pollard** received five years for her role in the spy ring.*

his complete lack of honour, he is a very dangerous man.'

Defence Secretary Caspar Weinberger said Pollard himself 'specifically identified more than 800 U.S. classified publications (many containing hundreds of pages) and more than 1,000 classified messages and cables which he sold to Israel'. In a secret memo to the judge hearing the case, Weinberger said that he wanted to 'dispel any presumption that disclosures to an ally are insignificant; to the contrary, substantial and irrevocable damage has been done to this nation'.

ADMISSION OF GUILT

At his trial, Pollard pleaded guilty and believed he would get a lesser sentence as part of his plea bargain arrangement. However, in March 1987, he was convicted and sentenced to life in jail for selling classified intelligence documents to Israel, while his wife received a five-year term as an accessory.

Pollard, who pleaded guilty to the charges of espionage, sold more than 1,000 classified documents to the Israelis over a period of 15 months. Pollard pleaded guilty to receiving embezzled government property and being an accessory after the fact to the possession of classified documents.

In 1991, renowned American journalist Seymour Hersh claimed that among Pollard's stolen secrets were top-secret U.S. intelligence details on the Soviet Union, and that Israeli Prime Minister Yitzhak Shamir gave his approval to pass on some of it to Moscow. According to Hersh, Pollard gave Israel information on the location of Soviet military targets, as well as data on Moscow's concealment of the sites. He also gave Israel information on Soviet air defences, a copy of the CIA's top secret analysis of Soviet nuclear weapons programmes, and codes of U.S. diplomatic communications. Some information was then 'sanitised' by Israel and given to the Soviet Union as a gesture of Israeli goodwill. Tel Aviv called the report 'total nonsense'.

Pollard is currently serving his time in the maximum-security prison in Marion, Illinois, America's toughest correctional institution and home to such notorious criminals as Mafia Godfather John Gotti.

THE
UNEXPLAINED

THE SECRET SEARCH
The Great UFO Cover Up

In the years since World War Two, there have been reported sightings of UFOs all over the world. But instead of investigating the truth of these matters, governments often appear more concerned with flatly denying the existence of such phenomena.

O n the afternoon of 24 June 1947, Idaho businessman Kenneth Arnold was flying his light aircraft over Washington State when he reported seeing nine 'saucer-like things' flying in formation at speeds he would later estimate at an astounding 1200 miles an hour. His sensational report, still not fully explained, gave birth to the term, 'Flying Saucer'.

But the Arnold sighting gave birth to something else – the start of an intensive, top secret search by the United States government into the UFO phenomenon which even today remains an ongoing assignment, despite repeated official denials. Initially, the investigations were either publicly dismissed as misidentifications or the products of overly-fertile imaginations, but inside the secret meeting rooms of the Pentagon military leaders were as baffled as anyone and set up a top-secret unit called Project Sign, later dubbed Project Bluebook, to look into the phenomenon.

In those files, which have recently been opened, researchers found a wealth of unexplained sightings, but nothing that could finally offer conclusive proof of the claims that UFOs were not of this Earth. It is now known why: the most explosive cases of possible extraterrestrial visits to our planet never made it into Project Bluebook. Indeed, many researchers now claim that Project Bluebook was itself a cover-up, a top secret government ruse to help hide the real facts. Even those associated with the official projects were kept in the dark. As early as

September, 1947, Lt General Nathan Twining wrote a top secret report to his commanders that flying discs were real and infinitely more sophisticated that anything humanly engineered. Less than 12 months later, a report from the Air Technical Intelligence Centre concluded that UFOs were real and of extraterrestrial origin.

And yet, behind the guise of Projects Sign and Bluebook a much more secretive search was underway. Evidence of this is widespread, but for our purposes we need to look at a few of the most glaring cases, including the spectacular incident at Rosewell, New Mexico.

This occurrence, which never made it into Project Bluebook, occurred over the tiny desert town on 2 July 1947, just over a week after the Arnold encounter. It remains one of the most sensational and document-

Above: *Arnold in the light aircraft he was flying when he saw 'saucer-like things' speeding past him.*

Opposite: *Businessman Kenneth Arnold – it was his close encounter with alien life that gave birth to the term 'flying saucer'.*

ARNOLD REPORTED SEEING NINE 'SAUCER-LIKE THINGS' FLYING IN FORMATION AT ESTIMATED SPEEDS OF 1200 MPH

Above: *The incident at Rosewell, New Mexico. Did the US Government really find the wreckage of an extraterrestrial craft?*

Above: *US President Harry Truman set up the top secret MJ-12 group.*

ed cases ever of the existence of extraterrestrial life – and there is eyewitness testimony, including that of an Army major who actually handled some of the UFO wreckage, to back up the claims that we are not alone.

According to previous research, residents of the town spotted a huge, disc-shaped object flying over their homes. As they continued to watch in transfixed awe, they noticed that the craft seemed to be in some difficulty. A few hours later, a local ranch owner, William Brazel, reported hearing a tremendous explosion, but gave it little thought because there was a violent thunderstorm in the area that same night. However, the next morning, as he was making the rounds of his property, he found the wreckage of an object scattered for more than a mile. He called the local sheriff, and Major Jesse Marcel, stationed at nearby Rosewell Army Air Field, was soon on the scene to co-ordinate the investigation. Major Marcel collected some of the pieces of wreckage and returned to his base. Years later, the Major described what he found: metallic columns with strange hieroglyphics on them; pieces of very light metal that couldn't even be dented by repeated blows from a sledgehammer; and metal that would not burn.

After his initial reconnaissance of the area, Marcel, an intelligence officer, returned to the crash site and began the task of collecting every fragment of wreckage he could. Once his mission was done, he was ordered to fly it directly to Wright

Field in Ohio, and was then told to return to New Mexico. A few days later, military officials called a press conference and said the wreckage had been that of an experimental balloon. Rancher Brazel, who had been held by the Army for almost seven days, refused to speak about the incident later, only to say that the government had 'scared the hell out of me'. But years later, in the mid-1980s, Marcel came forward and adamantly denied the wreckage was that of a balloon and, at the time of the press conference, was so angry at his superiors for the cover-up that he demanded a full military hearing, which was denied.

Why was this incident never recorded in Project Sign accounts, when other incidents, clearly hoaxes or cases of misidentification, were? Because it was neither. If it was a hoax, why would Major Marcel – a respected intelligence officer – lie? Why would there be a record of the flight to Wright Field? If it was a misidentification, what was it? The answer, which became the official version, was that the wreckage was that of a secret Skyhook balloon. But in the years since the incident, a former US Air Force sergeant told UFO investigators that he and others in service, were ordered into the area to tell local officials that the wreckage was, indeed, a Skyhook. It was all a lie, of course, as he himself later admitted. Whatever crashed outside Rosewell was no balloon.

UNWORLDLY WRECKAGE

Clearly, then, some unworldly wreckage was found. Where did it go, and what has become of it? The answers to those questions are buried deep within the inner sanctums of the US Government. But it is known that shortly after the Rosewell incident, President Harry Truman formed a top secret group called MJ-12, which some researchers claim was the real investigative body which controlled what went into – or was omitted from – Project Sign and Bluebook. In later years, the name is believed to have been changed to Project Aquarius and today goes by the title of The UFO Working Group. The Working Group, which was set up by the Pentagon's Defence Intelligence Agency, began operations in 1987. It comprises 17 members from the US intelligence and military communities. It, like its predecessors, oversees investigations into UFO sightings that cannot be easily explained away.

Yet regardless of the name, the mission is still the same – to discredit every attempt at verifying the existence of UFOs while keeping the real evidence confined to the inner circle. Witnesses have been harassed, evidence changed and concocted. Why? No one knows for certain, but the fact is that since the Rosewell incident, the US Government has known all along about the existence of UFOs, and done everything in its power to keep that reality a top secret.

There are numerous examples of the government cover-up: let's look at some of the more alarming incidents – cases which leave little doubt about the existence of UFOs.

One of the most detailed is the Kinross Case, which dates back to 23 November 1953, over the clear night skies of Lake Superior. Earlier that evening, a radar operator at the Traux Air Force Bass noticed that an unidentified blip on his screen was flying over restricted air space. The information went up the chain of command, until senior military officials ordered an F-89 jet, piloted by Lieutenant Felix Moncla, to intercept the unknown craft. He sped after the UFO at speeds in excess of 500 miles an hour, and after a 10-minute chase, had gained on the craft. Radar control on the ground then showed he had actually caught up with the UFO.

PANIC STATIONS

But seconds later, the two blips on the screen merged into one, and then a single blip flashed off the radar screen. Frantic ground crews tried to contact Lt Moncla by radio, but all they heard was static. A massive search was ordered and, even though the Air Force knew where the F-89 should have gone down, no trace of any wreckage was ever found. Not even an oil slick, let alone Moncla's body. To stave off a curious

THE AIR FORCE KNEW WHERE THE F-89 SHOULD HAVE GONE DOWN, BUT NO TRACE OF ANY WRECKAGE WAS EVER FOUND

Below: *Crews aboard several US Air Force planes have had dangerously close encounters with visiting space craft.*

*Above: **Retired wharf worker John Reeves claimed the American Government altered evidence that would have proved the existence of UFOs. Local police backed his story.***

public and clamouring media, top Air Force officers said Moncla had been mistakenly chasing a Canadian DC3 and, that after identifying it as such, had broken off the intercept mission and run into engine problems on his return to the base.

The Air Force never explained why he didn't radio that report in. Stranger still is the fact that the Canadian government quickly denied the story of an errant DC3. Not to be panicked, the USAF then claimed that the mystery craft had been a Canadian Air Force jet – only to be again rebuked by the authorities in Ottawa, who said it was no such thing. The USAF never explained the contradiction and later changed the story again to say that Moncla's jet had simply exploded at high altitude. In the files on the case, the disappearance of the F-89 was listed as an accident, and they never mentioned that Lt Moncla had been ordered into the air in search of a UFO Interestingly, however, many officers, navi-

gators and pilots all agreed that Moncla and his plane had indeed been taken by an alien craft. Years later, it was revealed that the reason the Air Force records made no mention of the UFO search was because it was simply not placed in the file.

TENSION IN THE AIR

Moreover, shortly after Moncla disappeared without trace, other USAF pilots reported being followed by a large UFO, which joined their formation as they sped across the skies on a training mission. After several tense minutes – both fighter pilots remembered Moncla's disappearance all too well – the UFO broke off and vanished. When they landed back at the base, the two officers filed a report which, according to regulations, should have been forwarded to Project Bluebook. The report never made it into Bluebook. It should also be noted that Moncla's disappearance was not the first – or the last – time an American Air Force man has vanished while pursuing a UFO.

When an encounter with an alien craft was reported by a military man, the US government could quickly deal with the incident and file it away inside the secret documents of Project Aquarius. But when a civilian had the close encounter, it was more difficult to cover up. Many civilian witnesses were discredited and harassed. But in the case of John Reeves, government officials simply changed the evidence to fit their story.

It was 2 March 1965. Reeves, a retired wharf worker, was taking a late night stroll in the forest outside his home in Brooksville, Florida, when he spotted a landed UFO. He recalled that a robot-like creature was walking near the craft, and began to take what Reeves believed were pictures of the area. Soon afterwards, the strange robot returned to the ship, which then lifted off and quickly disappeared into the night sky. The stunned Reeves collected his thoughts, then went over to the clearing where the craft had been. He began searching the ground, and found what looked like two sheets of paper covered with strange, hieroglyphic symbols. A short while after the incident, investigators from the Air Force arrived on the scene and, after interviewing Reeves, took the pieces of paper with them. Two weeks later, they contacted

Reeves again to return the items, telling him they had decoded the bizarre symbols. They told him it was a message from the Planet Mars ordering the space traveller back to base, and that it was obviously part of some hoax.

But unknown to the Air Force, two sheriff's deputies had also seen the mysterious sheets of paper, and they claimed that the documents returned to Reeves were not the same as those he had given them. And they had photocopies of the originals to prove it! Further, when Reeves first showed the deputies the sheets, one of them sliced off a corner of a page and lit it. It burned with little smoke, and very little ash. The documents returned to Reeves burned like ordinary paper. Despite the protests, however, the Air Force denied ever pulling a switch.

It was not the first time the Air Force had been accused of tampering with evidence to cover up the facts. In August, 1950, Nick Mariana, a baseball team manager in Great Falls, Montana, took a graphic film of what appeared to be UFOs.

He and his secretary saw two brilliantly-glowing objects appear over a park in broad daylight. The strange crafts moved in unison across the sky, and both eye witnesses recalled that they had never seen anything like them.

VISUAL EVIDENCE

After observing them for some time, the quick-thinking Mariana then ran to his car where he grabbed his 16mm home-movie camera. He managed to catch more than 15 seconds of the spectacular aerial display before the two craft disappeared. Later, he handed the film over to the Air Force but, when it was returned to him, more than 25 frames had been removed.

Needless to say, Mariana said the missing part of the film was where the craft had dipped slightly, highlighting their strange, elliptical shape. The Air Force denied editing the film, and then claimed it showed nothing but two jets anyway.

But the cover-up was not always as simple as doctoring evidence or explaining away UFO crash sights as experimental balloon mishaps – especially when dozens of citizens, air traffic controllers, military pilots and police officers were privy to the sighting. That is exactly what occurred in

July 1952, when America's capital, Washington, D.C., was buzzed for several nights by a fleet of UFOs! A newspaper headline of the time captured the furore perfectly with a headline that screamed: 'Saucers Swarm over Capital'.

Unlike most cases of sightings, the Washington incident is remarkable for the fact that several UFOs were picked up on radar scopes at both civilian and military installations. Even Air Force officials, knowing they could not deny this incident or sweep it under the rug, publicly conceded that the blips had appeared on screens at at least two bases in the region and that they were at a loss to explain them. Dozens of saucers were spotted, some travelling as fast as 8,000 miles an hour. Some would hover over the city, while others streaked back and forth across the sky. Some excited citizens even watched USAF jets trying to intercept the mysterious visitors.

And yet, almost laughably, the Air Force eventually changed its original statements to declare that the lights in the sky might have been nothing more than a strange weather phenomenon – no wonder the scrambled fighters couldn't catch that! Shortly afterwards, however, several meteorologists came forward and denied the weather could have had anything at all to

Above: *John Reeves claimed these were aliens' footprints.*

Below: *Reeves' impression of his other-world visitors.*

do with the sightings. Then, a Harvard astronomer came forward, claiming that the sightings could all be explained away by a mixture of high altitude balloons, meteorites, planes and hallucinations. Yet even the USAF was unimpressed with those explanations... and quietly labelled the sightings unexplained, while publicly still trying to blame the weather!

Four years later, in November 1957, the Air Force had another mass sighting to explain away. The small town of Levelland, Texas, had suddenly become a hotbed of UFO sightings and landings. The first sighting came on 2 November, when two men, driving on a lonely highway outside town, saw a huge, red UFO hovering nearby. Suddenly, their engine and car lights died. The men, Pedro Saucido and Joe Salaz, were stunned, but that shock turned to terror when the craft landed in front of them. They observed the craft, which they described as cigar-shaped, for several minutes until it sped off into the darkened sky. A short time later, another panicked man also called police with a strange report of a UFO in the area. Within a few hours, at least seven calls had been recorded by police.

Finally, a sceptical sheriff, Weir Clem, decided to check out the reports for himself. About an hour later, he and Deputy Patrick McCullough knew the sightings were real, for there, above them, they saw a glowing, red UFO. Unbeknown to them at

Above: *A purported UFO retrieval at Fort Riley, Kansas, in 1964.*

THE SMALL TOWN OF LEVELLAND, TEXAS, HAD SUDDENLY BECOME A HOTBED OF UFO SIGHTINGS AND LANDINGS

THE UFO WAS DESCRIBED AS LARGE AND OVAL-SHAPED, TRAVELLING AT MORE THAN 750 MILES AN HOUR

the time, three other policemen also spotted the craft. Military officials at Project Bluebook were promptly notified by Reese Air Force Base in nearby Lubbock. Almost immediately, the officers at Project Bluebook blamed the sightings on ball lightning, because there were reports of a thunderstorm in the area!

RELIABLE WITNESSES

But there was a problem with that scenario. Two hours after the spate of sightings, two men on patrol at the top secret White Sands missile base also reported seeing a UFO. They described it as egg-shaped, and said it bobbed up and down. They reported it to base commanders, but no one seemed interested in what they had just witnessed. However, back at Project Bluebook, there was deep concern. It was one thing to write off the civilians as mistaken, but two highly reliable guards at a top government military installation were something else. However, that, too, was eventually explained. The guards were young, impressionable men who had been taken in by the rash of sightings in Levelland. Case closed.

But two days later, across the border in nearby Orogrande, New Mexico, James Stokes, who was stationed at Holloman Air Force Base, was driving to El Paso when his engine came to a sudden halt. He looked up and down the highway, and spotted a UFO as it passed over his car. He described it as large and oval-shaped, and estimated that it was travelling at more than 750 miles an hour. As it passed over him, he could feel the heat emanating from the craft, and later noticed his face and hands began to itch and turn red, as if he had been sunburned. Unlike the impressionable young guards at White Sands, Stokes was a 24-year veteran of the military, but still the USAF wrote off his encounter as another weather phenomenon.

Not everyone allowed the Air Force to simply reject their encounter out of hand, however. Such was the case of Ray Rosi, who was driving near Mansfield Dam, outside Austin, Texas, on 24 June 1967, when he saw a bright blue light in the sky. He pulled over to the side of the road, and watched in amazement as the craft moved overhead. He grabbed his binoculars, and saw that the craft was cigar-shaped. After

the UFO sped off, he went to a nearby public phone and immediately called the Air Force to report the sighting.

After the usual brief investigation, the encounter was filed away and stamped 'Insufficient Data For Scientific Analysis'. Weeks later, when Rosi contacted the Air Force to ascertain what had been done about his report, he was furious when he found out how casually his sighting had been treated. He then wrote a report outlining the incident again. He then included a scathing condemnation, stating that the investigation 'leads me to believe that the accusations of negligence heaped upon you by some independent investigations in recent years may NOT be entirely unfounded'.

CHANGED REPORTS

Finally, after reviewing his statement again, and checking into his background – which showed he was a reliable witness – the Air Force was obliged to change the report to note that the object Rosi had seen was indeed 'unidentified'. Yet despite – or probably because of – their admission, the powers that be behind Project Bluebook never made public the incident.

In more recent times, we also see the shadowy hand of government cover-up. After several UFO sightings, the small Wisconsin town of Elmwood was so confident of the existence of aliens that the townspeople decided to build a landing

Above: *This remarkable photo – taken over Vancouver Island, Canada, in 1981 – clearly shows a saucer-shaped object.*

Below: *Another amazing photo of a possible alien space ship, taken in New Jersey in 1952.*

strip in a soya bean field to welcome the space creatures. The strip was to be designed in the shape of a man and an alien shaking hands.

The proposed £30,000,000 landing site attracted the curiosity of the Working Group, which could not brush off the sightings as weather balloons or low-flying aircraft. In the mid-1980s, it decided to send undercover agents to investigate.

The agents turned in a report to the Working Group with no explanation of what the people of Elmwood had seen. But instead of trying to solve the riddle, many residents claimed that the agents had harassed them.

Given all the evidence, it is now apparent that the US Government has known – for almost 50 years – of the existence of extraterrestrial craft. Why the official silence, the cover-up, the ridicule?

No-one knows for certain. There could be military reasons, or it could be that officials are just too afraid to tell us what they know. Whatever the reason, they continue to deny any interest in or active search for UFOs.

It is a denial that rings more and more hollow as we head into the new millennium. For too long, too many people have seen too many strange sights for the cover-up to continue indefinitely. It is only a matter of time before the web of secrecy is finally pierced.

ANCIENT TRAVELLERS
Early Visitors to Earth

The latter half of the 20th century has seen an explosion in the number of reported sightings of Unidentified Flying Objects. But outer-world travellers may have been coming to Earth for many centuries.

Probably the most fascinating instance of possible early UFO contact surrounds the centuries-old Dogon tribe, a hardy, primitive band of people who live in the arid desertscape of West Africa on the Bandiagara Plateau in what is now the Republic of Mali. Even today, as the 20th century comes to a close, the Dogons live just as they have always done, in huts made from mud and straw or caves, they use only the most primitive of tools.

And yet this backward, rudimentary tribe to whom electricity, cars and televi-sion are unknown, living some 250 miles south of Timbuktu, has an astounding grasp of the universe, familiar with the workings of planets and stars that only in relatively recent years became known to the most brilliant astronomers. Take, for example, the strange story of Sirius, the brightest star in the heavens. Sirius, which is also known as the Dog Star because it is located in the Canis Major constellation some eight light years – 47 trillion miles – away from Earth, is so bright that a companion star close to it was not discovered until 1862. That lesser star, called Sirius B, is completely outshone by its more brilliant neighbour, which is 20 times as radiant as our own sun, and wasn't photographed by the most modern tele-scopes until 1970.

Yet somehow, these primitive natives of the Dogon tribe knew of its existence hundreds, perhaps thousands of years beforehand. Moreover, the Dogons, who migrated to West Africa sometime between the 13th and 16th centuries, also knew that the world was round, that it spun on an axis running north to south, that it and the other planets revolved around the sun, that the Moon was a barren wasteland 'and dead like dry blood', and that our Milky Way galaxy was elliptical in shape! Even more oddly, they also knew that Saturn was surrounded by rings, and that Jupiter had four main moons.

THE PRIMITIVE DOGON TRIBE HAS AN ASTOUNDING GRASP OF THE UNIVERSE AND THE WORKINGS OF PLANETS AND STARS

Opposite: *The huge stone carvings on Easter Island could be the work of alien life forms.*

Below: *The ancient Babylonians wrote of alien visits more than 2,000 years ago.*

Above: *The Mayan civilisation of pre-Colombian Mexico had a startling knowledge of mathematics, science and astronomy.*

HOW COULD A PEOPLE LIVING IN MUD HUTS IN AFRICA KNOW SO MUCH ABOUT THE WORKINGS OF THE GALAXY?

INCREDIBLY, THE DOGONS BELIEVED THAT THEY HAD BEEN VISITED IN ANCIENT TIMES BY EXTRATERRESTRIALS

They also have four calendars – one for the Sun, the Moon, Venus and Sirius.

How could a people living in mud huts in darkest Africa, without any telescopes or other astronomical aids, possibly know so much about the make-up and workings of our galaxy? The answer might lie in their ancient myths, tales of superhuman beings who came down from the heavens to protect and nurture them.

Their remarkable knowledge of space was first reported by the French anthropologists Marcel Griaule and Germaine Dieterlen, who studied and lived among the Dogons for many years in the first half of this century. Although Griaule was roundly criticised when he wrote a study of the Dogons' astronomical knowledge in the 1930s, it has since emerged that he had indeed been telling the remarkable truth.

According to studies conducted on the tribe, the Dogons' religious beliefs centre on Sirius, and their knowledge of the Dog Star is simply astounding. With no scientific equipment whatsoever, they not only charted all the stars that passed within its orbit, but they also knew the path of Sirius B, which as we have noted earlier, wasn't

even 'discovered' by scientists until the last century! Further, the Dogons also knew that Sirius B, which they call Po Tolo, is a white dwarf, and that it is so incredibly dense that scientists estimate that just a single cubic metre of it weighs in excess of 20,000 tonnes!

UNWORLDLY KNOWLEDGE

The Dogons said it was so heavy 'that all earthly beings combined cannot lift it'. They also had somehow known that Sirius B revolves around its more brilliant neighbour every 50 years in an elliptical orbit. In their native tongue, Sirius B consists of the word for star, tolo, and po, which is the name of the smallest seed known to them. Incredibly, the Dogons believed that they had been visited in ancient times by extraterrestrials from a planet revolving around Sirius B, and that these alien visitors had shared with them their knowledge of the constellation.

Strangely, the Dogon tribesmen also insisted to the French anthropologists that there was yet another star revolving around Sirius, or a 'Sirius C,' and that it was four times lighter in weight than Sirius B. At the time Griaule and Dieterlen compiled their reports, there was no evidence to suggest the existence of such a star, which the Dogon called Emme Ya, which means 'sorghum female'. They claim a planet revolves around Sirius C.

But today, some scientists believe there is documentation to indicate that a third star, most likely a dwarf star, is indeed orbiting around Sirius. Conclusive proof has yet to be found, but some years ago, scientists at the prestigious London University produced a computer analysis of Sirius which suggested that a third star might be orbiting the giant every 400 years or so – just as the Dogon tribesmen had long ago insisted.

UNEXPLAINED WISDOM

As Griaule and Dieterlen wrote, 'the problem of knowing how, with no instruments at their disposal, men could know of the movements and certain characteristics of virtually invisible stars has not been settled'.

After World War Two, American scholar Robert Temple picked up where the French anthropologists left off – and he might have found the answer to the astounding riddle of the Dogons. He believed that their background might prove to be an important clue, so he began to trace the origins of the tribe. We now know that the Dogons arrived at their present location no more than 700 years ago. It is believed that they may have originally come from what is now Libya, meaning that the Dogons might have been influenced by the great Egyptian civilisation which flourished nearby for thousands of years.

However, Temple could not find any evidence that would suggest any such influence. But the ancient mythology of the Greeks and Babylonians did offer a hint. In both civilisations, there are stories of beings from other worlds who came to Earth and imparted their amazing knowledge of the Universe to man. Temple firmly believed that the Dogons worshipped extraterrestrials who had landed in the Persian Gulf region thousands of years ago. He says they called the visitors Nommos, who were amphibious, and described them as 'the monitor of the universe, the father of mankind,

guardian of its spiritual principles, dispenser of rain and master of water'. Ancient drawings done by the Dogons indicate that these Nommos, taken from the Dogon word meaning 'to take drink,' arrived in a whirling spacecraft or ark.

In his book, *The Sirius Mystery*, Temple wrote that 'the descriptions of the landing of the ark are extremely precise. The ark is said to have landed on the Earth to the north-east of the Dogon country, which is where the Dogon claim to have come from originally. They describe the sound of the landing of the ark. They say the 'word' of Nommo was cast down in the four directions as it descended, and sounded like the

Below: *The Mayans' culture and architecture was more advanced than those of many European civilisations in the same era.*

Above: *Controversial explorer Erich von Daniken claims that there are many examples throughout the ancient world that prove early man had contact with aliens.*

A MACHINE WITH FOUR LEGS APPEARED AND DRAGGED THE SPACE SHIP TO A HOLLOW IN THE GROUND

echoing of four large stone blocks being struck with stones by the children, according to special rhythms, in a very small cave near Lake Debo. Presumably, a thunderous vibrating sound is what the Dogon are trying to convey. One can imagine standing in the cave and holding one's ears at the noise. The descent of the ark must have sounded like a jet at close range.'

The craft landed and 'displaced a pile of dust raised by the whirlwind it caused,' wrote Temple. 'The violence of the impact roughened the ground.' The Dogons also described the landing as scorching the ground and 'spurting blood', which could possibly be a reference to a rocket's fiery exhaust flame.

After the craft landed, a machine with four legs appeared and dragged the spaceship to a hollow in the ground, which was then filled with water so that the vessel now floated.

It was after this 'arrival' of the space craft, say the Dogons, that the Nommos, who seemed more like fish than men, walked among them, teaching them the mysteries of the Universe. As preposterous as it might seem, is it as preposterous as a primitive tribe knowing about the existence of stars unseen by the most powerful telescopes until hundreds of years later?

Or knowing that one of those unseen stars took 50 years to revolve around its neighbour? Something remarkable did happen to the ancient Dogon tribesmen, but they were not alone.

In fact, the ancient Babylonians also wrote of a very similar alien visit. They called these amphibious beings Oannes, and, like the Dogons, believed the extraterrestrials had come to the world to help man. According to a 3rd century BC historian called Berossus, the Oannes arrived some thousands of years ago, and landed in the Red Sea.

SOMETHING FISHY

According to him, the strange creatures 'had the shape of a fish blended with that of a man... a complicated form between a fish and man. The whole body of the animal was like that of a fish; and had under a fish's head, another head and also feet below, similar to those of a man, subjoined to the fish's tail. His voice, too, and language, were articulate and human.

'This Being in the daytime used to converse with men, but took no food at that season; and he gave them an insight into letters and sciences, and every kind of art. He taught them to construct houses, to found temples, to compile laws, and explained to them the principles of geometric knowledge...in short, he instructed them in everything which could tend to soften manners and humanise mankind. When the sun set, it was the custom of this Being to plunge again into the sea, and abide all night in the deep, for he was amphibious.'

The Greek historian Helladius also told the story 'of a man named Oe who came out of the Red Sea having a fish-like body but the head, feet and arms of a man, and who taught astronomy and letters. Some accounts say that he came out of a great egg (a flying saucer?), whence his name, and that he was actually a man, but only seemed a fish because he was clothed in "the skin of a sea-creature".'

Could it be that both the Dogon and the ancient Babylonians were privy to the same visit? We will probably never know. But it is known that the Babylonians were also great astronomers, just like their African neighbours. More than 3,000 years before the great Polish astronomer Nicolaus Copernicus first outlined his heretical belief that the world was round and revolved around the Sun, the Babylonians already knew the make-up and workings of our solar system. Their predecessors, the Sumerians, also had great knowledge of the heavens, and their calendar, which they developed more than 3,000 years before the birth of Christ, is the basis for our calendars today. Incredibly, the Sumerians could also measure the distances between stars with great accuracy.

Even more amazing, they said the solar system comprised 12 heavenly bodies – the Sun, the Moon and ten planets. Today, we know of 11 – and it wasn't until 1930 that we discovered the ninth planet, Pluto. Could there be a tenth planet lurking somewhere in the outer reaches of the solar system? Science is yet to discover one, if it does exist, but it is interesting to note that in 1972, a Californian astronomer discovered a slight wobble in the orbit of Halley's comet which he believed could only be caused by a huge planet – roughly the size of Jupiter – that makes an orbit around the sun once every 1,800 years!

And what of the Efe pygmies of Central Africa? They have long referred to Saturn as 'the star of the nine moons'. The ninth moon was only discovered in 1899 by the American scientist William Pickering. Although astronomers now know that Saturn has more than a dozen moons, the Efe knowledge is still mystifying since all the other satellites of Saturn are invisible to the naked eye. And the Efe, like the Dogons, had no conception of what a telescope was.

HEAVENLY VISITS

Many other ancient cultures share similar myths and stories which tell of visitors from the heavens, and centuries-old carvings and paintings have been found throughout the world depicting what some believe are aliens, such as the alien-like rock drawings of the ancient aboriginals of Australia and the astounding carvings in China, on an island in the province of Hunan. The Chinese etchings, which show cylindrical objects, are believed to be the oldest depiction of possible alien spacecraft. They have been dated at almost 50,000 years old!

One of the most remarkable examples of alien depictions is the famous stone relief

MANY ANCIENT CULTURE SHARE SIMILAR MYTHS AND STORIES WHICH TELL OF VISITORS FROM THE HEAVENS

CHINESE ETCHINGS ARE BELIEVED TO BE THE OLDEST DEPICTION OF POSSIBLE ALIEN SPACECRAFT

Below: *The Mayan calendar was so accurate that when compared to the modern measurements of time it was found to be just a few seconds off the current scientific measure of a solar year.*

found at an ancient site in Palenque, Mexico, in 1935. In his controversial bestseller, *Chariots of the Gods*, researcher Erich von Daniken, whose theories of extraterrestrial visits in ancient times still fuel debate, describes the relief: 'There sits a human being, with the upper part of his body bent forward like a racing motorcyclist. Today, any child would identify his vehicle as a rocket.

'It is pointed at the front, then changes to strangely grooved indentations like inlet ports, widens out and terminates at the tail into a darting flame. The crouching being himself is manipulating a number of undefinable controls and has the heel of his left foot on a kind of pedal.

His clothing is appropriate: short trousers with a broad belt, a jacket with a modern Japanese opening at the neck and closely fitting bands at arms and legs. The relief also shows the being wearing a 'space helmet', which von Daniken describes as having indentations and tubes 'and something like antennae on top.

'Our space traveller – he is clearly depicted as one – is not only bent forward tensely, he is also looking intently at an apparatus on his face.'

Throughout Latin and South America, several advanced Indian civilisations knew a great deal about science and mathematics that went beyond anything the Europeans of the same era were capable of comprehending. Indeed, while Europe was awash

*Above: **The mysterious lines on the plains of Nazca may have been used by extraterrestrials to guide their space craft.***

ONE OF THE MOST
ASTOUNDING ANCIENT
ARTEFACTS KNOWN TO MAN
IS THAT OF THE NAZCA
LINES IN PERU

*Right: **The lines are hardly discernible from the ground – but at a great height their patterns become clear.***

in the ignorance and superstition of the Middle Ages, the mysterious Mayan Indians of Mexico had a deep understanding of maths, and even worked out planetary orbits and devised a yearly calendar that was so accurate that even when it was compared to the most modern measurements of time, it was found to be just a few seconds off the current scientific measure of a solar year.

Among the most advanced of the Indians which populated South America were the Nazcas, whose name is given to the famous Nazca Desert of Peru – site of one of the most astounding ancient artifacts known to modern man.

The Nazca Lines, which depict giant drawings and bizarre lines etched into the parched expanse of the desert, lay hidden from the world for more than 1,500 years until they were re-discovered in 1941 by an American archaeologist, Paul Kosok.

One can imagine his awe when he saw the tableau stretched out before him like some giant jigsaw puzzle – thousands of lines, all dead straight, and carvings drawn all over the floor of the desert. Some of the lines, which run for miles, literally cross over mountains while others plunge dramatically into the Pacific Ocean.

Realising that the full scope of the Nazca Lines could only be appreciated from a great height, Kosok hired a plane to fly over the desert. He was stunned as the artistry of these ancient people came into breath-taking focus. There were giant drawings, hundreds of feet long and all perfectly in proportion, of spiders, birds, fish and a monkey, as well as mathematical shapes like triangles and squares. Also, on the face of a hill rising from a plain further to the north, there was a strange, three-pronged carving known as the Trident of Paracas, which stretches for more than 600 feet.

According to the best dating methods, the Nazca Indians carved these magnificent shapes around 500 A.D., as European civilisation was crumbled into the dust by the hordes of Vandals, Goths and Huns. Kosok, who spent the rest of his life trying to fully understand what the lines might mean, called Nazca 'the largest astronomy book in the world'. He came to that conclusion one afternoon when he and his wife Rose, noticed that a major line pointed directly to the setting sun on the exact day of the winter solstice, 22 June, the shortest day of the year.

'With a great thrill, we realised at once that we had apparently found the key to the riddle,' he later wrote. 'For undoubtedly

Above: *The vast statues of Easter Island, which line the tiny island, are made from hard volcanic rock.*

THE NAZCA INDIANS CARVED THEIR MAGNIFICENT SHAPES AS EUROPEAN CIVILISATION CRUMBLED INTO DUST

THERE HAVE BEEN MANY THEORIES ABOUT THE NAZCA LINES, BUT NONE HAS EVER SOLVED THE RIDDLE

the ancient Nazcans had constructed this line to mark the winter solstice. And if this were so, then the other markings might very likely be tied up in some way with astronomical and related activities... With what seemed to us "the largest astronomy book in the world" spread out in front of us, the question immediately arose: how could we learn to read it?'

THE UNSOLVED RIDDLE

It was a question never answered. Until his death in 1959, Kosok worked alongside Maria Reiche, a renowned German scientist, who carried on the research after his death. She had many theories about what the Nazca Lines meant, but none has ever fully solved the riddle. The most scientific explanation is that the Nazca Indians carved the lines and drawings for purely religious purposes. But that does not in any way explain why the drawings can only be recognised from a height of at least 300 metres.

More controversial is the theory that the Nazca Lines are symbols left behind by a race of extraterrestrials, who used the desert as a sort of landing field and that the intricate lines act as guidance of some sort. When the aliens eventually left this planet, the Indians, believing them to be mighty gods, added to the design by drawing the intricate animal shapes in the hope that they might one day entice the visitors back to Nazca.

Two thousand miles to the west of Chile and the Nazca Lines in the middle of the Pacific Ocean lies the famed Easter Island, site of some of the most bizarre statues of ancient times. These vast carvings, which line the island, are made from hard volcanic rock. How could an ancient people, working with the most primitive of tools, have hewn these vast monoliths? Moreover, how could they have been moved across the desolate terrain? The statues themselves depict creatures with long noses, low foreheads and thin lips – characteristics which no islanders, even in ancient times, ever possessed.

> TALES OF SPACE CRAFT SIGHTINGS AND LANDINGS ARE TO BE FOUND IN SOME OF MAN'S OLDEST LITERARY WORKS

Again von Daniken makes the argument that extraterrestrials were responsible. He claims that the aliens somehow became stranded on Earth, and the statues are actually an elaborate 'SOS' design. He also notes that because some of the carvings remain unfinished, the rescue must have been sudden.

No-one, of course, really knows all the answers behind mysteries like the statues of Easter Island, the Nazca Lines or the remarkable astronomical ability of the primitive Dogon tribesmen. And even the best scholars admit the enigmas of these

Above: *Erich von Daniken claims the statues on Easter Island were carved by extraterrestrial castaways, stranded on our planet.*

and other strange relics of the past defy explanation.

But it is worth noting that tales of space craft sightings and landings are to be found in some of man's oldest literary works. Around 1,500 BC, for instance, during the reign of Egyptian Pharaoh Thutmose III, an unknown historian wrote on a piece of papyrus the following account:

A BIZARRE VISION

'In the year 22, of the third month of winter, sixth hour of the day... the scribes of the House of Life found it was a circle of fire that was coming in the sky. It had no head, the breath of its mouth had a foul odour. Its body one rod long (about 16 feet) and one rod wide. It had no voice. Their hearts became confused through it; then they laid themselves on their bellies... Now after some days had passed, these things became more numerous in the skies than ever. They shone more in the sky than the brightness of the sun, and extended to the limits of the four supports of the heavens... Powerful was the position of the fire circles. The army of the Pharaoh looked on with him in their midst. It was after supper. Thereupon, these fire circles ascended higher in the sky towards the south... The Pharaoh caused incense to be brought to make peace on the hearth... And what happened was ordered by the Pharaoh to be written in the annals of the House of Life... so that it be remembered for ever.'

Later, in the Bible, the prophet Ezekiel speaks of a strange vehicle coming down from the sky. He recounts that it landed in 592 BC in what is now Iraq: 'As I looked, a stormy wind came out of the north, and a great cloud, with brightness round about it, and fire flashing forth continually, and in the midst of the fire, as it were gleaming bronze.

'And from the midst of it came the likeness of four living creatures. And this was their appearance: they had the form of men, but each had four faces, and each of them had four wings. Their legs were straight, and the soles of their feet were like the sole of a calf's foot; and they sparkled like burnished bronze. Under their wings on their four sides they had human hands...each had the face of a man in front; the four had the face of a lion on the right side... the face of an ox on the left side and... the face of an

eagle at the back… And the living creatures darted to and fro, like a flash of lightning.'

Four hundred years after the birth of Christ, the Roman historian Julius Obsequens compiled an anthology of strange events for his book *Prodigorium liber*. He cites many examples of what would now be called UFO sightings.

In 216 BC, he writes that 'things like ships were seen in the sky over Italy… At Arpi (east of Rome), a round shield was seen in the sky. At Capua, the sky was all on fire, and one saw figures like ships.'

Then, in 99 BC, 'there fell in different places… a thing like a flaming torch, and it came suddenly from the sky. Towards sunset, a round object like a globe or round or circular shield took its path in the sky, from east to west.'

Nine years later, in Umbria, he recorded that 'a globe of fire, of golden colour, fell to the earth, gyrating. It then seemed to increase in size, rose from the earth, and ascended into the sky, where it obscured the disc of the sun with its brilliance. It revolved towards the eastern quadrant of the sky.'

Could it be that long ago, beings from other worlds really did visit our planet? If

Above: *Every ancient culture spoke of UFO visitations, including the highly-advanced Egyptian civilisation.*

THE ROMAN HISTORIAN JULIUS OBSEQUENS CITES MANY EXAMPLES OF WHAT WOULD NOW BE CALLED UFO SIGHTINGS

Right: *The prophet Ezekiel recorded his close encounter with a UFO in the Bible.*

we accept the evidence accrued in the past 50 years, when the number of sightings of UFOs exploded, and admit that maybe we are not alone in the universe, why then could not our ancestors also have been touched by the emissaries of another planet? One day, if these visitors do really exist, they might return. Then we shall all finally know the real truth.

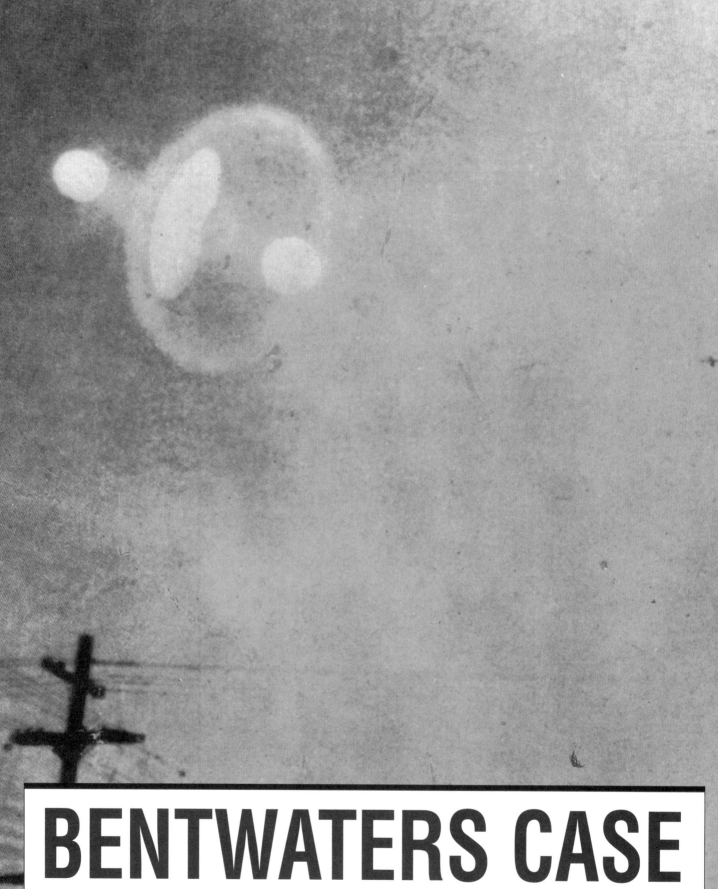

BENTWATERS CASE
Christmas visitors

It was on a quiet Boxing Day that the peace and tranquillity of part of rural England was shattered by an unexpected, unexplained visitation from space. Witnesses saw alien beings, but officialdom remained silent on the matter.

O f all the UFO mysteries in Britain, none can compare in detail or credibility with the bizarre happenings in and around the Rendlesham Forest in late December, 1980 – for the mysterious phenomena which descended from the cold night skies upon the area were not only witnessed by several civilians, but by a team of highly-trained American military personnel as well. Moreover, several radar screens in the region and in London detected the unidentified craft, sensational physical evidence was found at a landing site, and a top United States Air Force colonel even made a revealing tape recording as he and his party of veteran airmen watched the eerie events unfold right before their very eyes!

The story of the amazing encounter with visitors from another world began shortly after midnight, on 26 December 1980, when Suffolk farmer Gordon Levett walked outside his house to put the family dog into its kennel for the evening. But on this cold winter's night, the animal was behaving strangely, and was obviously scared of some unknown intruder. Suddenly, as Levett turned his head, he saw an astounding light move silently over his house. Hardly able to believe his eyes, Levett stood there transfixed as the light, which he later reported was shaped like a giant mushroom, stopped and hovered over his head. He was no stranger to flying craft – his farm was near the RAF base at Woodbridge and the US base at Bentwaters – but he had never seen anything like this

before. After a short while, the craft gracefully flew away, leaving Mr Levett and his dog very shaken.

Less than an hour later, a military radar installation in Norfolk picked up a strange blip on its screen which could not be attributed to any known aircraft in the region. According to the radar operators, the craft was about the size of a Boeing 737, but it was doing more than 1,500 miles an hour, almost three times the cruising speed of a passenger plane. Several other bases in the area – and even the tower at Heathrow Airport – had also tracked the strange craft until it went off the screen. Given its trajectory, it was computed that the object must have gone down somewhere over Rendlesham Forest, near Bentwaters. At around 2a.m., two military security police at Woodbridge reported seeing a bright, oval light hovering over the trees. They quickly dismissed the notion that it was the nearby Orford Ness lighthouse, because it suddenly dipped below the tree line. The senior security man radioed in to base, and an officer then informed them that they had no idea what they might have seen. There was no incoming air traffic, he said, and the base had received no reports of a downed plane, military or civilian.

The two men were ordered to stay at the perimeter of the base, while three servicemen were sent into the area to conduct a

HE STOOD TRANSFIXED AS THE LIGHT, WHICH WAS SHAPED LIKE A GIANT MUSHROOM, STOPPED AND HOVERED OVER HIS HEAD

Opposite: *The incident at Bentwaters remains the most credible sighting of a UFO in Britain.*

Below: *The gate outside the NATO base where several airmen claimed to have seen a UFO above a nearby forest.*

Above: *The UFO was picked up by radar all over the south-east, including that used by air traffic controllers at Heathrow Airport.*

THE OBJECT WAS ABOUT THE SAME SIZE AS A CAR. IT WAS BRILLIANTLY WHITE AND DOTTED WITH ROWS OF RED AND BLUE LIGHTS

THE CRAFT BEGAN MANOEUVRING BETWEEN THE TREES AND THEN IT SHOT RAPIDLY INTO THE NIGHT SKY

search. They took a jeep and, following directions given to them by the security police, made their way along one of the many dirt tracks winding deep into the forest. They had to continue on foot when the path became too treacherous to drive any further. A short time later, two of the men saw some red and blue lights flashing through the trees. They tried to radio HQ, but the walkie-talkie was inexplicably not working. They decided to press on regardless, and began inching their way forward until they came to what looked to them like a recently-cleared opening.

Both were puzzled by the strange clearing, but they didn't have time to dwell on it because suddenly, they saw an object. They would later describe it to military investigators as about the same size as a car, though roughly triangular in shape. It was brilliantly white, though dotted by rows of red and blue lights. One of the men overcame his amazement, and walked up to the object. He was less than ten feet away from it when suddenly the three legs which were protruding from the craft were withdrawn, and it began to lift gently upwards into the air. The men watched in a mixture of fear and awe as it gracefully began manoeu-

vring between the thick clumps of trees. The servicemen decided to give chase, and followed the craft as it made its way over a field. Without warning, it then shot rapidly into the night sky.

A few hours after making their report, the commander at Bentwaters, USAF Colonel Ted Conrad and a group of his men decided to make a thorough search of the area where the object had reportedly touched down. There they found three depressions in the moist soil. They made a perfect triangle, about 12 feet apart. Traces of radiation were also detected by instruments they carried with them.

STRANGE LIGHTS

That night, the deputy base commander at Bentwaters, Lt Colonel Charles Halt, was informed of yet another bizarre incident. A group of security police had again seen mysterious lights coming from within the forest. Immediately, he decided to organise another thorough search of the area. Together, he and about 30 of his men combed through the thick woods, and again heat radiation was detected and pod marks were found. As the team continued the search, farm animals in the area could now clearly be heard. Something was disturbing them. It was then that the men first spotted it – and Col Halt turned on his tape recorder: 'It's a strange, small red light – looks to be maybe a quarter, half mile, maybe further, out.'

As the party moved into a clearing to get a better view, Col Halt continued his amazing description: 'The light is still there and all the barnyard animals have gotten quiet now… I'm through to the clearing about 110 degrees from the site. Still getting a reading off the meter… I think it's something on the ground. I think it's something very huge. We're about 150 to 200 yards away from the site. Everything else is just deathly calm. There's no doubt about it. It appears to be moving a little bit this way. It's brighter than it has been.' Suddenly, the edge in his voice changes: 'It is definitely moving this way.'

For the next few seconds, Col Halt and his group of highly-trained American servicemen watched something they had never seen before. The object glided quietly past them, spewing a flood of bright, glowing colours. 'Pieces of it are shooting off!' Halt blurted into the tape. 'There's no doubt about it – this is weird!' Several hundred yards away, another group of his men was having an even more bizarre experience. A huge glowing light passed over them, and seemed to explode all around them – there was no sound, but after the flash they saw an object resting on the ground right in front of them. They had never seen anything like it – it was domed on top, and flat at the bottom. It glowed brilliantly. It then began to lift back into the sky, and the men were ordered to follow its path. A short time later, Col Halt and his party began to see two other lights flying near the one that had just given them such a spectacular show. 'There's something very, very strange,' he recorded. 'Pieces are falling off it again.'

AN AMAZING SIGHT

The party then moved across the clearing where the smaller search group had seen the object. Halt again recorded this amazing sight: 'We're looking at this thing and we're probably about two to three hundred yards away. It's like an eye looking at you, winking. It's still moving from side to side… it sort of has a hollow centre – a dark centre – like the pupil of an eye looking at you, winking.' The airborne spectacle continued unabated for more than another hour. 'We've passed the farmer's house and crossed into the next field and now we have multiple sightings of up to five lights with similar shaped orbits,' said

A HUGE GLOWING LIGHT PASSED OVER THE SERVICEMEN, AND SEEMED TO EXPLODE ALL AROUND THEM

THE OBJECT ON THE GROUND GLOWED BRILLIANTLY… THEY SAID IT WAS LIKE AN EYE WINKING AT THEM

Below: *The military radar at Norfolk picked up a strange blip on the screen.*

Halt. Later, the Colonel continued his dramatic commentary: 'We're at the far side of the farmer's – ah, the second farmer's field. Made a sighting about 110 degrees. Looks like it's clear out towards the coast – right on the horizon. Moves about a bit and flashes from time to time. Still steady and red in colour.'

The events of that night then changed considerably: '0105 we see strange strobe-like – very sporadic, but there's definitely something out there – some kind of phenomenon... We've got two strange objects. Half-moon shaped, dancing about with coloured lights on them. Appears to be

about five or ten miles out – maybe less. The half-moons have now turned into full circles – as if there was an eclipse there for a minute or two.'

As they watched transfixed, they caught sight of a big object: 'Now we've got an object about ten degrees directly south. But the ones to the north are moving away from us... Hey!... Here he comes from the south. He's coming towards us now!' Suddenly, the object began firing some sort of beam near them. 'Now we observe what appears to be a beam coming down towards the ground...this is unreal,' said Halt.

It was a little after 4a.m. on Saturday, 27 December, that the stunned search party returned to their Bentwaters base. What they had witnessed is being debated to this day, but to the men who were there – all of them, trained Air Force personnel – these

Opposite Top and Bottom: *Forester Vincent Thurkettle said the holes made by the UFO's landing pods were actually the work of rabbits.*

THE TRAINED AMERICAN AIR FORCE PERSONNEL RECOUNTED THE MOST ASTONISHING FEW HOURS OF THEIR LIVES

Above: *The Ministry of Defence suppressed the memo detailing the encounter.*

A RED, SUN-LIKE LIGHT WAS SEEN THROUGH THE TREES. IT MOVED ABOUT AND PULSED. IT APPEARED TO THROW OFF PARTICLES

---

were the most astonishing few hours of their lives. After returning to the base, Col Halt told his superiors what he had seen. They advised him to write a memo outlining the details, which would then be sent on to the Ministry of Defence in Whitehall. The Ministry had jurisdiction because the incidents had occurred outside the US base, on British soil.

The memo read:

'SUBJECT: Unexplained Lights.
1. Early in the morning of 27 December 1980, two USAF security police patrolmen saw unusual lights outside the back gate at RAF Woodbridge. Thinking an aircraft might have crashed or been forced to down, they called for permission to go outside the gate to investigate. The on-duty flight chief responded and allowed three patrolmen to proceed in the forest. The individuals reported seeing a strange glowing object in the forest. The object was described as being metallic in appearance and triangular in shape, approximately two to three metres across the base and approximately two metres high. It illuminated the entire forest with a white light. The object itself had a pulsing red light on top and a bank(s) of blue lights underneath. The object was hovering or on legs. As the patrolmen approached the object, it manoeuvred through the trees and disappeared. At this time the animals on a nearby farm went into a frenzy. The object was briefly sighted approximately an hour later near the back gate.
2. The next day, three depressions one and a half inches deep and seven inches in diameter were found where the object had been sighted on the ground. The following night the area was checked for radiation. Beta/gamma readings of 0.1 milliroentgens were recorded with peak readings in the three depressions and near the centre of the triangle formed by the depressions. A nearby tree had moderate (0.05 – 0.07) readings on the side of the tree toward the depression.
3. Later in the night a red, sun-like light was seen through the trees. It moved about and pulsed. At one point it appeared to throw off glowing particles and then broke into five separate white objects and then disappeared. Immediately thereafter, three star-like objects were noticed in the sky, two objects to the north and one to the south, all

However, he would occasionally grant interviews, and always maintained that what he had seen was consistent with the memo that had been sent to the Ministry of Defence. Halt also reportedly indicated that photographs had been taken of the objects, as had plaster casts of the strange indentations, but nothing has ever been released by authorities.

Interestingly, a later US television report about the sightings reported that an anonymous serviceman claimed to have driven an officer at Bentwaters onto the runway where he handed something to a pilot who was about to take off for West Germany. When the driver sheepishly asked the officer what it was he had just handed over, he was told 'we actually have pictures of the UFO there'.

BEYOND COMPREHENSION

Other airmen backed up their commander's amazing story. Larry Warren, who was just 18 at the time of the incident, claimed that one of the objects he saw was 'just beyond comprehension'. 'It was solid and this had to leave some traces... it had a reddish, I won't say light... The closest I could put to it is a neon light. Just the top part was a bright red, but you could see the structure of the ship through the red.'

of which were about ten degrees off the horizon. The objects moved rapidly in sharp angular movements and displayed red, green and blue lights. The objects to the north appeared to be elliptical through an 8-12 power lens. They then turned to full circles. The objects to the north remained in the sky for an hour or more. The object to the south was visible for two or three hours, and beamed down a stream of light from time to time. Numerous individuals, including the undersigned, witnessed the activities in paragraphs two and three.'

The memo was signed Charles Halt, Lt Col USAF.

For several years, the memo was suppressed by both the US and British governments and Halt, understandably, was reluctant to discuss the events with anyone other than fellow military investigators.

Another serviceman, who was a witness to the events of the first night in the forest and who spoke to researchers only on condition that his name was not revealed, claimed that the object he saw was definitely 'triangular... and it stood on three legs. I would say it was about ten feet, maybe 12, and eight feet in height. The colour was a strange sort of offish white. It actually

Below: *An artist's impression of the strange beings seen by the US servicemen and a map highlighting the area where the sightings were reported.*

looked pretty dirty. There were lights of different colours. When it moved it was so slow you could walk after it.' Another had told researchers that 'I do not know any technology, certainly not in 1980, probably not even now, that could do the things this did. It was just like magic. I think that's what freaked most people out. Not what it was, but the crazy, unbelievable things it could do. I just stood there in awe.'

There were many civilian witnesses as well. They reported seeing huge lights gliding silently overhead, then suddenly dart off into the night sky at astonishing speeds. Even workers in the forest saw things they could not explain. Foreman Donald James refused to comment on what might have happened, but said 'something definitely did occur in the forest that night'.

Exactly what did happen that night has never been established beyond doubt. The governments of both the United States and Britain have maintained a steady silence on the matter, while others have come forward claiming the entire incident could be blamed on the local lighthouse! But surely trained military men, who lived and worked on the base, would know the differ-

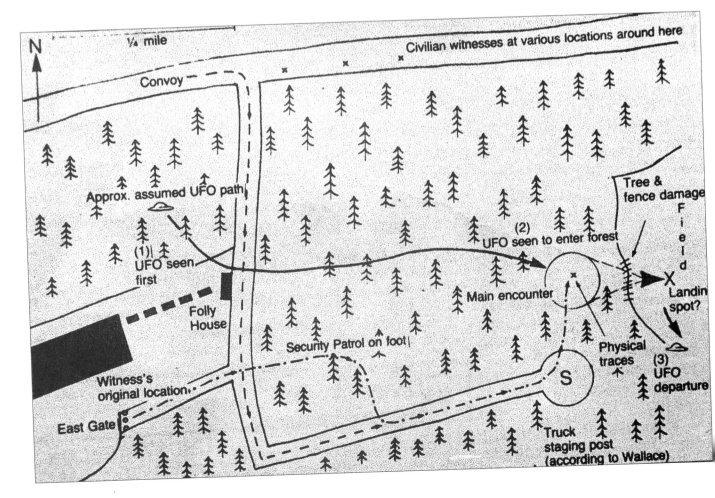

Traffic Control Centre had seen an object pass directly over the landing field at a speed estimated at some 4,000 miles an hour! The UFO, which had also been picked up on radar both at the Centre and on several planes flying nearby, then began making a series of manoeuvres which lasted for more than two hours.

A Royal Air Force jet was ordered into the air to investigate, and visual sighting was confirmed. The pilot reported the UFO then began tailing his jet and that he was unable to evade it. The craft played cat-and-mouse with the RAF interceptor until the fighter pilot was forced to return to base because he was low on fuel. A subsequent report issued by an independent US inquiry concluded that the probability was 'fairly high' the UFO was real.

It is interesting to note that in the wake of the Bentwaters case, there have been numerous others reports of strange, triangular-shaped objects in the night skies over Britain. Those reports continue to this day. No-one really knows for certain what they are or what their mission might be. The answers may come in a decade, or tomorrow. But somewhere up in that dark sky, there may be those who do know. But for now, we can only wait and marvel at the possibilities of what occurred that Christmas over Bentwaters.

ence between a lighthouse they saw almost daily and the strange glowing objects they sighted on the nights in question.

Besides, the United States Air Force still thought enough of Col Hart to make him commander of the Bentwaters base. Indeed, the servicemen's story was so detailed that even some notable figures, including Lord Peter Hill-Norton, the former Admiral of the Fleet, concluded: 'I myself think it is very difficult indeed to discount the almost certainty that something landed,' though he added he had no idea where the craft had originated. 'I wish I did,' he said.

Some sceptics even maintained that the strange objects might have been some top-secret new weapon or craft designed by the US military. Yet even veteran Air Force men who saw the objects observed they had seen nothing to even remotely compare with them.

The facts are clear – the Bentwaters incident is truly one of the most remarkable encounters in history, and goes far beyond the remarkable Lakenheath occurrence some 24 years earlier. On the night of 13 August 1956, over Lakenheath, Radar Air

Above: *Drawings of the crafts which were seen near the base.*

VETERAN AIR FORCE MEN WHO SAW THE OBJECTS OBSERVED THEY HAD SEEN NOTHING TO REMOTELY COMPARE WITH THEM

Right: *UFO sightings continue to be reported over England and the continent.*

GHOST SHIP
The Flying Dutchman

Nothing strikes fear into a sailor as much as the sighting of a dreaded ghost ship, condemned to sail the world's oceans for all eternity. And of all the tales of accursed ships, none has remained as mysterious or as terrifying as that of the Flying Dutchman.

The Flying Dutchman, which was immortalised by the German writer Heinrich Heine and composer Richard Wagner in his opera, *Die Fliegende Hollander*, many years later, was a 17th century brig which plied the sea lanes between Holland and the East Indies, at the centre of the lucrative spice trade. The full story of the ship's tortured journey through time was first recounted by the French writer, Auguste Jal, in about 1832.

In his book, Jal wrote that the vessel was rounding the Cape of Good Hope on its way to the East Indies, when it was struck by a frightful storm. The Dutch sea captain, a greedy, ill-tempered tyrant who was infamous for his cruelty, refused to listen to the pleas of his panicked crew who begged him to turn back for home lest the ship sink. But the captain only laughed at them and their terror, and he began singing blasphemous songs and drinking beer. As the raging storm worsened, it tore the sails and snapped the masts, leaving the Flying Dutchman completely at its mercy. But still the captain, now further emboldened by drink, laughed and ridiculed his terrified crew.

Then suddenly, at the height of the tempest, the clouds began to part, and a ghostly presence, said in Jal's account to have been God himself, appeared on the quarter deck for all to see. The crew was stricken with fright, but the evil Captain began to blaspheme the presence when it offered safety.

'Who wants a peaceful passage?' the captain shouted. 'I don't. I'm asking nothing from you, so clear out of this unless you want your brains blown out.'

According to Jal, the ghostly presence just shrugged its shoulders, so the Captain grabbed a pistol and fired a bullet into the spectre. But instead, the gun misfired, injuring the Captain's hand. Angrily, he rushed towards the apparition, and went to strike it. But his arm went limp, as if paralysed. In his wild rage, the Captain began to curse and blaspheme even more 'and called the presence all sorts of terrible names'.

By now, the apparition had had enough, and gravely spoke: 'From now on, you are accursed, condemned to sail forever. For you shall be the evil spirit of the sea. You will be allowed no anchorage or port of any kind. You shall have neither beer nor tobac-

Above: *Composer Richard Wagner immortalised the ghost ship in his opera,* **Die Fliegende Hollander.**

Opposite: *Of all the eerie tales of the sea, none strikes fear into the heart of sailors more than that of the Flying Dutchman.*

THE DUTCH SEA CAPTAIN WAS A GREEDY, ILL-TEMPERED TYRANT WHO WAS INFAMOUS FOR HIS CRUELTY

Above: *The Cape of Good Hope off South Africa. The area continues to play a strange role in the story of the Flying Dutchman.*

them. For you shall be the evil spirit of the sea. You shall travel all latitudes without rest, and your ship shall bring misfortune to all who sight her… And on the day of atonement, the Devil shall claim you.'

Then the presence vanished, leaving the Captain alone, save for his cabin boy, who by now had the horns and the face of a tiger. From that moment on, Jal wrote, the Flying Dutchman was the bane of the seven seas, forever doomed to its miserable existence.

AN INFAMOUS INDIVIDUAL

Strangely, Jal never names the malicious and heretical captain, but history indicates that it may have been Cornelius Vanderdecken, who apparently had the same vile temper and cruel demeanour as that attributed to the unnamed skipper. Moreover, Vanderdecken frequently sailed the seas off Africa, and was known to pass the Cape of Good Hope every four to six months. He was also notoriously greedy, and never let the safety of his crew stand in the way of making good time. And he was notorious for his blasphemous language.

Likewise, another Dutch captain, Bernard Fokke, has also been linked with the legend of the doomed ship. Like Vanderdecken, Fokke, too, was a foul-mouthed despot, who often made the passage between Holland and the East Indies in 90 days, regardless of the weather or the mutterings of his crew. Interestingly, Fokke was also accused of making a pact with the Devil to ensure his trips were speedy. Eventually, there was a falling out between the two, and Fokke was said to have been damned for all eternity.

Of course, it doesn't really matter which of the two brutes was at the helm of the Flying Dutchman. After all, say the sceptics, the very idea of a ship being condemned by God or the Devil is proof enough that the entire legend is nothing but a joke or a story to frighten young children. But upon further examination, it becomes clear that while Jal must have embellished on the story, there is ample evidence to suggest that there is much more to the Flying Dutchman story than just myth. It cannot simply be dismissed – because a vessel matching its description has been seen by sailors all over the world, and many of those ships which have come into

co. Gall shall be your drink and red hot iron your meat. Of your crew, your cabin boy alone shall remain with you; horns shall grow out of his forehead, and he shall have the muzzle of a tiger and skin tougher than that of a dogfish.

'It shall ever be your watch, and when you wish, you will not be able to sleep, for directly you close your eyes, a sword shall pierce your body. And since it is your delight to torment sailors, you shall torment contact with it have been hit by a bizarre spate of mysterious mishaps.

Indeed, it was once even seen by the future King of England! In July 1881, Prince George, who would later become King George V, was serving as a midshipman aboard the HMS Inconstant, a heavily-armed frigate and one of Her Majesty's most modern ships.

On 11 July, his log would recount, the ship was sailing between Melbourne and Sydney when suddenly he and 12 other crew members noticed an eerie light coming from over the horizon.

In his private journal, the Prince wrote: 'At 4a.m. the 'Flying Dutchman' crossed our bows. A strange red light, as of a phantom ship all aglow, in the midst of which light the mast, spars and sails of a brig two hundred yards distant stood out in strong relief as she come up on port bow. The look-out man on the forecastle reported her as close on the port bow, where also the officer of the watch from the bridge clearly saw her, as did the quarterdeck midshipman, who was sent forward at once to the forecastle; but on arriving there, no vestige nor any sign whatever of any material ship was to be seen either near or right away to the horizon, the night being clear and calm. Thirteen persons saw her.'

UNEXPLAINED TRAGEDIES

Incredibly, the so-called 'curse' of the Flying Dutchman soon followed. The seaman who had first reported seeing the vessel fell from the top mast to his death later that very same day. Then, a few days later, the Admiral of the Fleet also died, and many of the crewmen became gravely ill. It was never fully explained why.

There have been numerous other sightings recorded throughout the years. A full 15 years before the young Prince reported seeing the haunted ship, those aboard the American vessel, the General Grant, had an equally horrible encounter with the doomed Dutchman. In early May 1866, the General Grant left port in Melbourne for the long voyage to England. Everything seemed routine for the first two weeks, until the winds slackened, sending the Grant drifting helplessly away from the normal shipping lanes. On 13 May, the ship was pulled by the currents towards Auckland Island, a dismal, rocky outcrop in the middle of nowhere. The Grant was driven along the coastline until it was eventually forced into a huge cave. Its masts scraped along the top of the cavern, sending a shower of rocks crashing onto its deck. Almost miraculously, no-one was injured, but the seafarers' ordeal wasn't over yet.

Because of its position, the cave was subjected to sudden onrushes of waves,

Below: *Prince George (right) with his brother Prince Albert Victor, was a young naval midshipman when he saw the Dutchman. He later wrote of it as 'a phantome ship, all aglow'.*

which forced the Grant deeper and deeper into its bowels. Eventually, the masts became so wedged that one of them was forced through the hull.

The Grant began to take on water and, in a panic, some of the 46 passengers dived overboard to their deaths.

Those who remained joined the crew in frantically lowering three life-boats. Unfortunately, one of the lifeboats was then dashed against the rocks and broke up. All but three of the 40 people aboard were killed. Those in the other two boats, 14 in all, were luckier. They made it out of the cavern, and decided to row towards nearby Disappointment Island.

After a break, they continued their slow journey to the Auckland Islands, where they lived a desperate existence for more than 18 months until they were rescued by another vessel.

According to accounts of the time, the General Grant was actually lured to disaster by the spectre of the Flying Dutchman. As the ship drifted helplessly in the still

*Above: **Prince George's ship, HMS Inconstant. It was sailing between Melbourne and Sydney when the future King had his eerie encounter.***

ACCORDING TO ACCOUNTS OF THE TIME, THE GENERAL GRANT WAS ACTUALLY LURED TO DISASTER BY THE FLYING DUTCHMAN

winds another ship, said to be the Dutchman, suddenly appeared on the horizon and led the Grant to its watery grave.

The crew of the whaling steamer Orkney Belle also had an eerie experience. This one took place in January 1911, as the Orkney Belle ploughed through the frigid seas off the coast of Iceland.

A second mate later recounted the sighting to the *London Daily News*: 'The captain and I were on the bridge and a thin mist swirled over everything. 'Suddenly, this thin mist thinned out... to our mutual horror and surprise, a sailing vessel loomed up virtually head on.

'I rammed the helm hard aport and we seemed to escape the collision by a hair's breadth. Then, with startling suddenness, old Anderson, the carpenter, bawled out: 'The Flying Dutchman'.

'The captain and I scoffed at him, for we thought that oft-fabled ship existed in the minds of only superstitious sailors.

'As the strange vessel slowly slid alongside within a stone's throw, we noticed with amazement that her sails were billowing, yet there was no wind at all. She was a replica of a barque I once saw in a naval museum. Meantime, practically all the crew rushed to the ship's side, some in terror, but unable to resist their curiosity. Not a soul was to be seen aboard this strange vessel, not a ripple did her bows make.

'Then, like a silver bell, so sweet was the tone, three bells sounded, as if from the bows of the phantom ship, and as if in answer to a signal, the craft heeled to starboard and disappeared into the fog…'

A GHOSTLY APPARITION

The second mate's story echoes that of dozens of others, some of whom claim to have seen the ghostly ship well into this century, still sailing aimlessly across the seven seas.

In January 1923, its apparition appeared off the Cape of Good Hope and was seen by at least four veteran seamen. One of them, N.K. Stone, later wrote of the

THERE ARE DOZENS OF SIGHTINGS OF THE FLYING DUTCHMAN, SOME OF THEM WELL INTO THE PRESENT CENTURY

Below: *The crew of a whaling ship, the Orkney Belle, saw the Dutchman off the frigid seas of Iceland.*

encounter: 'At about 0.15a.m., we noticed a strange 'light' on the port bow… it was a very dark night, overcast, with no moon. We looked at this through binoculars and the ship's telescope, and made out what appeared to be the hull of a sailing ship, luminous, with no distinct masts carrying bare yards, also luminous; no sails were visible, but there was a luminous haze between the masts.

'There were no navigation lights, and she appeared to be coming close to us and at the same speed as ourselves.

'When first sighted, she was about two to three miles away, and when she was about a half-mile of us, she suddenly disappeared. There were four witnesses of this spectacle, myself, the second officer, a cadet, the helmsman and myself. I shall never forget the second officer's startled expressions – "My God, Stone, it's a ghost ship".'

Later, during World War Two, there were numerous sightings, and even Germany's Grand Admiral Karl Donitz

Above: King George was just one of many distinguished persons who have come across the haunted vessel.

HIS WIFE WATCHED HIM
CHANGE INTO A BROODING,
SILENT MONSTER. HE
WOULD LOOK AT HER WITH
THOSE EYES...

when they watched as an old sailing ship passed by them. All four of them later said that they viewed the ship for more than 15 minutes, until it vanished, leaving behind only a bright glow in its wake.

Since then, there has been at least one more sighting. In 1957, again off the coastline of South Africa, a group of people reported seeing an old vessel drifting eerily across the horizon, only to disappear without trace.

Of course, not every claimed sighting of the Dutchman can be taken at face value.

admitted 'that certain of my U-boat crews claimed they saw the Flying Dutchman or some other so-called phantom ship on their tours of duty east of Suez. When they returned to their base, the men said they preferred facing the combined strength of Allied warships in the North Atlantic to knowing the terror a second time of being confronted by a phantom vessel.' Even Hitler's 'supermen' were afraid of ghosts!

Incredibly, the Flying Dutchman has also been seen by people fortunate enough to be on dry land when the eerie apparition appeared. In 1939, more than 100 startled swimmers at South Africa's Glencairn Beach in False Bay, near the Cape of Good Hope, claimed to have seen the Dutchman at full sail gliding gently across the water, even though there was no discernible wind that day. The stunned bathers were mystified at the sight, but when it suddenly vanished, they were absolutely baffled.

Three years later, this time near Cape Town, a South African family was relaxing on the terrace of their ocean-front home

The oceans, particularly at night, can play tricks on tired eyes and nervous dispositions. But in the end, there are just too many credible sightings – many by respectable men like Prince George, other Royal Navy officers and German U-Boat commanders – to simply reject the story of the Flying Dutchman out of hand. The mystery, like the ghost ship itself, will most likely go on forever.

While the Flying Dutchman is the most notorious of all shipbound ghost stories, it is by no means the only one. Consider the case of the large American vessel, the St Paul, which was involved in two tragic accidents, including a disastrous collision with the British cruiser, HMS Gladiator. Even today, the story of the St Paul continues to mystify, and dozens of 'earthly explanations' have been dismissed.

It was Thursday, 25 April 1918. The Great War was still waging across Europe, and America, which by now had thrown its full military muscle into the all-out conflict against the Kaiser's Germany, was busy re-fitting its cruise line ships into troop trans-

> THE OCEANS, PARTICULARLY AT NIGHT, CAN PLAY TRICKS ON TIRED EYES AND NERVOUS DISPOSITIONS

Below: *Sightings have terrified crews for hundreds of years.*

port vessels. One such ship was the St Paul, a massive steamer which had once been the pride of the America Fleet. Early that morning, when the lengthy conversion work had been completed, the vessel set steam from its mooring at the Brooklyn docks for the short sail to Pier 61 on the Hudson River, on the west side of Manhattan. As the ship swung into the Hudson, Captain A.R. Mills noticed she was listing slightly to her port side.

AN UNEXPLAINED INCIDENT

He gave it little thought, however, assuming the crew was still filling the ballast tanks. When the ship approached the pier, two cables leading from the bow and the stern were thrown to the dock and secured. But as the St Paul's giant winches began to pull in the cables, the vessel began to list further. Suddenly and inexplicably, tons of water began to pour into her lower decks, forcing the boat onto her side, her towering masts scraping along the pier. Men began pouring over the sides, but fortunately, several tugs and a number of barges were

THE ST PAUL WAS FORCED ON HER SIDE, POSSIBLY TIPPED OVER BY THE WORK OF THE SINISTER GHOST OF A DEAD SAILOR

Below: The ghost ship has been blamed for several bizarre mishaps over the years, including shipwrecks.

close by, and rescued hundreds as they scrambled to safety. The incident could have been a major disaster if not for that stroke of good luck, and as a result, just four of the 400 men aboard were lost.

Initially, the investigation into the accident centred on German sabotage, but it was quickly ruled out. So, too, were dozens of other theories offered by everyone from old salts to the local newspapers. The real cause, however, was a shocker – when divers were sent into the river, they found that one of the ash ports close to the water line had not been closed! Every member of the crew was quizzed by the investigators, yet no-one was ever blamed for the error and to this day, the mystery of the open port has never been solved.

However, there was one other possibility – it might have been the sinister ghost of a dead sailor! To those who believe this to be the case, the timing of the disaster is the key. Because exactly ten years earlier – to the very day and to the very hour – the St Paul had been involved in a fatal collision with HMS Gladiator. Did a malevolent spirit chose that day, the tenth anniversary

of the collision, to strike back? The accident involving the British cruiser occurred off the still waters of Southampton, when the St Paul was still a passenger liner.

The fog was so heavy that the two ships remained invisible to each other until they were less than half a mile apart. Once it was realised that a disaster was about to strike, Captain Walter Lumsden ordered evasive action, as did the pilot of the St Paul. Tragically, there was a miscalculation. Captain Lumsden ordered his ship hard-a-starboard, which left the St Paul heading directly towards her. A few minutes later, the inevitable occurred, as the mighty steamer ripped into the cruiser's starboard side. Twenty-seven of her crew were lost. At the inquiry that followed, Captain Lumsden was severely reprimanded by an Admiralty court martial, even though many considered his actions to have been the correct ones given the circumstances that day.

As we said earlier, ten years later to the hour of the disaster, an unseen hand opened the ash port aboard the St Paul, sending her to the bottom of the Hudson River. Mere coincidence?

Above: *Even Hitler's 'supermen' were terrified of the Flying Dutchman.*

Right: *Rear Admiral Donitz, Nazi Germany's supreme sea lord, reported that his U-boat crews had seen the haunted vessel.*

TEN YEARS LATER, TO THE HOUR OF THE DISASTER, AN UNSEEN HAND OPENED THE ASH PORT OF THE ST PAUL

SPACE KIDNAPPING
Travels with Aliens

Many people claim to have spotted UFOs, but some have gone a step further and insist that they have been taken aboard space visitors' craft. Their tales of their subsequent adventures are always fascinating.

While controversy continues to rage about the existence of alien UFOs hovering over our air space, those who claim to have seen them are satisfied that their eyes did not deceive them. Some have even gone so far as to take lie-detector tests to prove their assertions against the flood of incredulity. Yet still there are many who doubt them, and over the years numerous witnesses to close encounters of the first kind, or sightings, have been ridiculed as crazy or lambasted as hoaxers.

But if those who claim to have 'merely' seen a UFO can be subjected to such scorn, what then of those who actually claim to have been abducted – a close encounter of the fourth kind – by an alien being? One can sympathise with their plight, because even the less sceptical, and indeed even some UFO believers themselves, have grave doubts about their stories of genuine kidnappings by extraterrestrials.

There have been numerous incidents in recent times of purported close encounters of the fourth kind, and several of them have withstood every effort to discredit their veracity. There is the 1975 case of Carlos Diaz, an Argentinian waiter, whose claim of being taken on board an alien craft for a physical examination could not be debunked even by a team of more than 40 doctors, psychiatrists and police officials. And Brazilian farmer, Antonio Boas, who made similar claims more than 15 years before Diaz's encounter, was actually found to be suffering from radiation poisoning, something that could rightly be considered a rare disorder for a farmer living and working in the remote hinterland of South America!

But the most astonishing example of actual alien contact is the one that we now refer to as the Whitfield Abduction. It is remarkable not only because of its very nature, but because one of the people who were taken, Betty Hill, later drew a map of a star system which the aliens had pointed out as their home on an astral chart. It was part of the universe that was not chartered by the best telescopes on Earth until several years later!

Betty Hill, a white social worker and her husband Barney, a black post office employee, were returning to their home in Portsmouth, New Hampshire, after a short vacation across the border in Canada.

Shortly before midnight, on 16 September 1971, as they approached the tiny hamlet of Whitfield along US Route 3, Betty saw what she thought was a very large and bright star. But when it continued getting bigger, they realised it was no natural heavenly body – especially when the bright ball of light began to move erratically across the dark sky.

Neither had an explanation for the strange glow and though puzzled, they decided not to stop and continued on their homeward journey.

Opposite: *Barney and Betty Hill had one of the strangest encounters ever with extraterrestrials. Even today, their story fascinates people all over the world.*

Below: *The face of one of the UFO occupants, as described by Barney Hill while under hypnosis.*

A short time later, however, they noticed that the mysterious light, which had grown much brighter and larger, seemed to be following them along the lonely road. As they later recalled, the object was 'jumping all over the sky and making right-angled turns'. By now their curiosity was aroused, and Barney pulled the car over to the side of the road for a better look at the eerie radiance. He reached for his binoculars, and got out of the car. What he saw next will live vividly in his memory for the rest of his life. Inside the rowed portholes of the craft, he spotted some 11 human-like beings! He could even make out their sinister, dark eyes and later recalled the aliens as being dressed in shiny black uniforms and visored caps. He also recalled that they moved with military precision. As Barney continued to watch the unworldly sight with a mixture of fear and awe, he repeatedly shouted: 'I don't believe it! I don't believe it! This is ridiculous!'

By now, the oval-shaped craft was less than 25 yards away from him, and Barney began to sense danger. He broke off his gaze, and raced back into the car, screaming to his terrified wife: 'They are going to capture us!' He started the engine, and sped off as fast as he could hoping to put as much distance as he could between him and his wife and the strange craft. But their mysterious encounter with beings from another world was just beginning.

The car began to shake and rattle, and the last thing Barney and Betty heard before falling into unconsciousness was a loud 'beeping' noise. It was almost two hours later before they came to. Inexplicably, they found themselves more than 35 miles away from where they thought they should have been. Although very upset and thoroughly bewildered by the bizarre experience, they managed to continue the journey and reach their home. 'All the way home, we were in a sort of post-hypnotic state, only we didn't know it at the time,' said Betty.

Because the incident was so fantastic and bordered on the realm of science fiction, the Hills decided they would not tell a soul about what had happened – something which is clearly not the strategy of a would-be hoaxer. 'If people find out,' said Barney, 'they're going to think we're crazy.' But even though they tried to put it out of their minds, for the next ten days both suffered inexplicable pains and sweated through bizarre nightmares. Although the physical pain would eventually subside, for the next two years they would be plagued with problems related to their nervous systems and experience horrifyingly real dreams.

FRIENDLY ALIENS

Barney began to suffer from anxiety, insomnia and a recurrent ulcer, while Betty became increasingly convinced that they had been taken aboard an extraterrestrial space craft. In her dreams, she saw eight to 11 men, dressed in matching uniforms and 'military caps', standing in the middle of the highway to stop their car. The 'leader', she said, would always assure them they would not be harmed.

Then, she and her husband would be led on board the glowing craft and medically examined. She recalled that the aliens would take samples of her hair, fingernails and skin. Afterwards, they would be allowed to leave the ship and continue their drive home to Portsmouth.

Eventually, the couple were unable to cope any longer with the horrible nightmares, and they decided to tell their tale to two scientists who were intrigued by their experience. They recommended that the Hills visit Dr Benjamin Simon, a prominent Boston psychiatrist who specialised in treating disorders and amnesia through hypnotherapy.

Beginning in January 1964, Dr. Simon subjected them to repeated sessions of hypnotherapy. During the course of the next six months, the Hills gradually began to remember every detail of their incredible experience. 'The doctor hypnotised us individually,' Betty recalled. 'This way we relived the whole experience.'

Convincingly, both told identical tales of that strange night, and their descriptions of the aliens were incredibly similar. After Dr

---

THE ALIENS HAD SINISTER, DARK EYES AND WERE DRESSED IN SHINY BLACK UNIFORMS AND BLACK, VISORED CAPS

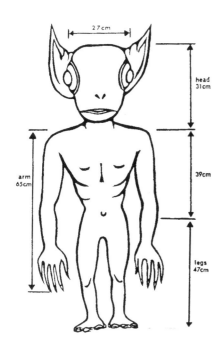

Above: Strange creatures like the one in this artist's impression, based on an actual case, have been spotted throughout the world.

Simon replayed the tapes from the sessions, Barney and Betty sat stunned as they learned the full extent of their nightmare. For some reason they had left the highway and driven up a side road. Their car had then somehow been forced to stop, and they were met by 'short grotesque' men who took them aboard the 'silver metal' craft. They described the extraterrestrials as being less than five feet tall, with triangular heads and grey skin. Their eyes were large, slanted, and their mouths were nothing but tiny slits. Somehow, their language was translated into English in the Hills' minds. They took their two 'guinea pigs' aboard the craft, where they were given a thorough physical examination, then released.

Betty recalled that the creatures' eyes were 'very dark black... they didn't have any ears'. During the examination, she was also placed on a table like one at a doctor's office, where the visitors performed a pregnancy test. When they had finished with her, the aliens moved into the room where Barney was being held. Under hypnosis, Barney remembered that he had also been examined physically and that a circular instrument was placed over his groin.

A SOUVENIR FOR HOME

However, Betty recalled that the 'leader' stayed behind with her when the others went to examine her husband. She said to him: 'When I get home, no one is going to believe me, so I need something to prove this actually happened.'

'What do you want?' the leader replied.

Betty then remembered that she saw a book, with rows of strange symbols on it, and told the alien she wanted that.

'Fine,' he replied. 'You may have it.'

Suddenly, their brief conversation was interrupted when the startled examiner rushed back into the room, holding Barney's false teeth. He looked baffled, and began tapping Betty's teeth. She explained that hers were real, but added that some humans eventually lose their teeth.

A short time later, an argument broke out among the aliens, and the leader returned to where Betty was lying and told her that she could not take the book with her as proof of her strange experience. 'It has been decided that you're going to forget the whole thing,' he said.

However, under Dr Simon's careful guidance, Betty recalled something else – something which continues to amaze and baffle UFO experts. When she asked the leader of the aliens where they were from, he pointed to a 'star map', which she later reproduced under hypnosis. The heavy line, he told her, represented places where they visited often, and the lighter one showed places where they went only occasionally. It wasn't until several years later, based on new astronomical data that was not available in 1961, that it was learned Betty had drawn an amazingly close map of a newly-discovered cluster of stars called Zeta Reticuli! How a social worker living in a small American city could know of its existence is beyond a worldly explanation.

Above: *Lumberjack Travis Walton claimed he was kidnapped by aliens and subjected to days of bizarre tests.*

SHORT, GROTESQUE MEN, WITH TRIANGULAR BEARDS AND GREY SKIN, TOOK THEM ABOARD THE SILVER METAL CRAFT

Above: *Walton remembers waking up and seeing three tiny aliens staring at him.*

Right: *Various descriptions of these alien visitors are remarkably similar.*

There have been dozens of other well-documented cases of alien abduction, and hypnosis has become the accepted technique for recovering the hours of missing time from when the UFO observer first saw the craft to their next clear memory. A majority of abductees have only a vague sense of their experience without hypnosis: they remember images of a strange, brightly-lit room; a feeling of being naked on a table; and have recurrent dreams of humanoid faces. But under hypnosis, which probes the subconscious, some UFO witnesses, like the Hills, have been able to recall the full story of their very close encounters.

TRAVIS WALTON

Such was the case of Travis Walton, a lumberjack working in an national forest outside Snowflake, Arizona. On 5 November 1975 he and six of his fellow tree-trimmers were returning to base after a day's work when they noticed an object hovering near the ground less than 30 yards away. Over the protests of his work mates, Walton got out of the lorry and walked towards the saucer-shaped craft, which began to emit a 'high-pitched, buzzing sound'. As he moved even closer, a blue and white beam suddenly shot out from the craft, knocking him to the ground. His terrified friends were so startled that they sped away in the lorry to find the nearest police station. Needless to say, the police officers were more than a little sceptical, and originally wondered whether or not Walton's friends might have done him in.

A massive search was organised, and although police and volunteers combed through every inch of the forest, they found no trace of Walton or even a clue to his possible fate. For five days, Walton had simply vanished, literally from the face of the Earth. Then, out of the blue, his sister received a telephone call from him. Later, under hypnosis, he recalled his incredible experience. After he was knocked out by the beam, he remembered coming to in a metallic 'hospital' room. When he looked around, he saw three tiny aliens standing there in the room with him.

He described them as having pale, white skin, bald heads and small eyes, noses and mouth. When they saw him regain consciousness, they left, and soon a being closely resembling a 'human' – a man, some six feet tall, with blond hair, wearing 'a clear, bubble-type helmet' – came into the room. The tall alien did not speak, but simply led the terrified wood-cutter down a hall into another room, where he eventually lost consciousness again.

'I know people won't believe me, that they'll call me a freak or a crackpot,' Walton said. 'But I was in their spaceship and I met those creatures. We all saw the saucer that night... when I woke up, I

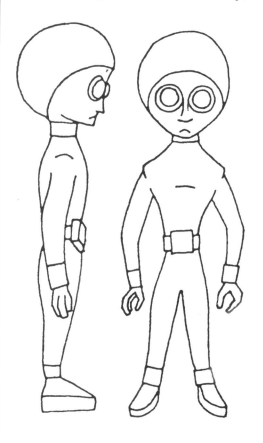

thought I was in a hospital. I was on a table on my back and as I focused I saw three figures. It was weird. They weren't humans. They looked like foetuses to me, about five feet tall, and they all wore tight-fitting, tan brown robes. Their skin was white like a mushroom, but they had no clear features. I guess I panicked. I picked up a transparent tube and tried to smash it for use as a weapon, but it wouldn't break. I was petrified. They just scampered away. Then another man suddenly appeared a few feet from me. He seemed human, but he just smiled at me through a kind of helmet, like a fish bowl.

'He led me through a corridor into another big, bright room, where there was a high-backed chair in the centre of the

room. There was a lever on one arm and buttons on the other. The man left as suddenly as he arrived, and I began to play with the buttons. I pushed the lever. The scene outside suddenly changed. I felt we were moving. I knew we were in a spaceship. Then things went black again. When I woke I was shaky. I was on the highway. It was black but all the trees were lit up because just a few feet away was the flying saucer. I saw no-one, and was still wearing my work clothes. I just ran. I recognised I was in a place a few miles from my home in Heber, and called my sister.'

Walton thought he had been inside the craft for a matter of only hours, and was startled to learn that he had been missing for five days. Throughout the years since, many people have tried to explain Walton's experience as some sort of fantasy. Yet through it all, he has remained adamant that he was abducted.

HICKON AND PARKER

Then there is the case of two shipyard workers, Charles Hickon and Calvin Parker. On the evening of 11 October, 1973, in Pascagoula, Mississippi, the two friends were doing some night fishing on the local river. Out of the chilly, quiet blackness came a strange sound, followed quickly by the appearance of a bright, seven-yard-long object which hovered menacingly above them. Three creatures, no more than five feet high, emerged from the craft and literally floated across the water towards the two terrified fishermen. Both men would later recall that the aliens were grey in colour and that their skin was wrinkled like an old person's. Their hands, they said, were claw-like, with only two fingers on each, and their eyes were mere slits.

Parker was so overcome by their ghastly appearance that he fainted on the spot. But Hickson, who remained conscious, remembers that he was somehow 'floated' into the craft, while one of the creatures carried his unconscious mate. Like others who have had similar experiences of alien abduction, the two men found later themselves in a

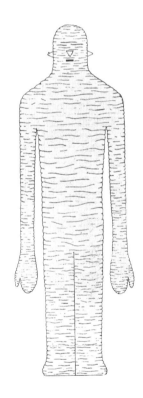

Above and Above Left:
Charles Hickson recalled that the aliens he saw were grey and that their skin was wrinkled.

Top: *Hickson (left) and Calvin Parker recall their amazing encounter with extraterrestrials.*

very brightly-lit room where they were examined by what Hickson later described as an 'eyelike' device. During the examination, Hickson said he was totally numb, and that he literally could not even lift a finger. Once they had been examined, he and Parker were then 'floated' back out of the craft, and laid to rest on the riverbank. The beings then went back to their craft, and disappeared into the night sky.

WHITLEY STRIEBER

Finally, consider the case of Whitley Strieber, the renowned American author of

books such as *The Hunger* and *The Wolfen*, who, under hypnosis recalled in vivid detail the eerie events of October 1985, at his home in upstate New York. He had seen a huge light pass by his bedroom window, then remembered seeing 'a dark shape, about three foot tall' standing in the corner of his bedroom.

'It's like a little man with a hood on or something,' he recalled under hypnosis. 'He looks mean. Got big eyes. Big slanted eyes. And comes over to my bed and he starts like sticking something in – not into my head, you understand, but like it was sticking into my mind. It was terrible!' Later, Strieber recalled seeing several more of the creatures, who then 'carried' him outside into the woods.

'I just shot right up out of the woods. In this chair, this thing. I must have gone up about a hundred feet. Up past the trees, just like that. (Then) I'm sitting on a bench in a

ONCE THEY HAD BEEN EXAMINED, THEY WERE 'FLOATED' BACK OUT OF THE CRAFT AND LAID TO REST ON THE RIVERBANK

HE SAW A HUGE LIGHT PASS BY HIS BEDROOM WINDOW, THEN THERE WAS A DARK SHAPE STANDING IN THE CORNER OF THE ROOM

Left: *Famed author Whitley Strieber has joined the growing number of Americans who claim to have been abducted by UFOs.*

'SHE LOOKS LIKE A LITTLE PERSON MADE OUT OF LEATHER. SHE'S GOT A BIG HEAD AND HER EYES HAVE BULGES

little room. And it smells funny. There is somebody talking to me. She's wearing a tan suit. She looks like a little person made out of leather. She's got a big head and her eyes have bulges. And when she opens her mouth her lips are all – she hasn't got lips exactly – but it flops down. Her lips are floppy. You know, the truth is, I don't know what that is. I don't know whether it's a bug or what. And I also don't know if it's a woman or not.'

BIZARRE TESTS

The creatures then conducted some bizarre tests on the author, and the next thing he knows he is back in his living room. 'I had no memory of where I had just come from.' After Strieber wrote his account of the experience in his best-seller, *Communion*, hundreds of people began to come forward claiming similar experiences. It was as if his book had opened the floodgates for people who had previously been too afraid to reveal their experiences.

Whatever happened to Whitley Strieber, the Hills and literally thousands of other ordinary people cannot be explained away by snorts or laughter. Something did happen to these people. Their belief, that aliens are indeed among us, may well be the truth.

Today, many psychologists believe that something truly bizarre did happen to these people. One researcher, Dr John Mack, from the prestigious Harvard Medical School, has been treating, for many years, patients who claim to have been abducted by aliens. He says that he knows of cases involving everyone from a top administrator at a U.S. naval base to businessmen and housewives. Indeed, the problem is so widespread in the U.S. that victims have formed self-help groups in five cities.

Dr Mack admitted that when he first began counselling abductees, he thought they were mentally unbalanced. Their bizarre tales of bug-eyed aliens were just too much for science to treat seriously. But now, even he agrees that not one of his dozens of patients is mentally ill. A colleague, John Bowman, from the New York State University, said that he has come to a similar conclusion. 'I'm not a fanatic who says I know exactly what happened to these people,' he said, 'but I can tell you this: they are not wackos.'

History professor David Jacobs, who is considered an authority on the subject and recently completed a book on alien abductions, said a vast majority of the victims – despite their dissimilar backgrounds – give almost identical descriptions of their abductors and what occurred to them while under alien control. Interestingly, he notes, many of the male victims give a similar description of a very complex instrument which the aliens use to obtain sperm samples. Yet before his book was published, early in 1993, the device had not been described publicly. 'There's no way every abductee could be making this all up,' he said.

Many researchers into the field also note that some victims are left with identical scars after their experience, including puncture marks which they recall under hypnosis were caused when the aliens' took blood samples. And Dr Mack reports that one man even found seven fresh scars on his upper arm where he said aliens had conducted a series of tests. Incredibly, the man was a quadriplegic, and could not possibly have inflicted the wounds on himself.

'In my 40 years of psychiatry, I have never encountered anything like this abduction phenomenon,' said Mack. 'I don't know how to explain it, except that it is a real event of some kind. God knows what it is.'

Budd Hopkins, a renowned US investigator who has spent years delving into UFO sightings and alien abductions, says he gets more than 20 letters a week from people claiming to be victims. The abductees are taken from a wide gamut of locales, he said, including one woman, who wrote she had been snatched from the 12th floor of her Manhattan skyscraper!

Despite his mass of files and testimony, however, even Hopkins concedes that he has no concrete proof of alien kidnappings. 'The aliens are not going to give us a smoking gun,' he said. Yet even without that solid evidence, Hopkins says the case for abductions is beyond doubt. He asks –

Below: UFO investigator Budd Hopkins (below and below right) remains adamant that abductions cannot be explained away as the product of imagination.

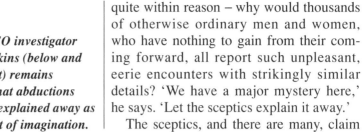

quite within reason – why would thousands of otherwise ordinary men and women, who have nothing to gain from their coming forward, all report such unpleasant, eerie encounters with strikingly similar details? 'We have a major mystery here,' he says. 'Let the sceptics explain it away.'

The sceptics, and there are many, claim 'victims' have been led on by hypnotists to recall alien kidnappings. Yet researchers, like Professor Jacobs, maintain that they are very careful not to influence their patients in any way, and point out that many abductees cannot be led under hypnosis, anyway. As evidence, they point to the case of Barney and Betty Hill. During their sessions with Dr Simon, he spent hours trying to convince them that the abduction did not occur. Yet whether under a hypnotic trance or not, the Hills continued to insist that it had.

It is likely that the mystery of these so-called encounters of the fourth kind will one day be finally solved. No one can say when that day might come. But one thing is certain – between now and then, hundreds, even thousands of ordinary men and women will have experiences similar to those outlined above.

ABRAHAM LINCOLN
Ghost of a President

The ghostly shape of Abraham Lincoln, America's 16th and most acclaimed president, is said to still walk the corridors of power inside the White House to this very day! The assassinated Lincoln is a particularly distinguished ghost

While the settings for many hauntings often involve gloomy buildings, fog-shrouded nights and isolated surroundings, there are some ghosts that would seem to prefer a more crowded, more open environment.

Indeed, everyone from Winston Churchill to presidents and visiting heads of state have claimed to have seen the ghost of 'Honest Abe' at 1600 Pennsylvania Avenue. Former President Ronald Reagan's eldest daughter, Maureen, recalled just a few years ago that she, too, had seen it. 'I'm not kidding,' says Maureen. 'We've really seen it.' She and her husband, Dennis Revell, often slept in Lincoln's bedroom when they visited her parents in Washington, and claim to have seen the apparition, which sometimes glows a bright red, sometimes orange. Maureen and her husband claim that it is Lincoln's ghost. 'When I told my parents what I saw, they looked at me a little weirdly,' she admitted.

Eleanor Roosevelt, the wife of President Roosevelt, often thought she could feel Lincoln's presence when she was up late at night, writing in her diary. And President Harry Truman, who served from 1945 to 1952, also claimed to have heard Lincoln's ghost walking through the building.

The most detailed sighting, however, came from Dutch Queen Wilhelmina, who stayed as a guest at the Roosevelt White House. One night, after hearing footsteps outside her bedroom, she opened the door and, to her amazement, there stood Lincoln, complete with his trademark top hat. Queen Wilhelmina was so overcome by the sight, that she fainted to the floor with a heavy thud! With the exception of Maureen Reagan, there have been few sightings in recent years, though Nancy Reagan recalled that Rex, the family dog, would often sit outside the haunted bedroom and bark at the door for no apparent reason – and the pooch steadfastly refused ever to set paw in it.

In real life, Abraham Lincoln was a dedicated follower of the paranormal for much of his adult life, attending numerous seances and several times he had chilling premonitions and nightmares of his own assassination. His wife, Mary Todd, whom he married in 1842, was also a firm believer in seances, and that same year Lincoln wrote to a friend explaining that 'I have always had a strong tendency to mysticism,' and often felt that he was controlled 'by some other power than my own will.' However, it wasn't until the death of his favourite son, Willie, several years later, that he became a devotee of seances. He tried on many occasions to contact his dear departed son, but he never succeeded.

When he became President in 1860, he was often a guest at seances, and one medium, Cora Maynard, a friend of his wife, even claimed that she was responsible for Lincoln's landmark emancipation procla-

ABRAHAM LINCOLN WAS A DEDICATED FOLLOWER OF THE PARANORMAL. HE ATTENDED NUMEROUS SEANCES

Opposite: *Abraham Lincoln's ghost is said to still haunt the White House.*

Below: *Visitors to the White House, including Winston Churchill, have claimed to have seen Lincoln's ghost.*

Above: *An artist's impression of President Abraham Lincoln's murder.*

mation of 1 January 1863, which ordered the release of every slave in the United States! Mrs Maynard maintained that Lincoln issued the order after spirits told him to do so. While American historians doubt that a man of Lincoln's convictions would have issued so important an order simply to placate the spirit world, some agree that it might have bolstered his long-held belief that slavery was morally wrong.

It was a belief that would eventually cost him his life. On 14 April 1865, just three months into his second term of office and just five days after the southern Confederate forces surrendered to end the bloody Civil War, Lincoln attended the opening of a new play, *My American Cousin*, at the Ford Theatre in Washington, DC, with his wife and several dignitaries. Shortly after the curtain went up, a disgruntled Southerner, John Wilkes Booth, calmly walked into the presidential box and shot Lincoln in the head. He died the next morning.

Yet incredibly, Lincoln had had numerous 'forewarnings' of his own death, and on the very day he was shot, he had remarked to his chief bodyguard that he had been having nightmares about his murder. His first premonition, however, came just prior to his election in 1860, when he saw a strange image of himself in a mirror. Next to his reflection was another image of himself, deathly pale in colour. When he tried to stare at it, it vanished. This was to happen several times during the course of his time in the White House, and wife Mary concluded that it meant he would serve two terms, but not survive the second!

Then, in the days leading up to his ill-fated trip to the Ford theatre – which he had only attended because Mary had wanted to – he had a series of macabre, disturbing dreams. In his diary, he wrote about one of those vivid nightmares:

A DREAM OF DEATH

'I retired late. I soon began to dream. There seemed to be a death-like stillness about me. Then I heard subdued sobs, as if a number of people were weeping. I thought I had left my bed and wandered downstairs. There the silence was broken by the same pitiful sobbing, but the mourners were invisible. I went from room to room; no living person was in sight, but the same mournful sounds of distress met me as I passed. It was light in all the rooms; every object was familiar to me; but where were all the people who were grieving as if their hearts would break?

'I was puzzled and alarmed. What could be the meaning of all this? Determined to find the cause of a state of things so mysterious and so shocking, I kept on until I arrived at the East Room, which I entered. Before me was a catafalque, on which rested a corpse wrapped in funeral vestments. Around it were stationed soldiers who were acting as guards; and there was a throng of people, some gazing mournfully upon the corpse, whose face was covered, others weeping pitifully.

'"Who is dead in the White House?"' I demanded of one of the soldiers. "The President," was his answer. "He was killed by an assassin." Then came a loud burst of grief from the crowd, which awoke me from my dream. I slept no more that night; and although it was only a dream, I have been strangely annoyed by it ever since.'

On the very day prior to his death, Lincoln even confided to one of his Cabinet members that he had had premonitions of the murder, and told his head body-guard, W.H. Cook, that he had dreamed of his assassination for three straight nights. The startled guard begged the much loved President not to attend the opening, but Lincoln simply sighed and said he had promised Mary they would go. He never came out alive.

Following the state funeral service in Washington, Lincoln's body was transported by train to his home state of Illinois. But more than 100 years later, there are still some people who claim to have seen a phantom train, draped in black bunting, slowly wending its way along the same route to Illinois. Many years ago, an account of this sad phenomenon was recorded in an article carried in the *Evening Times*, a newspaper in Albany, New York.

'Regularly in the month of April, about midnight, the air on the tracks becomes very keen and cutting. On either side of the tracks, it is warm and still. Every watchman, when he feels the air, slips off the track and sits down to watch. Soon the pilot engine of Lincoln's funeral train passes along with long, black streamers and with a band of black instruments playing dirges, grinning skeletons all about.

'It passes noiselessly. If it is moonlight, clouds come over the moon as the phantom train goes by. After the pilot engine passes, the funeral train itself with flags and streamers rushes past. The track seems covered with black carpet, and the coffin is seen in the centre of the car, while all about it in the air and on the train behind are vast numbers of blue-coated men, some with coffins on their backs, others leaning upon them.

STRANGE OCCURRENCES

'If a real train were passing, its noise would be hushed as if the phantom train rode over it. Clocks and watches always stop as the phantom train goes by and when looked at are five to eight minutes behind. Everywhere on the road about 27 April watches and clocks are suddenly found to be behind.'

It is also interesting to note that some months after the president was assassinated by Booth, his wife posed for a photographer – when the plate was developed, there was a foggy resemblance of Lincoln standing right there next to Mary.

For almost 60 years after Lincoln died, there were no known reports of his ghost inside the White House. But when Calvin Coolidge became the 29th President in 1923, following the death of Warren Harding, the ghost made its first known appearance. Coolidge's wife, Grace, recalled seeing Lincoln's shadow standing at the window inside the Oval Office, which is the presidential seat of power. It was only visible for a few seconds, and seemed to be looking forlornly towards the Potomac River, which wends its way into the distance. Incredibly, during Lincoln's term of office, he had once stood at that very same window, and was described by Army chaplain E.C. Bolles as looking thoroughly despondent. 'I think I never saw so sad a face in my life, and I have looked into many a mourner's face,' Bolles later recorded in his journal.

Following Grace Coolidge's experience, many other powerful and important people also claimed to have seen or heard the spectre of President Lincoln. But there have been no reported incidents since Maureen Reagan's encounter in the late

Above: *Lincoln's wife, Mary Todd, shared his interest in the paranormal.*

Below: *Lincoln's ghost continues to wander the corridors of power.*

1980s. That is not to say, however, that Lincoln has finally given up the ghost on the White House! Maybe we will have to wait until Bill and Hillary Clinton leave office to know if they, too, heard or saw anything of Honest Abe.

HAMPTON COURT

Like President Lincoln, some other ghosts also prefer a more crowded environment than the traditional haunt. Such is the case with the spirits of Hampton Court, in Middlesex, which has been home to a series of unexplained events for centuries. Various ghosts have been sighted within its surrounds, including the puzzling case of the fair-haired boy. Before World War Two, the Old Court House, which was home to Sir Christopher Wren while he supervised renovations to the palace, was owned by a man called Norman Lamplugh. On a lovely summer's day, as guests mingled on the lawn, Norman's brother Ernest and another man, who were looking out across the gardens from a staircase, suddenly spotted a young boy aged about eight walking across the lawn. They looked at each other quizzically, for not only had Norman not invited any children to the garden party, but the

fair-haired lad was clad in a page boy suit from the time of King Charles II, who died in 1685! His costume was authentic right down to the big silver buckles on his shoes!

The mysterious youngster then entered the house, and walked up the stairs right past the two startled guests. He said nothing, and seemed to not even notice them. He then walked down the hall, entering a room which had only one entrance, the one leading off the hall. The two men quickly followed the young guest into the room, but could find no trace of him!

But there are said to be ghosts at Hampton Court which predate even a 17th century page boy. During the reign of Henry VIII, the king's third wife, Jane Seymour, gave birth to a son, in October 1537, at Hampton. Tragically, the baby died just seven days later. For hundreds of years ever since, people have reported seeing Queen Jane's ghost, clad all in white, gliding through the Court, her way lit by a taper, on the anniversary of the child's death. Many have seen her presence come from a doorway in the Queen's Old Apartments, then wander silently down the stairway where she disappears into a gallery. Two servants who saw the apparition described her as 'a tall lady, with a long train and shining face'.

Then there was the case of the two Cavaliers who haunted Fountain Court.

SOME GHOSTS PREFER A MORE CROWDED ENVIRONMENT TO THE TRADITIONAL SOLITARY HAUNT

Right: *Sir Christopher Wren, who renovated the ghostly Hampton Court.*

Below: *The palace has been home to ghosts for more than 400 years.*

They were seen earlier this century by Lady Hildyard, who complained about their appearance and the strange noises she heard from her apartment which overlooked the Court. A short time later, a work crew was sent down to install new drains in the Court, and workers discovered the remains of two Cavaliers, buried just a few feet below the pavement. They were disinterred and given a proper burial, and that was the last anyone ever heard from them.

Not so the so-called White Lady of Hampton Court who was spotted by fishermen as recently as the 1960s. There are also said to be ghosts of the headless Archbishop Laud, who has been spotted walking quietly inside the hallowed halls of the Court, and Mrs Sybil Penn, who was the nurse of Edward VI. Mrs Penn, a kindly soul who tended like a mother to the sickly young prince, retired to an apartment inside Hampton Court after her service was done. She caught smallpox, and died in November 1568. She was buried at St Mary's Church, close to the Court, and remained there at rest for more than 250 years, until the church was struck by lightening and destroyed in 1829. Her tomb was taken to the site of the new church, but tragically her grave was vandalised and her remains scattered.

A short while later, her ghost was seen back at the apartment she had once lived in. At that time, a family was living there and they often heard the sound of a woman's voice and a spinning wheel. After making complaints, a team of workmen were brought in to check out the noises. They found a secret chamber leading off one of the rooms in the apartment – and inside, they found a spinning wheel, which was thought to be one used by Mrs Penn some 300 years earlier! After the chamber was discovered, the ghost of Mrs Penn was itself seen for the first time. A guard on duty outside her apartment looked up one day to see a woman, dressed in a long robe and hood, coming from inside the rooms. The ghostly figure then vanished. He later

*Below: **Jane Seymour's ghost mourns the death of her infant son every October.***

THE GHOST OF KATHERINE HOWARD APPEARS EVERY 11 NOVEMBER, RUNNING AND SCREAMING THROUGH THE HAUNTED GALLERY

claimed that the woman bore a striking resemblance to the stone replica of Mrs Penn. Princess Frederica, of Hanover, who had heard nothing about the ghost, also claimed to have seen Mrs Penn, this time in a long grey robe with a hood over her head. Since then, her ghost has been known as the Lady in Grey.

In the years since, many others have had brushes with the Royal nurse. Servants have been woken in the dead of night by an icy hand touching their heads; they've heard footsteps and crashing sounds with no earthly explanation. Once, servants claimed they entered the vacant apartment and found it awash in 'a ghastly, lurid light'.

But of all the ghosts said to inhabit Hampton Court, none has achieved the notoriety of the one believed to be the spirit of Lady Katherine Howard, Henry VIII's fifth wife, who was 19 when the King was first captivated by her charms. Lady Katherine was a tiny, waif-like girl, but no stranger to romance. She had had numerous suitors before she married Henry in July 1540, and continued her affairs even after she became his wife and Queen. Indeed, her love life was so hectic that enemies later chided her for living 'an abominable, base, carnal voluptuous and vicious life,' and branded her 'a harlot'.

She was eventually arrested on 12 November 1541, for her wayward lifestyle, but on the very night before she was taken away to the dreaded Tower of London for eventual execution by beheading, she begged Henry to spare her life. Her pleas fell on deaf ears, and Henry even watched in stony silence as she was dragged away by his sentries to meet her horrible fate. Over the centuries, her ghost is said to every appear 11 November running and screaming through what is today known as the Haunted Gallery. Numerous people have seen the ghastly apparition, and all describe it as a woman with long, flowing locks.

In the mid-1800s, the Haunted Gallery was closed and its space used for storing

AN ARTIST WAS STUNNED
TO SEE A DISEMBODIED
HAND APPEAR RIGHT IN
FRONT OF AN
OLD TAPESTRY

Right: *King Henry VIII…
several of his wives and
servants are said to still call
Hampton Court home!*

Below: *A 19th century
sketch of Mistress Penn, the
nurse of Edward VI, who is
known as the Lady in Grey.*

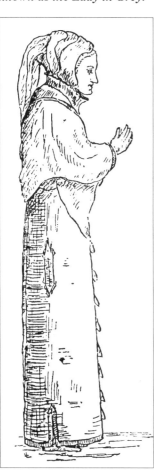

pictures. But a lady living in an apartment next door claimed that one night she was awoken from a sound sleep by a hideous scream which seemed to be coming from inside the Gallery. A short time later, a friend staying with her also heard the blood-curdling shriek.

But probably the most eerie story concerning Queen Katherine came after the Haunted Gallery was eventually re-opened. An artist, who was doing a sketch of an old tapestry hanging on the wall, was stunned to see a disembodied hand appear right in front of it. The quick-thinking artist drew the free-floating hand, and the ring which it wore. Incredibly, the ring was later identified as one often worn by Katherine.

Yet another of Henry's wives, Anne Boleyn, is said to haunt Hampton Court. She was spotted about 100 years ago by a servant, who recognised her from her portrait. She was dressed completely in blue, and vanished within seconds. Her ghost has been spotted at several other sites around England, including the Tower, Hever Castle, Rochford Hall and Salle Church.

There have been other reports of hauntings at Hampton Court, though none of the ghosts could be identified. During World War Two, a policeman on duty saw 11 people on the palace grounds simply vanish into thin air, while stage actor Leslie Finch, who had just completed a play at the site, saw a Tudor-clad figure that vanished, leaving behind only a sudden iciness in the air. Similarly in 1966, a member of the audience viewing a light and sound display saw the ghost of Cardinal Thomas Wolsey, who gave the palace to Henry VIII, standing under one of the archways.

VERSAILLES

Although not as overrun by ghosts as Hampton Court, the great palace of Versailles, just outside Paris, has some of the most intriguing tales of haunting ever recorded. In fact, this monument to the grandeur of pre-Revolutionary France was the site of a major investigation into psychic phenomena. Since 1870, there had been reports of 100-year-old apparitions not only of people, but also of buildings (!) within the Petit Trianon at Versailles, but it wasn't until 1902 that a painstaking analysis of the sightings was finally undertaken.

In 1762, Louis XV ordered the Petit Trianon built for his mistress, the beautiful Marquise de Pompadour, but she never lived to see its completion. However, when the house was finally finished in 1770, the King had by then taken another mistress, Madame Dubarry, who lived inside the estate occasionally. A carriageway led from the house to the King's farm at Versailles, called the Allée de la Managerie. Over the next few years, further work was carried out on the site. In 1773 a chapel was added, but its construction meant the carriageway had to be closed, and some of it was wiped out. Following Louis's death in 1774, the Petit Trianon was given to Marie Antoinette by the new king, Louis XVI, and she used it until the bloody Revolution ended the royal reign of the Bourbons for the next 25 years.

Our story really begins on 10 August, 1901, when Eleanor Jourdain and Annie Moberly, both British scholars and the daughters of respected clergymen, were visiting the Palace of Versailles during a holiday stay in France. Although both were well-educated, neither had any particular knowledge of the royal compound which could account for the stunning developments to come.

After wandering through the Grand Trianon where the Age of Kings has been

resplendently captured in time, the two friends began walking towards the Petit Trianon. Given the vast size of Versailles, it is not surprising to learn that the two women soon found that they had become completely lost. However, they eventually came to the garden, which they entered. Moberly would later recall that when they did so, she felt 'an extraordinary depression'. Jourdain, too, was somehow aware of a strange feeling inside the garden, and both ladies felt a little ill at ease.

STRANGE FIGURES

Oddly, they later recounted, there had been a strong breeze blowing that day, and yet when they arrived at the Petit Trianon, the air had turned deathly still. Not a leaf moved. As they walked onwards, they suddenly noticed two strange-looking men. The women believed them to be gardeners, although they thought it a little odd that both men were dressed in 18th century costumes, with greenish coats and tricorn hats. Later, Moberly recalled that 'I began to feel as if I were walking in my sleep; the heavy dreaminess was oppressive.'

Undaunted, the British holidaymakers asked the men for directions, and were told to continue their trek straight ahead. As

they did, they saw a bridge and a kiosk. Sitting near the kiosk, they observed a curious looking man in a slouch-hat and coat. Both women felt a little put off by his appearance. Suddenly, they heard footsteps behind them. They turned and a man with 'a curious smile' and strange accent gave them more directions. They believed him to be one of the gardeners they had just met. He vanished as suddenly as he had appeared.

As they neared the house, Moberly saw yet another figure, this time a woman, who was sitting on a small seat on the grass. She, too, was dressed in authentic period costume. A few seconds later, they watched as a young man, also smiling strangely, walked from the house using a solid door – a door they would later discover had been broken and left in ruins for many years. They also noticed the carriageway, which had been obliterated more than 130 years earlier!

The bizarre experience lasted for some 30 minutes, and afterwards both women concurred that the Petit Trianon had to be haunted. For the next ten years, these two well-educated ladies returned several times to the site in the hope that they could finally solve the mystery that had so disturbed them. Jourdain made a second visit a year later, and once more she felt the same oppressive atmosphere that seemed to

A MAN WITH A CURIOUS SMILE AND A STRANGE ACCENT VANISHED AS SOON AS HE HAD APPEARED

A YOUNG MAN, SMILING STRANGELY, USED A SOLID DOOR – A DOOR THAT HAD BEEN BROKEN AND IN RUINS FOR MANY YEARS hover over the area. As she crossed the small bridge that led to the former house of Marie Antoinette, she came across two workmen who wore the costumes of 18th century French labourers, right up to their pointed hoods. She also remembered hearing the sound of distant music. However, she was no closer to solving the mystery.

Moberly joined her for yet another visit, this time on 4 July 1904. Oddly, they could no longer find the paths they had earlier taken, and there was no sign of the kiosk or the bridge! Both had literally vanished into thin air. Moreover, the spot where they had seen the woman sitting was now occupied by an old bush, which had been obviously growing there for many, many years.

A CAPTIVATING RIDDLE

The two women were by now completely enthralled by the riddle of the Petit Trianon, and for the next six years, they researched its entire history, firmly believing they had somehow 'seen' the site as it had appeared in the late 1700s. Upon completing their research, they wrote a book, *An Adventure*, in which they came to deduce that the woman they had seen sitting on the grass had in fact been Marie Antoinette herself! They came to this conclusion when they discovered that that particular spot had been a favourite of hers.

They also identified the two gardeners as the Bersey brothers, who had been employed to work on the estate by the Queen. Despite their years of research, however, the women were treated with scorn and derision upon the release of their book. However, the book was a popular success, and it prompted other holiday makers to come forward with similar bizarre tales of Versailles.

One such visitor was Englishman John Crooke who had taken his wife and young son to Versailles in the summer of 1908. However, their ghostly encounter came in the Grand Trianon, where they saw a woman sketching on some paper. She wore a long, cream skirt and a white hat. Crooke recalled that she paid no attention to them until he tried to get a peek at what she was drawing so intently. She grabbed her sketch so he couldn't see it, and then shot him an angry look. Suddenly, she disappeared. A short time later, the Crooke family saw two

Above: *Marie Antoinette, whose ghost was spotted at Versailles.*

THEY COULD NO LONGER FIND THE PATHS THEY HAD TAKEN, AND ALL THE OTHER LANDMARKS HAD DISAPPEARED

more strangely-dressed people, who similarly vanished into thin air.

There were many other sightings to come over the years, some as recently as 1955. In 1928, two women, Clare Burrow and Ann Lambert, both English, went on a trip to Versailles. Neither had read the book written by Moberly and Jourdain, and yet they reportedly had a similar adventure. As they walked towards the Petit Trianon, Burrow, like Moberly 27 years earlier, suddenly felt an eerie languor. As they got closer, they saw an elderly, sinister-looking man, dressed in an 18th century uniform. Despite his appearance, they asked him for directions, but ran off when he began shouting at them in guttural French. When they looked back at him, he had vanished. Throughout the course of the afternoon, they saw several other people all dressed in period clothes.

Ten years later, Elizabeth Hatton was strolling alone through the same grounds when from out of nowhere a man and woman, dressed like peasants, walked past her, pulling a wooden cart. When she turned to watch them, they slowly vanished before her very eyes. Many others have had similar experiences with vanishing people. In October 1949, Jack Wilkinson, his wife Clara, and their young son were touring the Grand Trianon. They noticed a woman, in 18th century attire, holding an umbrella on the steps of the Grand Trianon. A few seconds later, she was gone.

One of the last recorded sightings came in May 1955, when a British lawyer and his wife walked towards the Petit Trianon. Like others before her, the woman felt a sudden depression, and then she and her husband spotted two men and a woman. Each was clad in the clothing suitable for French aristocracy before the Revolution. The men wore knee-length coats, black breeches, black shoes with silver buckles and black hats. The woman looked dazzling in a long yellow dress. Like other apparitions seen over the decades, they vanished into thin air without a trace to mark their appearance.

Sightings like these prompted much speculation about the existence of ghosts and other phenomena at Versailles. Many were sceptical, espousing the belief that all the startled visitors had simply seen people

A MAN AND A WOMAN WALKED PAST ELIZABETH, BUT WHEN SHE TURNED TO WATCH THEM, THEY SLOWLY VANISHED

THE APPARITIONS SEEN OVER THE DECADES VANISHED INTO THIN AIR WITHOUT A TRACE TO MARK THEIR APPEARANCE

Below: *English tourists Eleanor Jourdain and Annie Moberly wrote of their 'time travel' experiences at Versailles.*

clad in the often-unfamiliar costumes of their native lands! Later, French writer Philippe Jullian would also claim that there was nothing sinister at all about the sightings. He said the poet Robert de Montesquiou, and his friends would often dress up in period costume when they visited the Petit Trianon around the turn of the century. Yet Jullian's theory does not explain why there were sightings well into the second half of this century, or how Montesquiou and his party could simply vanish without a trace.

Famed psychic researcher G.W. Lambert, who later wrote a book on the Versailles hauntings, believed in their validity. Using historical data available on Versailles, he concluded that the two gardeners first seen by Moberly and Jourdain were not brothers, but a father and son, Claude Richard and Antoine. However, he felt that the two English women had somehow seen Versailles as it would have appeared in 1770, and therefore the woman they saw sitting on the grass could not have been Marie Antoinette. Of course, the actual date is of little significance. After all, seeing something literally from out of the past is still incredibly bizarre, whether it dates back to 1770 or post-1774 when Marie Antoinette first came to the Petit Trianon.

In the final analysis, the hauntings of Versailles must be considered a puzzling mystery to this day.

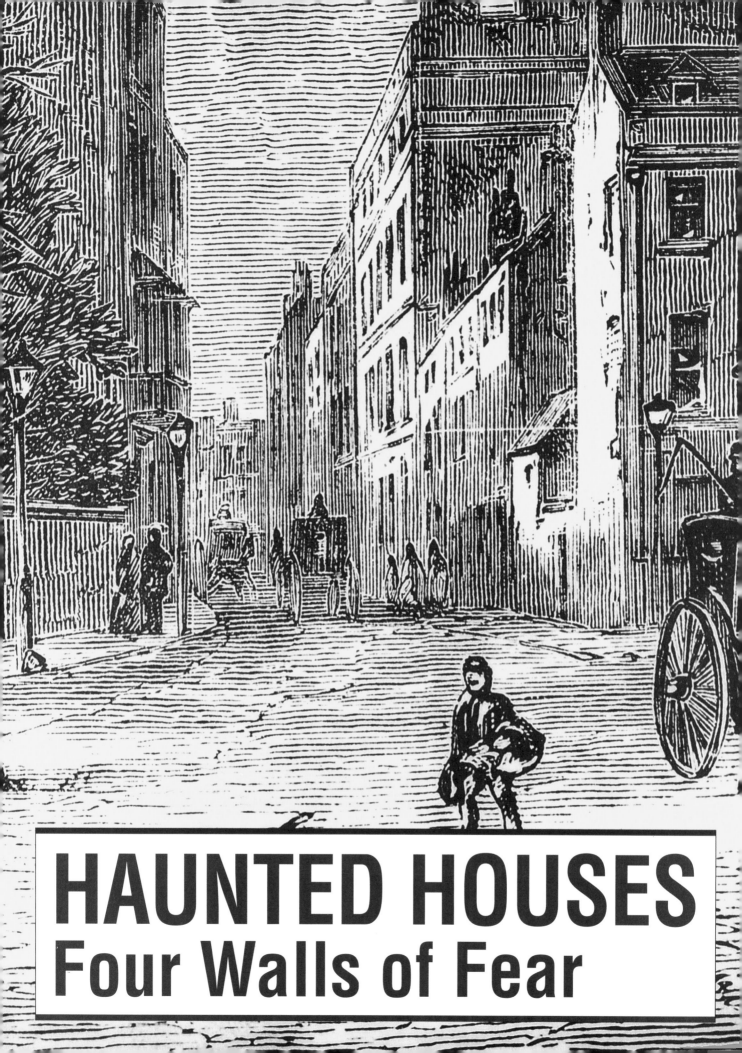

HAUNTED HOUSES
Four Walls of Fear

Few ghost stories are more terrifying or bone-chilling than those of spooky addresses… because a ghost in the house can strike anyone at anytime. Even now, some of the most notorious haunted houses in history remain legendary

Today, the site at 50 Berkeley Square is not unlike other buildings in that fashionable area of inner London. Now a bookstore, with its stately elegance intact, it was once a grand old home, and even the residence of short-term Prime Minister George Canning, who owned it until his death in 1827. But 100 years ago,

young children would cross the street to avoid it. Women, and even men, would walk quickly past it, lest some unseen force somehow reach out onto the street and grab them. All over the capital, people feared and loathed the site as a place of evil and malevolence.

Fifty Berkeley Square, you see, was said to be haunted! And not just by some ghostly apparition that occasionally moaned or rattled the pots and pans, but by a real evil – a murderous malevolence so ghastly that as many as four people were said to have been literally scared to death by the very sight of it, while others were driven to total insanity, unable to ever fully explain what had so terrified them.

The story of 50 Berkeley Square begins in 1859, when a Mr Myers took over the house. According to reports at the time, the poor man was left standing at the altar by his one true love and from that day on he shunned society and turned into a bitter, cynical recluse, rarely seen in public or even outside the house. The story goes that he moved all his belongings into a cramped, tiny room in the garret, and would see no-one except his manservant

Opposite: *Berkeley Square in London as it appeared in 1865. The house at number 50 was the most feared in England.*

Below: *One of the most evil ghosts ever recorded in the annals of the paranormal lay in wait at number 50.*

Opposite Top and Bottom:
An evil presence hovered over Lord Lyttleton's bed when he spent a night at the haunted house. In his later years he devoted himself to study of the phenomenon.

who brought him his daily meals. At night, however, while the rest of London slept or partied into the late hours, Mr Myers would mournfully walk the cobwebbed corridors of the house, his way lit by a single candle. Over the years, as he became even more eccentric, the once-proud house fell into disrepair, its windows caked with thick black dust and grime.

In 1873, when Mr Myers failed to pay his local taxes, he was summoned to appear

Above: *Prime Minister George Canning, who owned the house at Berkeley Square until his death in 1927.*

before the city council. But the weird loner steadfastly refused to even answer it. Despite his refusal, however, local officials decided not to take the matter any further – because they had heard the house was haunted and felt sympathy for the wretched man so unhinged by his unrequited love. Matters grew steadily worse for Mr Myers and within six years the house had become so notorious that London newspapers began writing articles on it and its strange legend. After Myers' death, terrified neighbours claimed they could still hear loud

thumps, moans and sobbing coming from inside, and some reports claimed that even pieces of furniture would inexplicably move around the house.

One of the many tales surrounding the origins of the 50 Berkeley Square hauntings tells of a young child who was either tortured or frightened to death in the house's nursery. The tot's forlorn ghost, still sobbing and wearing a plaid skirt, is said to make periodic appearances. Another story claims that the ghost is actually that of a young woman, who shared the house with her lascivious, miscreant uncle. In a final, desperate attempt to at last free herself of his immoral advances, the young woman is said to have thrown herself from a window on the top floor to her death. For some time afterwards, people in the neighbourhood claimed to have seen her ghost, hanging on to the ledge, screaming for help. Eventually, there were so many sightings of various phenomena that the house actually became a tourist spot so widespread was its infamy!

A CLUB OF SCEPTICS

But not everyone was ready to concede that it was haunted by unseen forces, and many believed that the cause of all the commotion could definitely be explained. Sir Robert Warboys was one such sceptic and, on a challenge from some fellow members of his club, he reportedly offered to spend a night inside the vacant house to prove that the bizarre tales of ghosts and evil were complete rubbish.

But the owner at this time, a Mr Benson, was reluctant to allow the bet to go ahead unless Sir Robert promised to take some precautions, including arming himself. Warboys good-naturedly agreed, and also took with him a bell Mr Benson had given him, which he could ring if anything went awry. Still, Sir Robert thought it all one big joke, and as he bade his friends good night, he scoffed at Benson nevertheless: 'My dear fellow,' he said, 'I am here to disprove the bunkum of a ghost, so your little alarm will be of no use. I bid you good night.'

With that, Sir Robert went upstairs. It was the last time anyone ever saw him alive. According to the story, all was well for the next 45 minutes. But suddenly, the little bell began to ring furiously from inside the bedroom. Then a shot was heard. People dashed up the creaky stairs, thrust open the bedroom door and found the limp body of Sir Robert sprawled across the bed. He had not been shot, but rather he is believed to have been literally frightened to death. His death mask was a face of sheer horror. His eyes bulged, and his mouth was frozen in twisted terror. His death only fuelled speculation that an intense evil lurked inside the house.

GUARANTEED PROTECTION

Not surprisingly then, the old house remained closed for some time afterwards until, in 1878, another well-heeled citizen, Lord Lyttleton, decided to follow in Sir Robert's footsteps by daring to also spend a night inside the haunted house. He, too, vowed to get to the bottom of the mystery and won permission from the new owner to spend a night in the very bedroom where Warboys had died some time before. But as a precaution, he took along with him two rifles which he had loaded with buckshot and silver sixpences, which folklore dictated would guarantee protection against whatever evil dwelt inside the room.

During the course of that long, lonely night, Lyttleton got very little sleep as he tossed and turned, but once he did drift off he was suddenly awoken by a mysterious, grotesque shape that lunged at him from out of the dark. He managed to get off one shot at the apparition, which then vanished right before his startled eyes. Lyttleton was clearly shaken by his macabre experience, and wrote about his encounter in a book, *Notes and Queries*, which was published the following year.

SUPERNATURALLY FATAL

In it, the former sceptic conceded that 50 Berkeley Square was 'supernaturally fatal to mind and body'. For years afterwards, the aristocrat devoted much of his spare time to researching the macabre history of the house, and eventually located a woman who he said was driven insane after spending just one night inside the place. However, like so many others, Lyttleton could not determine why the ghost was so evil or what caused it to appear in such a hideous manner.

Another victim of that house of horrors was a new maid, whose terrifying ordeal was reported in *Mayfair* magazine. One night, after the household had long ago retired to bed, the owners were startled from their sleep by the maid's terrifying screams. They scrambled upstairs and entered her room, where they found her standing in the middle of her bedroom, 'rigid as a corpse, with hideously glaring eyes'. The poor girl was so overcome with terror, that she could not even utter a single word. She was taken to St George's Hospital, where doctors examined her and then asked her what had scared her so horribly. But the poor creature was too overcome to reply, and steadfastly refused to

Above: *Borley Rectory is rightly called the most haunted house in England. Over the years, many residents have fled from it in mortal fear.*

THE APPARITION WAS THAT OF A WHITE-FACED MAN, HIS MOUTH AGAPE IN EVIL. THE HIDEOUS SPECTRE CAME TOWARDS THEM

discuss the events of the previous night, saying only it was 'just too horrible' to describe. Her doctors never did get her to talk – because she died the very next day!

Yet another horrifying story of Berkeley Square concerns the macabre tale of two sailors, Edward Blunden and Robert Martin, who came to London on shore leave from the frigate HMS Penelope. It was Christmas Eve, and they had much trouble finding a room for the night. Freezing from the cold they eventually came upon 50 Berkeley Square, which was vacant at the time, so the two seamen forced open a window and decided to sleep there. They came across a bedroom, which had been at the centre of all the previous sightings, and unwittingly bedded down for the night.

Blunden, however, had trouble falling asleep. He was nervous that someone might discover that they had broken into the house and summon the police to arrest them. He thought his fears had come true when he soon heard footsteps coming up the stairs. He was beside himself with panic, fearing that a policeman must have discovered the forced window and that he would be spending the night in a cold, damp jail cell.

He quickly woke Martin, and both heard the footsteps moving ever closer to the bedroom door. Then, the door opened, and both saw a hideous spectre coming towards them. Blunden quickly leaped to his feet, and made a grab for a heavy object resting on the nearby mantelpiece. He wasn't quick enough, however, and the ghost moved to stop him. As it did, Martin made his escape, running down the stairs and fleeing into the street. He was later found unconscious on the footpath, and after he was revived he told a passing policemen that he had seen an apparition, which he described as that of a white-faced man, his mouth agape in evil.

PANICKED INTO DEATH

The policeman was highly sceptical about the sailor's claims, but agreed to accompany Martin into the house to find his friend. When they arrived, they found Blunden's broken body sprawled on the basement stairs. His neck had been broken, and his eyes bulged in eternal horror. Apparently he had been so panicked by whatever he had seen that he had fallen down the stairs to his death.

In the years since, many people have tried to explain the events inside 50 Berkeley Square, but no one has yet been able to offer convincing proof that the disasters which befell Warboys, the maid, Lord Lyttleton, the sailors and the others were not the work of some sinister supernatural force.

In 1924, however, author Charles Harper wrote in his book, *Haunted Houses*, that one of the owners of the house, a Mr Du Pre, kept his mentally retarded brother imprisoned in the house. Mr Harper claims that the wretched lunatic was terribly violent, and given to frenzied bouts of sobbing and anger, in which he would throw objects about and scream with rage.

However, Harper's theory does not explain why the witnesses were never able to fully describe the monstrosity they had all seen. Nor does it explain why the house was so often put up for let. After all, who in their right mind would move into a house that came complete with a demented madman as a permanent guest in the upstairs room? Moreover, if both Sir Robert and Lord Lyttleton had shot at this insane prisoner, why was no blood ever found, let alone a body? And lastly, could any human being, no matter how deranged, literally frighten to death a knight of the realm and two of Her Majesty's servicemen? One can only answer with a resounding, 'No'.

Whatever strange disturbances occurred inside 50 Berkeley Square is a mystery which lasts to this very day. Fortunately for the new tenants, there have been no supernatural incidents reported at the site for many years.

BORLEY RECTORY

That is not the case with the Borley Rectory, with good reason called 'the most haunted house in England'. The Rectory, which lies some 60 miles north-east of London in the county of Essex, is a grotesque looking building, isolated from surrounding houses by a lonely country road. The house, a gloomy redbrick monstrosity, has always had an eerie aura about it, and many visitors down through the years have remarked on its cold, forlorn appearance.

Below: *The church at Borley is said to have been haunted from when it was built, 130 years ago.*

The Rectory was said to have been haunted from the very time it was built, in 1863, and down through the passing decades everyone who ever lived in the house and hundreds of visitors have all claimed that some supernatural force is at work inside.

A HAUNTED SITE

The first occupants were the Rev Henry Bull, who built it, and his wife and family. Even when they moved in, all were aware of the local legend that a monastery had once occupied the site, and that a monk had tried to elope with a nun from a nearby convent at Bures. According to the story, the ill-fated lovers were captured soon after they fled. The monk was hanged, and the poor nun bricked up alive inside one of the walls. Every 28 July, it was said, the lonely figure of a nun could been seen almost gliding along a path, forever searching for

Above: *Ghost hunters and researchers have flocked to the site at Borley Rectory looking for evidence of the paranormal.*

BULL HEARD BELLS RINGING WITH NO POSSIBLE EXPLANATION AND CLAIMED TO HAVE SEEN A PHANTOM COACH AND HORSES

her long-dead lover. All four of the reverend's daughters saw the nun-like figure on 28 July 1900, and tried to speak with her. The apparition simply vanished into thin air. Numerous other people, including a local headmaster, also claimed to have seen the nun.

When the Rev Bull died in 1892 the Rectory was taken over by his only son, the Rev Harry Bull, who had also seen the nun. But there were many other mysterious intruders besides her. On many occasions, Harry Bull heard bells ringing with no possible earthly explanation, and he claimed to have seen and heard a phantom coach with horses. Once, he claimed to have seen the vehicle driven by two headless horsemen! Before his death in 1927 he told many people that he had no doubts that the place was indeed haunted.

For almost 12 months following his death, the Rectory remained vacant, largely because no fewer than 12 clergymen turned down the post and local folks avoided it as soon as nightfall approached. It was not until the Rev Eric Smith and his wife, both avowed non-believers in the paranormal, moved in in 1928 that the lights burned again inside the Borley Rectory. But soon after they arrived, their resolve weakened. They, too, began to see and hear strange, unexplainable things: Mrs Smith reported seeing the phantom coach and horses; lights inside the house would flick off and on by themselves; bells rang out; mysterious footsteps were heard. And on one occasion, Rev Smith said he heard a woman groan, then listened as she exclaimed: 'Don't, Carlos, don't!'

BLACK SHAPES

They also claimed to have seen black shapes wandering about the rooms and, on one occasion, they said that they saw the ghost of Rev Harry Bull! This is an astounding fact because sometime before his death, Harry said if he was not happy with his successor, he would come back to haunt the place.

The frightened couple finally decided that they had better get some professional help in to investigate the spooky occurrences, and soon famed ghost hunter Harry Price arrived on the scene to examine the paranormal happenings. Price quickly found volumes of evidence to support the Smiths' claims, including unexplained footsteps in the snow, terrified animals, knocks on doors and walls, objects flying about the rooms. Despite his assurances – or maybe because of them – that they were not imagining things, the Smiths had finally endured enough. One year after the sceptical couple first moved in, they were gone. But the ghosts remained!

In 1930, Rev Lionel Foyster and his wife Marianne arrived at Borley Rectory, and for the next five years, until they too left in panic, the hauntings not only continued, but increased in dramatic frenzy. Eerie messages – begging for 'Mass' and 'Prayers' – were found scrawled on pieces of paper and walls; Marianne was savagely struck across the eye by some invisible force; their three-year-old daughter, Adelaide, was locked in a room that had no key; objects were tossed violently around the rooms; bottles materialised from thin air, then vanished as they

Above: *Over the years, many experiments into the paranormal have been conducted at the Borley Rectory.*

MARIANNE WAS SAVAGELY STRUCK ACROSS THE EYE BY SOME INVISIBLE FORCE. ADELAIDE WAS LOCKED IN A ROOM THAT HAD NO KEY

had appeared. Many of these paranormal phenomena occurred in the presence of witnesses, including a Justice of the Peace, a military officer and numerous other reliable spectators.

CONTINUED INVESTIGATIONS

Like the others before them, the Foysters eventually moved out and the Rectory was again vacant until 1937, when Harry Price decided to lease the site for 12 months so that he could continue his investigation into the dramatic hauntings. During the first few nights, he and a companion, Ellic Howe, drew circles in chalk around the bases of many movable objects in the Rectory. Each morning, the objects had somehow moved!

Gradually, Price gathered together a large team of investigators – at one stage there were 40 in all – who set up various experiments to try and record the ghosts' movements. That was to no avail, but in subsequent seances, Harry Bull appeared and told medium S.H. Glanville that the bodies of the monk and the nun had been buried on the site. In March 1938, another medium was told that the Rectory would burn to the ground that very evening, and that the hauntings would cease. Nothing happened, but it's interesting to note that indeed the place was gutted by fire in February 1939. By that time, Captain W.H.

Gregson had owned the house for just three months. He was going through some books when a stack of them accidentally fell over, knocking an oil lamp to the ground.

SPOOKY REMAINS

However, shortly before the disaster, Rev Canon W.J. Phythian-Adams, who had recently read Price's book about the Rectory, discovered that a young French woman had been murdered at the site and that her remains were buried there sometime in the 17th or 18th century. At his suggestion, Price and his team excavated the cellar and found the remains of a long-departed young woman!

Towards the end of 1939, Dr A.J. Robertson organised yet another team of

investigators to pour over the burned out remains of the Rectory. For the next five years, he and his team recorded more strange occurrences including inexplicable noises and rappings, stones thrown by an invisible hand, temperature changes which could not be accounted for by the prevailing weather and sightings of an eerie, incandescent patch.

Similarly, in recent years other reliable witnesses, including a headmistress, another rector and a Sunday school teacher have all reported seeing or hearing evidence of the paranormal at the site. Organ music has been heard by many coming from inside the church, which is empty and locked; the nun has been sighted several times. One witness, who saw a female apparition in 1951, described the woman as sad and

Above: *Everyone from Sunday school teachers to rectors has seen the ghosts of Borley.*

Opposite Top: *Nothing prepared unknowing residents for the horrors of Borley.*

Opposite Bottom: *Searchers comb the grounds outside the Rectory looking for 'the phantom nun'.*

wearing a black hood, a white collar, a gold bodice and a long black skirt. Another witness, Peter Rowe, a retired official from the Bank of England, saw the nun running past the gate towards the former garden. Sightings of her have come as recently as the 1970s.

PECULIAR SMELLS

Incredibly, even though the Rectory itself is no longer still standing, peculiar smells can still be noticed emanating from where it once sat and the sound of furniture being moved about can also be heard. Others have reported hearing plates being smashed, while others have heard voices.

The ghosts of Borley Rectory, it seems, are still at play.

A GHOST IN FLIGHT
The Haunting of Tri-Star 318

Most encounters with ghosts occur in haunted houses or castles, but there is one remarkable story concerning a haunted passenger plane. This state-of-the-art commercial jet flew for many months with a very unusual passenger on board

The ghost of Tri-Star 318 is as bizarre an apparition as anything to be found in the fog-cloaked graveyards or Gothic castles of England and France. Indeed, even a US government agency was unable to solve the mystery or explain what it was that many experienced airline crews had seen and heard.

The first warning that something was amiss aboard Tri-Star 318 came in 1973, when Fay Merryweather, a senior stewardess of several years' experience and a respected member of the flight crew, was walking back towards the rear of the Eastern Airlines plane to prepare the lunch for the 180 passengers fleeing the snow of New York for the sun-baked beaches of Florida. But as she walked back into the galley to begin heating the food, she remembers feeling something – or someone – watching her every movement. She remembers feeling a little uneasy, then suddenly, she turned her eyes and saw it – the reflection of a face staring at her from the tinted glass door of the in-flight oven.

Merryweather remembered being shocked, but when she looked closer at the vision, she was somehow not frightened. The face wasn't some grotesque, contorted image. Instead, it was the one that looked worried! Then, the mouth began to move, but no sound came. The stewardess got the impression that it was trying to warn her about something. Not knowing what to do, she quickly but calmly walked up the cabin aisle to the cockpit, carefully ensuring she did not arouse the suspicion of her passengers, and informed the flight engineer of the strange sighting.

Puzzled, because he knew Merryweather to be an experienced flier and not one prone to fanciful hallucinations, the officer left the cockpit and his bank of instruments and followed her back to the galley to take

THE FACE WAS NOT A GROTESQUE, CONTORTED IMAGE. THEN THE MOUTH BEGAN TO MOVE, BUT NO SOUND CAME

Opposite: *The mystery of Tri-Star 318 has confounded sceptics – and thwarted even the US Government's bid to explain it away.*

Below: *An Eastern Airlines Tri-Star… identical to the one that became known as a ghost plane.*

Above: *It was in the galley that highly-trained airline personnel first saw a mysterious apparition.*

THE DISEMBODIED FACE BELONGED TO DON REPO, A FORMER COLLEAGUE WHO HAD DIED 12 MONTHS EARLIER IN A PLANE CRASH

a look himself. When he looked into the oven door, not only was the disembodied face still there – but the startled engineer recognised it! It was Don Repo, a former colleague who had died 12 months earlier in a tragic plane crash that occurred over the Florida Everglades! As both stared at the image in disbelief, they heard it whisper: 'Beware! Beware! Fire in the jet!' Strangely, there was nothing amiss on board the Tri-Star that day, but the ominous warning was to come true three months later on another Eastern Airlines flight.

A PUZZLING APPARITION

The puzzling apparition forced officials and Eastern crew members to recall that devastating night some months earlier, when tragedy struck the airline. Repo, an engineer, and pilot Bob Loft were killed along with more than 100 passengers while on the same run between New York and Florida on the night of 29 December 1972. The plane was

a new Lockheed L-1011, or Tri-Star, the pride of the Eastern fleet and one of the most sophisticated planes then plying the skies over America. It was the first of the new generation of wide-body 'jumbo jets' to crash. The death toll at the time was the highest of any one-plane accident in United States' civil aviation history, and its downing made headlines around the world.

According to the lengthy, official investigation into the horrible crash of Flight 401, the trip had been routine for most of the way. Indeed, with Miami in sight, Captain Loft had announced cheerfully to his passengers and crew: 'Welcome to sunny Miami', as the plane passed over the city. 'The temperature is in the low 70s, and it's beautiful out there tonight.'

But as Captain Loft made the remarks, Repo went through the pre-landing motions, activating the sign instructing passengers to fasten their seat belts, then flicking the switch which would lower the wheels. It was then that the cockpit crew noticed that the square green light on the control panel which should have indicated that the nose wheel was locked and secured into position had failed to come on.

Captain Loft immediately put the Tri-Star on automatic pilot to circle, while Repo scurried to an observation point to see whether or not the nose gear had activated. As he did, Loft then decided to see if the problem was not merely a faulty indicator light. The captain guessed, correctly as it turned out, that the nose wheel was all right and locked into position and that the light was faulty. However, he still called off the landing and flew away from other airport traffic to make certain. After that, everything seemed to go wrong. Tragically, Captain Loft somehow bumped the automatic pilot switch into the 'off' position while he continued to check his panel – and neither he nor Repo realised the error until the plane was plummeting into a swamp.

There was nothing they could do, because unavoidable disaster was just seconds away. The left wingtip hit first, and the jet ploughed into the murky waters of the Everglades, leaving 101 people dead, and 75 lucky survivors. Initially, both Repo and Loft survived the horrific crash. Unfortunately, Loft died about 60 minutes later, still trapped inside the doomed cockpit, while Repo, who paramedics say seemed terribly angry when they pulled him from the smoking wreckage, lingered for more than a day before finally succumbing to his extensive injuries.

DEATH COMES CALLING

Angelo Donadeo, an Eastern Airlines technical specialist on L-1011 aircraft, was returning to Miami that night from a trouble-shooting assignment in New York and remembers it well. Although he was a passenger, he rode in the cockpit with Loft, Repo and co-pilot A. Stockstill, who was also killed. 'That wasn't my first brush with death,' Donadeo recalled many years later. 'I was wounded in World War Two when the ship I was on was hit by a kamikaze. I had first, second and third-degree burns all over my body. That

UNAVOIDABLE DISASTER WAS JUST SECONDS AWAY AND THE JET PLOUGHED INTO THE MURKY WATERS OF THE EVERGLADES

Below: *The scattered wreckage of Flight 401 which went down on a landing approach outside Miami International Airport in December 1972: months later strange events began.*

Above: The crash of Flight 401 claimed more than 100 lives – at the time it was the worst single plane disaster in US history.

TWO OF THE AEROPLANE'S FUEL TANKS BURST OPEN, SENDING BURNING BODIES AND DEBRIS FLYING INTO THE AIR

REPO'S GHOST WARNED OF A FIRE WHICH EVENTUALLY TOOK PLACE ON THE PLANE THREE MONTHS LATER

---

doesn't haunt me either. I don't see any reason to worry about what fate has brought. I don't question what the Lord does.' According to the records, Flight 401 flew into the ground just 18 minutes before midnight, crashing into the Everglades 18 miles northwest of the airport.

A survivor, Richard Micale, told local reporters that it had all happened so quickly. 'I remember thinking "Shit! The plane's crashing," and before I got finished thinking it, it was over. You could hear the cry of death. Funny how people scream for God at a time like that. I probably did too, I'm sure.'

STUNNING STORIES

Witnesses recall that there was a huge flash of flame as two fuel tanks burst open, sending burning bodies and debris flying into the air and into the alligator-infested waters. Richard Marquis, a carpet-layer, was out that night on his airboat catching frogs with a friend, Ray Dickens. They headed towards the flash, and saw the lights of rescue helicopters, circling and searching over the black lagoon.

They were much too far to the east and south, Marquis recalled, so he began to wave his headlamp in circles, guiding the rescue pilots to the crash site. Afterwards, he and his friend spent most of the night taking doctors and paramedics to the

injured, and the injured to the levee where the helicopters were landing to whisk them away to the nearest hospitals.

Following the lengthy investigation, which took several weeks, maintenance crews managed to salvage parts of the doomed airliner, which were then installed into other Tri-Star craft. The galley was installed into Tri-Star 318, where stewardess Merryweather and the flight engineer encountered Repo's ghost. Although his warning of a fire never eventuated on that flight to Florida, it did come true three months later, when the plane was forced to turn back with engine trouble on a trip from Mexico to New York.

Repairs were ordered and, when completed, the Tri-Star was sent up on a routine test flight to check the servicing. Just as the pilot edged the nose into the air, one of the engines suddenly burst into flames. The official report issued some weeks later found that if it had not been for the experience and professionalism of the crew, the plane would have crashed.

THE CAPTAIN'S GHOST

Later, on another flight, Captain Loft's ghost was sighted. The plane was filled with Eastern Airlines' staff, returning to their home base in Florida from various destinations around the United States. Among those aboard was an off-duty pilot and a senior airline executive, who sat next to each other. Not long into the flight, the two men began chatting, and when the executive turned to look at his fellow passenger, he recoiled in horror – for sitting next to time was Captain Loft, who had been dead for more than 12 months! (Oddly, the third member of the flight crew of Flight 401, First Officer Stockstill, was never seen). The executive let out a scream, and a host of fellow workers and stewardesses rushed to his aid. They found him ashen and shaking – and the seat next to him very much empty. A short while later on yet another flight, Captain Loft appeared again, still dressed in his captain's uniform, sitting in the first class section of the plane. A stewardess came over to him, and asked why he did not appear on her passenger list. When he didn't reply, she went to see the captain, who accompanied her back to the first class cabin. He immediately recognised

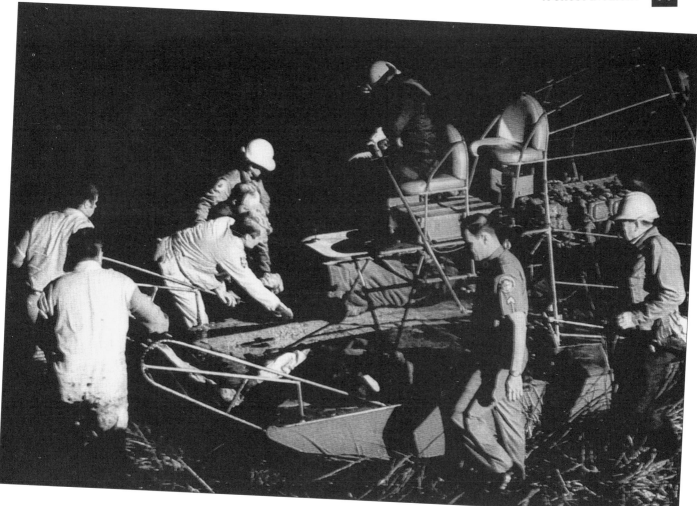

Loft, who then suddenly vanished into thin air right before their eyes.

There were several more sightings of the doomed fliers. A stewardess on another flight saw Repo's face appear on a luggage locker, while another spotted Loft near the bulkhead. In all, there were more than 20 sightings. One of the last came in 1974, when a pilot was conducting his routine pre-take-off check for a flight to Georgia.

As he inspected the complex bank of dials before him, the face of Dan Repo appeared. But this time, there were no warnings of near-disasters. Instead, the face whispered that he had already made the inspection, then added: 'There will never be another crash on an L-1011. We will not let it happen.' The voice had used the Lockheed serial number of the Tri-Star jet.

Still others claim to have had eerie encounters with the dead aviators. Some say they heard Repo's voice coming in over the public address system, while a few passengers say they felt inexplicable sudden rushes of cold air. During one haunting, in which Repo appeared yet again in the gal-

ley, he repaired an oven that had a circuit dangerously close to overloading. When the engineer assigned to the flight came to investigate the problem, he told the stunned air stewardess that he was the only engineer on the plane. Later, she looked up Repo's photo from his employment file and positively identified him as the man who had fixed the errant oven.

Above: Rescue teams scoured the swamp marshes looking for survivors.

Below: Witnesses recall bodies and debris hurtling into alligator-infested swamps.

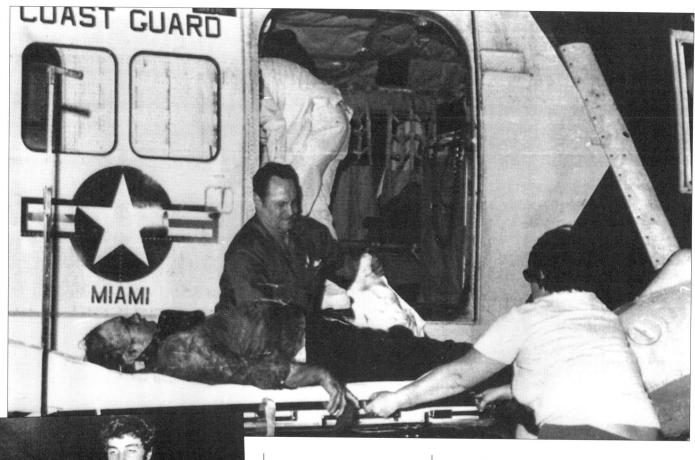

Above: *The crash and its aftermath prompted Eastern Airlines officials to even conduct an exorcism!*

Left: *A tiny survivor is rushed by a paramedic to a waiting ambulance.*

THE EXORCISM WORKED – THE TRI-STAR'S GHOSTS OF REPO AND LOFT WERE NEVER SEEN AGAIN. THEY SEEMED FINALLY AT REST

By this time the rash of apparitions had begun to worry crew members, but Eastern Airlines executives remained sceptical. Also, they didn't want the ghost stories made public, for fear that they could seriously erode the airline's passenger business. Those who reported seeing or hearing either Repo or Captain Loft were often urged to see a company psychiatrist, which was seen as the stage before getting fired. Eventually, however, as the number of sightings grew, Eastern management, which had no idea what could be causing the hauntings, called in an employee with devout religious leanings, and asked his advice. The man knew there could be just one way to rid the Tri-Star of its high-flying ghosts – an exorcism, which he did by splashing holy water about the plane. It worked, because the ghosts of Repo and Loft were never seen again. They were finally at rest – or so it seemed.

Shortly afterwards, details of the sightings were forwarded to the Flight Safety Foundation, which oversees airline safety in the United States. Its report, issued several weeks later, concluded: 'The reports were given by experienced and trustworthy pilots and crew. We consider them significant. The appearance of the dead flight engineer in the galley door was confirmed by the flight engineer. Later, records at the Federal Aviation Agency record the fire which broke out in that same aircraft. We published reports of the ghost sightings in our safety bulletin issued to airlines in 1974.'

died on Flight 401 roaming the Everglades late at night. Sadie Messina, whose husband was aboard the doomed craft, had a terrible premonition as she waited at the gate for the plane that would never arrive. 'My husband always had a distinctive little whistle, a code whistle,' she said.

'When I heard that whistle, I knew he was home. We were waiting at the gate, my two sons and I, and I heard his whistle. It sounded like he was right behind me. I turned around to look, but, of course, he wasn't there.' Sadie swears she heard the whistle at precisely the time Flight 401 crashed. Her husband, Rosario Messina, was among the dead.

Further, a secluded strip of land just outside Miami, which was once targeted to house the world's largest airport, is also said to be home to Don Repo's ghost. In 1969, it was envisioned as a massive hub for SSTs and 747s, but today it is a windswept piece of prairie, used for training airline pilots. But locals say that they have had several reports of his ghost in the area!

The bizarre hauntings remain a mystery to this very day.

But the Flight Safety Foundation never offered an explanation of the eerie apparitions, and to this day the hauntings remain a complete mystery.

Interestingly, some locals also claim to have seen the ghosts of some of those who

Above: *The mangled wreckage of Flight 401.*

Below: *A survivor tries to recall the events leading up to the crash.*

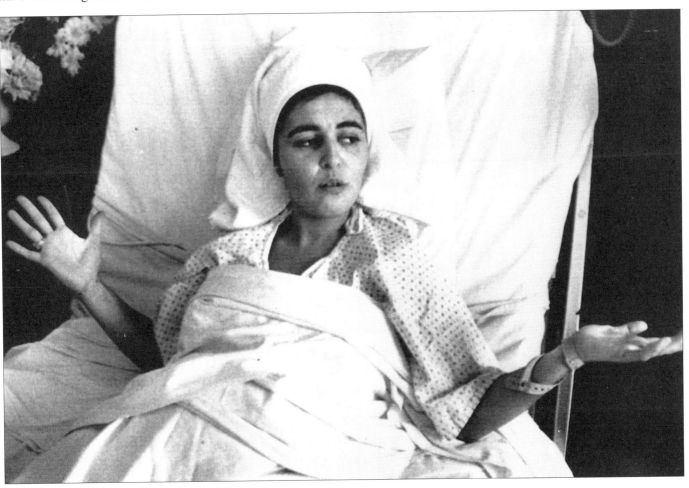

HAUNTED U-BOAT
Underwater Horror

It was the ghost from which there was no escape, the ghost that had its victims trapped – the ghost of U-boat 65. For the submariners in the German Navy, a posting onto that submarine was almost as terrifying as coming under attack from the enemy

Almost two years into the Great War, the battlefields of France and Belgium were literally running red with blood. Hundreds of thousands of young men were dying, an entire generation consigned to the mud and mayhem of trench warfare along the Western Front. The conflagration was so evenly matched that victories were measured in mere yards.

Neither side could muster the reserves for that one decisive thrust to punch through the other's defences, and the war developed into a grotesque stalemate – except that in this case, the pawns were the young men of England, Germany and France.

The only breakthrough in the war, it seemed, might come at sea where, by the summer of 1916, the Kaiser's navy, led by the wolf packs of U-boat submarines, was beginning to take a heavy toll on British shipping. Hundreds of thousands of tons were consigned to the bottom of the seas by the fast-moving U-boats. Particularly hard hit was the British merchant fleet, which carried supplies vital to the war effort in Europe.

The Kaiser and his navy warlords were convinced that this was the way to break the back of the British bulldog and so, with the war two years old, Germany was devoting much of its total war effort to producing more and more submarines to press the attack. That year, among the many U-boats which came down the assembly line ready for British blood was UB65, which would go down in naval lore as the host to at least one ghost, and the scene of many disturbing and tragic occurrences. Indeed, UB65 became so infamous, that even as the war raged on, its panic-stricken crew grew increasingly reluctant to sail on her.

UB65 PLAYED HOST TO AT LEAST ONE GHOST AND WAS THE SCENE OF MANY DISTURBING AND TRAGIC OCCURRENCES

Opposite: *Submariners aboard U-Boat 65 were as terrified of the ghosts on their vessel as they were of Allied attacks.*

Below: *When the Great War became bogged down on bloody battlefields, the Germans deployed more of their dreaded U-Boats.*

Above: *The Kaiser joins his naval sea lords for the test run of a U-Boat.*

Even before she was launched, the 'Iron Coffin' as she became known, seemed to attract disaster. She was built to join a fleet of submarines prowling off the Flemish coastline, gorging on the slow, heavily-laden ships crossing back and forward across the English Channel. But it seemed that everything that could go wrong during construction, did.

A HORRIFYING END

Not even seven days into her construction, as the hull was being laid, the first tragedy struck. As workers poured over the site, a giant girder hovering overhead on chains suddenly broke free, plunging into the hull. A hapless worker was horribly crushed under its massive weight, and lay there, in agony, for over an hour while frantic mates tried to rescue him. Tragically, he died just as the huge weight was finally lifted off him. An inquiry into the accident found there had been no faults in the chains used to hoist the girder, and officials were mystified as to what could have caused it to snap free.

Less than two months later, there was a second, more alarming tragedy. Three engi-

A HAPLESS WORKER WAS CRUSHED ON THE SUBMARINE JUST SEVEN DAYS INTO ITS CONSTRUCTION

neers who were assigned to the U-boat's engine room to test the submarine's dry cell batteries, were overcome by deadly chloride fumes. They died before anyone could rescue them and drag them into the fresh air. No-one ever determined why the batteries ever leaked the toxic fumes.

Thankfully, there were no more mysterious incidents during the remaining construction and shortly afterwards UB65 set sail for sea trials. But whatever dogged the boat seemed to follow it out of port because it quickly ran into a fierce Channel storm, and one hapless sailor was washed overboard to his death when the vessel came up to test her stability on the surface during rough seas.

After the man went overboard, the captain ordered the U-boat to dive. As she did, a ballast tank sprang a leak, flooding the dry-cell batteries in sea water and filling the engine room with the same deadly gas that had already claimed three lives while the boat was still on the slipway. After 12 nerve-racking hours the crew finally managed to get the ship to surface, where they flung open the hatches and breathed clean air. Amazingly, no-one was killed, and the

Left: A fleet of U-Boats waiting to set sail and gorge themselves on the slow, heavily-laden cargo ships in the English Channel.

Below: A direct hit! Thousands of tons of Allied shipping was lost to the German U-Boats.

bedevilled craft limped back to Germany for repairs.

After several days, the U-boat was again readied for sea and her first on-line patrol. But as a battery of torpedoes was being placed on board, a warhead suddenly exploded, killing the second officer and badly wounding several others. Yet again, an inquiry was conducted, but no explanation for the explosion was ever found. In the meantime, the second officer was buried, and another round of repairs made to the jinxed vessel. Her jittery crew, already worried about the U-boat's growing reputation for being accursed, were given a few days' much-needed shore leave to calm their shattered nerves before setting out on their first active patrol.

A GHASTLY APPARITION

Yet just moments before she was set to leave port, another bizarre incident occurred – this time, a panicked sailor swore he had seen the apparition of the dead second officer. 'Herr Kapitan!' he blurted. 'The dead officer is on board!' The captain, of course, refused to take the report seriously, believing the sailor had had too much to drink during his shore leave. However, even the stoic skipper was a little taken aback when a second member of his crew also claimed to have seen the ghost of the second officer coming casually up the gangplank! The seaman was sobbing from fear when he told the captain that the apparition had walked aboard, strolled up to the bow, then looked out at the inviting sea. He then vanished into thin air.

That two crew members had reported seeing the dead officer gave the captain some reason for pause, but nevertheless he knew his duty lay at sea and in sinking British ships. UB65 had some early successes on its maiden voyage, sinking three Allied merchant ships in quick succession. However, the rumours of the unwanted ghost had spread through the crew like wildfire, and their celebration over any direct hits was tempered by their belief that their vessel was haunted.

STARTLED SAILORS

Indeed, there was almost full-scale panic after UB65 recorded its second kill, when startled sailors in the engine room saw the dead officer observing the instrument panel as he had done in the trial voyage. By the time the submarine returned to base, rumours of its ghostly visitor were already spreading throughout the entire U-boat armada. The captain did his best to dispel the talk, claiming it was all poppycock, fearing that the ghost tales would only further erode the morale of the 34-man crew. But in their hearts, the men of UB65 knew something was terribly amiss with their craft.

Then in January, 1918 as the war dragged ever closer to its inevitable conclusion, even the captain could no longer dismiss the sightings as the rantings of some foolhardy seamen – for he, too, saw the apparition! It came as the U-boat was prowling in the Channel off Portland Bill. Because the weather was so foul and the seas extremely

Above: U-Boat 65 was forced to limp back to harbour after another mysterious disaster. The submarine was bedevilled by tragedy and death.

Below: A U-Boat crew pose on the deck of their submarine. Rumours about the ghost of U-Boat 65 soon became the talk of the German navy.

rough, the captain ordered the craft to surface. After breaking the surface, a lookout stationed on the starboard side was scanning the stormy horizon. He turned to look to port, when suddenly he spotted an officer standing on the deck, which heaved under the growing fury of the waves. At first, the crew man thought the officer foolhardy for taking such a risk, but then realised that all the hatches were still battened down, bar the one from which he himself had climbed onto the deck. He knew no-one could have come up through there without him immediately spotting him.

ALL-OUT PANIC

Suddenly, the crew man got a full look at the officer – and his face went white as the blood drained from it. There standing in front of him was the second officer, who had been buried with full honours back at home base. When he finally summoned the courage to move, the terrified seamen screamed to his shipmates that the ghost was on the boat. Below deck, the crew was close to all-out panic, and the captain had to act immediately lest a hysterical sailor put all their lives in jeopardy. He raced up the ladder, fully expecting to see nothing save a panicked crew man, when he, too, saw his dead comrade, his face a grotesque distortion. Seconds later, the ghost vanished, as if blown into the raging swell by the strong winds.

By the time the U-boat returned to port, navy authorities were already waiting. They were determined to get to the bottom of the mystery, fearing that the morale of the crew was so low that another disaster was just waiting to happen. With intense secrecy, each and every man assigned to UB65 was interviewed by a panel of high-ranking officers.

The reader must remember that U-boat crews were among the most reliable and hardiest in the navy. They were subjected to long periods of confinement deep below the ocean surface, and had to withstand

> THE KAISER'S SEA LORDS FOUND THE GHOST STORIES TOO CONVINCING TO SIMPLY LAUGH OFF OR DISMISS

ghost of the dead second officer too convincing to simply laugh off or dismiss as the talk of overwrought sailors. Instead, they decided to break up the crew of UB65, sending some to other submarines and others to destroyers.

But that still left the problem of what to do with the vessel itself. Eventually, the U-boat was decommissioned at the port of Bruges, in Belgium, and a Lutheran pastor was asked to perform the ancient Christian rite of exorcism! In surely what must be one of the most incredible wartime scenes ever, a Belgian civilian was taken on board

hours of nerve-racking pursuit by Allied destroyers. It was a fact that a submariner had only a 50-50 chance of ever returning from his mission, and that on a man-for-man basis, the U-boat force suffered the highest casualties of the war. So when these brave, innately fearless men, told navy officials that they were terrified of returning to their craft because of ghosts, then their story could not simply be dismissed as irrational rantings. And it wasn't. Although the Kaiser's sea lords could never admit to having a haunted ship – one could imagine the widespread effect on morale that would have on their other crews – they found the stories about the

Above: *On one exercise, the terrified sailors had to endure 12 hours below the water line, praying they would make it back to the surface.*

> THE NEW SKIPPER SCOFFED AT THE STORIES. HE WARNED HE WOULD NOT TOLERATE TALES OF GHOSTS OR GOBLINS

while German officers watched with a mixture of fascination and dread. Once the exorcism was completed, everyone breathed a sigh of relief.

A new crew and captain were assigned to the 'cleansed' ship, and it was business as usual for the next few weeks. The new skipper, a stern disciplinarian who scoffed at the stories of dead men walking the ship, warned his crew that he would not tolerate any renewed tales of ghosts or goblins. For the next two missions, it appeared as if everything was back to normal. There had been no sightings and no inexplicable accidents. But in May 1918, the ghost appeared again.

Right: *Bruges, where the haunted vessel was decommissioned and exorcised.*

Below: *Just four months before the Armistice was signed, U-Boat 65 suddenly exploded – killing everyone aboard.*

During the long voyage, in which UB65 was ordered to patrol the sea lanes off the Spanish coast as well as the English Channel, the dead officer was seen no fewer than three times. One of those who saw the ghost was the petty officer, who swore to God that he saw the man walk though a solid iron bulkhead and pass into the engine room! Another man, a torpedo handler, claimed the ghost visited him several times at night. The terrified soul became so disoriented that when the submarine surfaced to recharge its batteries, he leaped off the deck to his death in the seas.

On its final voyage – during July 1918, just four months before the Armistice was signed and peace returned to a ravaged Europe – the UB65 was spotted by an American submarine resting like a sitting duck on the surface. No one knows why. It was 10 July. The American sailors, who couldn't believe their good fortune, quickly armed their torpedoes and prepared to fire. But just before they did, the UB65 suddenly exploded, sending the remains of metal and men spewing out over a wide range of ocean.

Within seconds, all that remained of the submarine and her crew was a heavy oil slick and scattered debris. No-one aboard the American submarine ever gave the order to fire, and the crew swears no-one launched a torpedo. What happened? To this day, no-one knows. But it seemed a fitting, if bloody, end to the story of the haunted ship, which took its most enigmatic secret with it to its watery grave.